Ingo J. Timm   Christian Guttmann (Eds.)

Multiagent System Technologies

10th German Conference, MATES 2012
Trier, Germany, October 10-12, 2012
Proceedings

 Springer

Series Editors

Randy Goebel, University of Alberta, Edmonton, Canada
Jörg Siekmann, University of Saarland, Saarbrücken, Germany
Wolfgang Wahlster, DFKI and University of Saarland, Saarbrücken, Germany

Volume Editors

Ingo J. Timm
University of Trier
Department of Business Information Systems I
Universitätsring 15
54286, Trier
E-mail: itimm@uni-trier.de

Christian Guttmann
IBM R&D Laboratories
Level 5, 204 Lygon Street
Carlton, VIC 3051, Australia
and Etisalat British Telecom Innovation Centre (EBTIC)
Khalifa University, Abu Dhabi, United Arab Emirates
and School of Primary Health Care, Monash University
Melbourne, Australia
E-mail: christian.guttmann@gmail.com

ISSN 0302-9743   e-ISSN 1611-3349
ISBN 978-3-642-33689-8   e-ISBN 978-3-642-33690-4
DOI 10.1007/978-3-642-33690-4
Springer Heidelberg Dordrecht London New York

Library of Congress Control Number: 2012947928

CR Subject Classification (1998): I.2.11, I.2.8, K.4.4, H.3.4, H.4.1, I.6.5, I.6.8, I.2.3-4

LNCS Sublibrary: SL 7 – Artificial Intelligence

Typesetting: Camera-ready by author, data conversion by Scientific Publishing Services, Chennai, India

Printed on acid-free paper

Springer is part of Springer Science+Business Media (www.springer.com)

Lecture Notes in Artificial Intelligence   7598

Subseries of Lecture Notes in Computer Science

Preface

This volume contains the papers accepted for presentation at MATES 2012, the 10th German Conference on Multiagent System Technologies, held on October 10–12, 2012 in Trier, Germany. Over the past decade, the MATES conference series has established itself as a growing and important forum for researchers, users (members of business and industry), and developers of intelligent agents and multi-agent systems, in Germany and beyond. Current challenges in society require intelligent technologies like agents and multi-agent systems to enable companies and organizations to be more resilient, inter-connected, and collaborative. Hence, the conference investigates technologies for truly open distributed systems covering a wide spectrum of approaches from self-organization and autonomous systems to agreement computing.

This year's MATES conference celebrates two anniversaries: the 10th anniversary of MATES and the 20th anniversary of the German special interest group on Distributed Artificial Intelligence. MATES 2012 was organized by the German special interest group on Distributed Artificial Intelligence (Gesellschaft für Informatik e.V. Fachgruppe Verteilte Künstliche Intelligenz) together with the steering committee of MATES to promote theory and application of agents and multi-agent systems.

MATES 2012 received 39 submissions. Each submission was reviewed by at least three program committee members, who provided reviews to the authors and recommendations to the MATES chairs. Based on these recommendations, MATES decided to accept 7 full papers (18% acceptance rate), and also one invited paper. We also decided to include 6 short papers outlining preliminary work with promising future directions. We were pleased to host two prominent invited speakers in the agent community: Dr. Jeffrey Bradshaw (Florida Institute for Human and Machine Cognition, USA), and Prof. Dr. Stefan Kirn (University of Hohenheim, Germany). Both presented work on the advances of agent system technologies.

We would like to thank the authors and reviewers for their excellent work. Furthermore, we would like to thank Ralf Gerstner as well as the local staff of the University of Trier, including Ralf Schepers, Melanie Müller, Axel Kalenborn, and Tjorben Bogon, for their support in the organization of MATES 2012. As chairs of MATES 2011, Franziska Klügl and Sascha Ossowski provided support in starting up the MATES 2012 conference – thank you. The reviewing process and proceedings were organized using EasyChair. We are also grateful to the IBM R&D lab, Melbourne, Australia for their support of MATES 2012.

July 2012

Ingo J. Timm
Christian Guttmann

Preface

Conference Officials of MATES 2012

Conference Chairs

Christian Guttmann   IBM R&D Laboratories, Australia,
EBTIC – Etisalat British Telecom
Innovation Centre / Khalifa University,
United Arab Emirates and Monash
University, Australia

Ingo J. Timm   University of Trier, Germany

Doctoral Consortium Chair

René Schumann   University of Applied Sciences Western
Switzerland, Sierre, Switzerland

Steering Committee of the MATES Conference Series

Matthias Klusch   DFKI, Germany
Winfried Lamersdorf   University of Hamburg, Germany
Jörg P. Müller   Technische Universität Clausthal, Germany
Paolo Petta   University of Vienna, Austria
Rainer Unland   University of Duisburg-Essen, Germany

Organization

Program Committee

Klaus-Dieter Althoff	German Research Center for Artificial Intelligence (DFKI) / University of Hildesheim, Germany
Bernhard Bauer	University of Augsburg, Germany
Holger Billhardt	Universidad Rey Juan Carlos, Spain
Vicent Botti	Universitat Politècnica de València, Spain
Jeffrey Bradshaw	Florida Institute for Human and Machine Cognition, USA
Lars Braubach	University of Hamburg, Germany
Joerg Denzinger	University of Calgary, Canada
Juergen Dix	Clausthal University of Technology, Germany
Torsten Eymann	University of Bayreuth, Germany
Maria Ganzha	University of Gdańsk, Poland
Christian Guttmann	IBM R&D labs, Australia and Etisalat British Telecom Innovation Centre (EBTIC) / Khalifa University, United Arab Emirates and Monash University, Australia
Koen Hindriks	Delft University of Technology, The Netherlands
Benjamin Hirsch	Etisalat British Telecom Innovation Centre (EBTIC) / Khalifa University, United Arab Emirates
Tom Holvoet	Catholic University of Leuven, Belgium
Michael Huhns	University of South Carolina, USA
Samin Karim	Melbourne University, Australia
Stefan Kirn	University of Hohenheim, Germany
Franziska Klügl	Örebro University, Sweden
Matthias Klusch	German Research Center for Artificial Intelligence (DFKI), Germany
Daniel Kudenko	University of York, UK
Stefano Lodi	University of Bologna, Italy
Marco Luetzenberger	Technical University of Berlin, Germany
Beatriz López	University of Girona, Spain
Daniel Moldt	University of Hamburg, Germany
Joerg Mueller	Clausthal University of Technology, Germany
Eugénio Oliveira	University of Porto, Portugal
Andrea Omicini	Università di Bologna, Italy

Sascha Ossowski	University Rey Juan Carlos, Spain
Julian Padget	University of Bath, UK
Marcin Paprzycki	Polish Academy of Science, Poland
Mathias Petsch	Technical University of Ilmenau, Germany
Paolo Petta	Austrian Research Institute for Artificial Intelligence, Austria
Alexander Pokahr	University of Hamburg, Germany
Marco Schorlemmer	Artificial Intelligence Research Institute, Spain
René Schumann	University of Applied Sciences Western Switzerland, Switzerland
Frank Schweitzer	ETH Zurich, Switzerland
Akash Singh	IBM California, USA
Michael Thielscher	University of New South Wales, Australia
Ingo J. Timm	University of Trier, Germany
Denis Trcek	University of Ljubljana, Slovenia
Rainer Unland	University of Duisburg-Essen, Germany
Gerhard Weiss	University of Maastricht, The Netherlands
Cees Witteveen	Delft University of Technology, The Netherlands

Additional Reviewers

Ahrndt, Sebastian	Rocha, Ana
Bogon, Tjorben	Schüle, Michael
Bulling, Nils	Tanase, Dorian
Hermoso, Ramon	Ter Mors, Adriaan
Kaisers, Michael	van Lon, Rinde
Karänke, Paul	Zanetti, Marcelo
Koster, Andrew	Zhang, Dongmo
Patzlaff, Marcel	Zhao, Dengji

Table of Contents

Invited Talk
Human-Agent Teamwork in Cyber Defense

Jeffrey M. Bradshaw

Florida Institute for Human and Machine Cognition (IHMC), USA
jbradshaw@ihmc.us

Abstract. Despite the significant attention being given to the critical problems of cyber security, the ability to keep up with the increasing volume and sophistication of network attacks is seriously lagging. Throwing more computing horsepower at fundamentally-limited visualization and analytic approaches will not get us anywhere. Instead, we need to seriously rethink the way cyber security tools and approaches have been conceived, developed, and deployed. IHMC is taking advantage of the combined strengths of humans and software agents to create new capabilities for Network Operations Centers (NOCs). These capabilities are being implemented in a new cyber defense framework called Sol. Our objective is to enable distributed sensemaking, rapid detection of threats, and effective protection of critical resources. Specifically, we use agents, policies, and visualization to enact coactive emergence as a sensemaking strategy for taskwork and teamwork, and we implement capabilities for organic resilience and semantically-rich policy governance as a means of assuring effective and adaptive human-agent team response. IHMC has applied its long years of experience with software agents to the design of a new agent framework called Luna. Luna agents function both as interactive assistants to analysts and as continuously-running background aids to data processing and knowledge discovery. Luna agents achieve much of their power through built-in teamwork capabilities that, in conjunction with IHMC's KAoS policy services framework, allow them to be proactive, collaborative, observable, and directable. In order to support dynamic scalability and other features of the Sol framework, the Luna platform supports the policy-governed option of allowing the state of agents (vs. code of agents) to migrate between operating environments and hosts. We believe that the approach to cyber defense embodied in Sol is equally relevant to applications of distributed sensemaking for other kinds of complex high-tempo tasks such as real-time disease control or disaster management.

Biography

Jeffrey M. Bradshaw (Ph.D., Cognitive Science, University of Washington) is a Senior Research Scientist at the Florida Institute for Human and Machine Cognition (IHMC) where he leads the research group developing the KAoS policy and domain services framework. He co-leads the group developing IHMC's Sol Cyber

I.J. Timm and C. Guttmann (Eds.): MATES 2012, LNAI 7598, pp. 1–2, 2012.

Framework and the Luna agent framework. Formerly, Jeff led research groups at The Boeing Company and the Fred Hutchinson Cancer Research Center. Though his earliest publications were focused on memory and language, Jeff's research focus soon turned to a wide variety of topics relating human and machine intelligence. With Ken Ford, he edited the seminal volume Knowledge Acquisition as a Modeling Activity, and became well known for his role in helping develop a suite of successful methodologies and tools for automated knowledge acquisition. While at Boeing, he founded the emerging technologies group of the Aviation Industry Computer-Based Training Committee (AICC). Jeff helped pioneer the research area of multi-agent systems, and his first book on the topic, Software Agents, became a classic in the field and a best-seller for The MIT Press. Jeff served for over a decade on the Board of Directors of the International Foundation for Autonomous Agents and Multiagent Systems. Human-Agent-Robot Teamwork has been a central interest for many years. From 2002-2006, KAoS was used as part of a NASA series of annual two-week field tests of human-robot teams performing simulated planetary surface exploration at the Mars Desert Research Station in the Utah desert. Jeff was sponsored by DHS to undertake detailed simulation studies of the use of human-robot teams to secure facilities at Port Everglades. He has also led the ONR-sponsored NAIMT and Coordinated Operations projects where a team of humans and heterogeneous robots performed field exercises at the Naval Air Station in Pensacola, aimed at port reconnaissance, and robot-assisted detection and apprehension of intruders. Jeff co-founded and organized the Human-Agent-Robot Teamwork Workshop series (HART), whose most recent meetings were held at the Lorentz Center in Leiden, The Netherlands, and at the 2012 Human-Robot Interaction conference in Boston. He recently served as lead editor for a special issue of IEEE Intelligent Systems on HART (April-May 2012). In June 2012, he led an international workshop for the National Academies on Intelligent Human-Machine Collaboration. Jeff has been a Fulbright Senior Scholar at the European Institute for Cognitive Sciences and Engineering (EURISCO) in Toulouse, France; a visiting professor at the Institut Cognitique at the University of Bordeaux; is former chair of ACM SIGART; and former chair of the RIACS Science Council for NASA Ames Research Center. He served as a member of the National Research Council (NRC) Committee on Emerging Cognitive Neuroscience Research, was an advisor to the HCI and Visualization program at the German National AI Research Center (DFKI), and was a scientific advisor to the Japanese NEC Technology Paradigm Shifts initiative. He currently serves as a member of the Board on Global Science and Technology for the National Academies and as an external advisory board member of the Cognitive Science and Technology Program at Sandia National Laboratories. He is an Honorary Visiting Researcher at the University of Edinburgh, Scotland, a member of the Graduate Faculty at the Florida Institute of Technology, a faculty associate at the University of West Florida. With Robert Hoffman and Ken Ford, he serves as co-editor of the Human-Centered Computing Department for IEEE Intelligent Systems. In 2011, he received the Web Intelligence Consortium Outstanding Contributions Award.

Invited Talk
25 Years of Distributed AI in Germany: From the Very Beginnings to Multiagent Applications in Industry in Germany Today

Stefan Kirn

University of Hohenheim, Germany
stefan.kirn@uni-hohenheim.de

Abstract. *I.* The presentation starts with a brief report on the first steps of Distributed AI research in Germany, beginning in 1988, the year of the publication of the famous book of Bond / Gasser, followed by a stimulating discussion on Michael Huhns DAI mailing list (1991), and by a number of ambitious German PhD projects (Fischer, Klett, v. Martial, Kirn and others), and, finally, by the foundation of the German Special Interest Group on Distributed AI in the early 1990's.

II. From its very beginning, German DAI research has been driven by three main forces:

(1) **basic research:** developing towards well-defined concepts for distributed problem solving and multiagent systems, coordination and cooperation, situated behaviors, etc. in two 6 years basic research programs on Sòcionik (1999-2005), and cooperative intelligent agents (2000-2006).
(2) **industrial DAI/MAS applications** in lots of branches, e.g. banking and finance, production planning and control, logistics and others, and
(3) **the enrichment of other computer science technologies** like databases, knowledge based systems, distributed systems, grid computing, and cloud computing nowadays by proven concepts of the multiagent field.

This part of the presentation gives introductions into and examples of these projects and to the results achieved.

III. Nowadays it is well understood that the multiagent paradigm is an important cutting edge technology for innovative solutions in the field of smart objects. National and international research programs offer a lot of opportunities for ambitious multiagent research and development. The presentation introduces some up to date examples from fields like food security, material logistics, and civil engineering.

I.J. Timm and C. Guttmann (Eds.): MATES 2012, LNAI 7598, pp. 3–4, 2012.
© Springer-Verlag Berlin Heidelberg 2012

Biography

Prof. Dr. Stefan Kirn holds a chair in Information Systems at University of Hohenheim at Stuttgart/Germany. He obtained master degrees in management science (Munich, 1980) and in computer science (Hagen, 1989). He did his Ph.D. in Distributed AI in 1991, and his habilitation in Organizational Theories for Multi-Agent Systems in 1995. Stefan Kirn has been the initiator and coordinator of a 6 years German Research Foundation priority program on business applications of agent technology (2000-2006). From this research program originated the agent technology testbed Agent.Hospital, which has been successfully presented to an international audience the first time at Barcelona in February 2003. The most important results of this program have been published as a Springer book entitled "Multiagent Engineering Handbok". From 2001-2003 he has been Chief Scientist of IWT GmbH/Erfurt, a research company owned by the Association of the Industry of Thuringia/Germany. Since 2005, Stefan Kirn is CEO of the Hohenheim Research Center on Innovation and Services. In 2004, he founded Jesselle GmbH, an agent technology based university spinoff. Since 2004, he initiated a series of series of national and European projects on industrial applications of multiagent technology, e.g. Akogrimo, AutoBauLog, BREIN, MIGRATE!, ProBauDok, etc. Stefan Kirn has published more than hundred peer reviewed international publications, is on the editorial board of several journals in information systems, and acts as a consultant to governments, industry, and professional organizations.

Exploiting Dynamic Weaving for Self-managed Agents in the IoT

Inmaculada Ayala, Mercedes Amor Pinilla, and Lidia Fuentes

Departamento de Lenguajes y Ciencias de la Computación,
Universidad de Málaga, Málaga, Spain
{ayala,pinilla,lff}@lcc.uma.es

Abstract. Agents are a good option to develop Internet of Things (IoT) systems with self-management capacities. Current agent technology offers the necessary means to manage many of the requirements of self-management satisfactorily, however agent approaches for lightweight devices do not provide support for self-configuring agents' internal functionality adequately. This paper describes part of the Self-StarMAS approach for self-managing the IoT, which uses aspect-oriented mechanisms to model self-managing tasks. Aspect-orientation facilitates the adaptation and reconfiguration of the Self-StarMAS agents' internal architecture. This paper focuses on describing the internal composition of aspects, which is performed by an internal *weaver* at runtime.

Keywords: Agent Architectures, Self-management, Hand-held devices, Aspect-Orientation.

1 Introduction

The Internet of Things (IoT) envisions a world in which everyday objects collaborate using the Internet in order to provide integrated services for users. This vision defines the IoT as a dynamic global network requiring global self-managing capabilities, based on standard and interoperable communication protocols [1]. In general, IoT systems are characterized by being composed of a large variety of heterogeneous devices, able to observe, react and adapt to events occurring in the environment. Therefore, IoT devices not only must be aware of the physical world, they demand the reconfiguration of their internal functioning in response to external changes. Each IoT device should then be able to manage itself given a set of high level goals, without the intervention of human administrators. The distributed nature of IoT systems, the autonomy, awareness and adaptation properties make software agents a good option to develop self-managed IoT systems: software agents are reactive, proactive and their communication is supported by distributed agent platforms (APs).

In opposition to agent-based centralized solutions, we focus on novel decentralized solutions, more suitable to the highly decentralized and embedded nature of the IoT systems [2]. Concretely, in the Self-StarMAS Multi-Agent System (MAS), each IoT device has one agent in charge of both application specific and

I.J. Timm and C. Guttmann (Eds.): MATES 2012, LNAI 7598, pp. 5–14, 2012.

system-level goals. In IoT systems, system specific goals are mainly related to physical resources and network protocols, and it is essential to explicitly include them as part of any agent-based solution. For example, being able to change the communication protocol to consume less energy, is considered a system-level goal versus application-level goals. Achieving this goal may imply changing one or more agent internal components. Therefore, agents not only must be aware of the devices and the external context they are running at, but also be required to manage their internal components given a set of system-level goals. This is possible using standard agent frameworks, by designing a control loop customized to provide the self-management functions required by IoT devices. As part of this control loop, the agent developer has to implement a mechanism for endowing each agent the ability to be aware of their internal state and adjust their internal functioning in response to external changes occurring both inside the IoT device and in the global IoT system.

Agents have been previously used to implement self-managed systems in the area of Information Technology Systems (ITS) [3]. In contrast to our approach, in these approaches agents are used as external autonomic managers of the ITS, that have specific purposes in the self-management of the application (e.g. power manager), sometimes integrating Artificial Intelligence (AI) techniques as part of the self-management. The main limitation of these solutions is that they usually require a lot of computational resources and are unsuitable for more lightweight devices. There are other solutions that are specialized in devices that are typical of the IoT, Wireless Sensor Networks being one of the application areas [4,5]. However, these approaches also propose centralized solutions based on external agents, which means these devices are not able to be self-managing.

We have found three important limitations in current agent toolkits and APs (specially those that work in lightweight devices). Firstly, their representation of the agent's internal state is restricted to application specific elements (resources, data and behavior), making it difficult to be aware of the agent's internal state related to its internal architectural configuration (i.e. the set of components and their connections). Secondly, the adaptation of the agent internal functionality is also limited to the set of components developed specifically for the application; making it difficult to perform adaptations requiring the reconfiguration of the agent's internal components. The main problem is principally due to the poor modularization of the agent internal architecture, which normally has intermingled application and core components of the agent [6,7]. This makes the adaptation and reconfiguration required by some self-management activities (such as add or delete components) complex. And finally, the incorporation of the self-management tasks affects application-specific modules, complicating the development of some self-management activities in a non-intrusive manner. Moreover, the concerns related with the self-management of the system properties normally crosscut the core components of the agent architecture.

Therefore, the purpose of our work is to enhance the agent architectural configuration to overcome these limitations. One important challenge in order to address self-management functions, is to make it the least intrusive as possible, modeling the self-management related concerns in a modular way. Aspect Oriented Software Development (AOSD[1]) is a successful software development technology, which encourages the modeling of crosscutting concerns separately, by a new entity called *aspect*. In this paper, we will show how we benefit from Aspect-Orientation (AO) to facilitate the agent architectural reconfiguration at runtime. The proposed approach -by exploiting AO- gains in flexibility and modularity with respect to other agent-oriented frameworks for lightweight devices. This self-managed agent framework can be used to develop MAS for the IoT, which can benefit from their self-management capacities.

Currently, there are several approaches that use AO to provide different functions of self-management. For instance, the work presented in [8] uses AO to encapsulate self-management properties as crosscutting concerns. For the work in [9], aspects are specifically used to facilitate and enhance the monitoring function. The work presented in [10] also applies AO for providing a dynamic and reconfigurable monitoring system. However, none of these AO approaches are intended for lightweight devices and many of their AO mechanisms are difficult to adapt for these devices, resulting inappropriate for the IoT.

The content of this paper is organized as follows: Section 2 presents the aspect oriented architecture for self-management and the aspect composition process. Section 3 discusses our proposal. Section 4 summarizes our conclusions.

2   An Aspect-Oriented Architecture for Self-management

Self-management or autonomic computing [3] is a term used to describe systems that assume their own management (i.e. are self-managing). From this general definition, we consider a self-managed agent as an agent that is able to independently, and according to a set of rules or policies, take care of their own maintenance, configuration and optimization tasks, thus reducing the workload of the MAS's administrators. In order to develop a self-managed agent-based system, there are four so-called autonomic functions (AF) that each agent should support [11]: self-awareness, self-situation; self-monitoring and self-adjusting. Self-awareness is the capacity for introspection, while self-situation is related to the awareness of current external operating conditions; self-monitoring refers to the ability to detect changing circumstances in the agent environment. Finally, self-adjusting is the ability to accordingly adapt to these environment changes. In this paper we focus on highlighting the benefit of using aspect-orientation to implement these AFs, focusing on the dynamic weaving of the aspects at runtime.

So, modeling the AFs by aspects allows us to: (1) add or remove the possibility of self-management from the agent; (2) optimize the resource usage, by adding only those aspects of self-management required by the MAS; (3) improve the reasoning about each concern, since they are modeled separately; (4) reasoning on a limited number of aspects combined with the runtime weaving of aspects improving the scalability of the reconfiguration mechanism (5) explicitly model the context awareness concerns as aspects, able to be used differently by each of

---

[1] http://aosd.net/

the self-management properties (i.e. self-configuring, self-optimizing, self-healing and self-protecting).

The application scenario we have chosen for the case study is a typical application of the IoT, an Intelligent Museum. The building includes a considerable set of sensors and personal lightweight devices and mobile phones, which interact in order to provide provide context-aware services. Measures provided by the sensors help museum guides and security staff in their work, and additionally, bring location based services to the visitors. This system has different services for its target users: in the case of the guide, it provides support for the organization of the route inside the museum considering the presence of other groups in the halls and rooms of the museum, and helps share information between the guide and the group of visitors; in the case of the security staff, the sensor nodes application provides information on the presence of people in the museum and environmental conditions, and sends global notifications to the different groups of people that are in the museum; and in the case of the visitors, we take advantage of the fact that most people usually bring a mobile phone with them in order to provide location based information.

This case study is designed as a MAS whose agents are located in devices that people bring with them. The MAS has four types of agents: one for the guides (*GuideAgent*), another for security staff members (*SecurityAgent*), another for the visitors (*VisitorAgent*) and the last kind of agents that are running in the sensors of the museum (*SensorAgent*). All the agents of the MAS except *SensorAgents* are executed in hand-held devices. The architecture of the *SensorAgent* is different to the other agents of the MAS and is beyond the scope of this paper, more details on this kind of agent are given in [12].

2.1   The Agent Self-management Control Loop

The agent is conceived as a software system running in a lightweight device, capable of interacting with its environment and with other agents. Its behavior is goal-oriented, context-aware and deliberative; agent actions are organized in plans, being each plan associated with a goal to be achieved, to which it contributes. The achievement of goals depends on the current context and their internal state. Inside the agent architecture, agent functionality is encapsulated in both components and aspects. In our approach, this modularization makes it possible to enable, disable, configure and compose different agent properties at runtime. Aspects do not maintain any reference to other aspects of the architecture. Instead, their composition is performed by an *aspect weaver*, which captures certain agent execution points, and invokes aspects' behavior. This feature is crucial to incorporate the AFs in a non-intrusive manner, and to modify the agent configuration easily. Another distinguishing feature of our approach is that the agent maintains an explicit representation of its *architectural* context and the *system* context. The former captures the current state of the agent architecture by containing the set of components, aspects and relationships that are currently active (i.e. those which are instantiated and in use). The latter context refers to the data and information derived from the system the agent is running in (mainly the lightweight device), such as resource consumption. The maintenance of these contextual *knowledge bases* definitely contribute to self-awareness and self-situation of the agent.

Figure 1 shows the different elements involved in self-management that compose the control loop in the *GuideAgent*. The details are briefly outlined in following sections, stressing its relation with the AFs. Due to limitations of space the explanation of the self-adjusting (aspect) is beyond the scope of this paper, but some details about its design and functioning are given in [12]. At runtime, the agent behavior is determined by two control loops, one is application-specific and the other is for the self-management (which is the scope of this paper). The two loops generate goals that are processed at runtime by the Reasoning Engine.

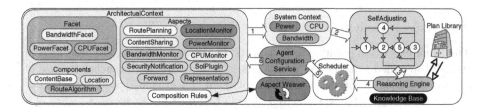

Fig. 1. Self-management loop for *GuideAgent*

2.2 Achieving Self-awareness and Self-situation

In most BDI agent architectures, there is a knowledge base that contains relevant information for the agent. In addition to the knowledge base of the application, in order to carry out self-management we need the information internal to the agent (self-awareness) and about the external world (self-situation). In our agent architecture, we consider that the internal information of the agent is its architectural configuration, i.e. running components, aspects, composition rules and their configuration. The current state of the external world is the other information that may be considered as context, this information can be about the physical world (e.g. location) or about computational resources (e.g. memory occupation). The self-awareness is achieved using an explicit representation of the agent architectural configuration, while the self-situation is achieved by modeling the environment as a set of context data elements.

Self-awareness is represented by the *ArchitecturalContext* element, which contains the set of aspects and components which compose the agent. For instance, the behavior of the *GuideAgent* (see Fig. 1) to plan the route inside the museum, to share contents with *VisitorAgents* and also, to receive notifications from *SecurityAgents*, is distributed in different components and aspects. All the functions required for communication are encapsulated by aspects (the *Aspects* box in Fig. 1), e.g. the support for a routing protocol (*Forward*) or the communication through an AP particularly well suited for the IoT (*SolPlugin*). Moreover, the application specific functionality is encapsulated in components, e.g. the information shared between the guide and the visitors (e.g. *ContentBase*). The *ArchitecturalContext* also contains a set of composition rules (*CompositionRules*) to support the aspect composition process that will be explained later.

Self-situation is represented inside the agent architecture by the *SystemContext* element (see Fig. 1). The elements of *SystemContext* has a time stamp that enables the quality of the context to be checked or failures to be detected. How the information of the system context is gathered will be explained in section 2.4. In the case of the *GuideAgent* that has to communicate with every the agents in the IoT system and has to ensure the device functioning during the tour, the communication and the power consumption are the main concerns for self-management. So, its *SystemContext* includes battery consumption, the bandwidth and the CPU.

2.3   Aspect Weaving

The agent execution points, where aspects' behavior is invoked, are described in terms of so called *interception* points. As seen in different approaches the use of aspects provides a better encapsulation of agent concerns [6,7], and in particular a natural way to compose unrelated objects by an *aspect weaver*.

In our approach an aspect is an entity with special methods that differ from common components in that they are never invoked explicitly by other components of the architecture. Instead, aspects behavior (accessed by methods called *Advices*) is only invoked by the aspect weaver. In our approach any aspect has a set of advices by default (*handleOutputMessage*, *handleInputMessage* and *handleEvent*), which coincide with the basic interception points. In order to compose aspects we use a variation of the mechanism approached by Malaca [6] that is based on interception points and composition rules.

The composition rules define how the aspects are composed in the interception points. We define three interception points by default: message reception and sending, and event throwing (these are identified by the tags *RCV_MSG*, *SND_MSG* and *THRW_EVNT* respectively). This means that every time a message is sent or received, or an internal event is thrown, agent execution is intercepted, aspects behavior is invoked and composed. Moreover, the user can define more interception points (e.g. the invocation of certain methods of a component) and the corresponding advices for the aspects to be applied in the user-define interception point. In order to do this it has to define a tag to identify the new interception point and extend the agent with the new method that represents the new interception point.

The aspect composition process is guided by a set of *composition rules*. The composition procedure is described in Algorithm 1. A composition rule is composed of a tag that identifies the interception point and a set of aspect descriptions. In line 1, aspect descriptions that correspond to the specific interception point (identified by input *tag*) are selected and stored in A. Aspect descriptions contain the necessary data to weave an aspect at a specific interception point, such as the restriction for the weaving of the aspect, the role that fulfills the

---

Algorithm 1. Aspect Composition

Input: the identifier the interception point *tag*, the aspect composition input *input*
Output: the output of the aspect composition process *output*

1: $A \leftarrow \{\forall AspectDescription \in CompositionRules|$
   $InterceptionPoint(AspectDescription) == tag\}$
2: $j \leftarrow 0;$
3: *Aspect aspect*;
4: **while** $j \leq size(A)$ **do**
5:   *Restriction rest* $\leftarrow A_i.getRestriction();$
6:   **if** $rest.holdRestriction(input)$ **then**
7:     **if** $A_i.getRole() == Role.COORDINATION$ **then**
8:       $aspect \leftarrow getRequestAspectForMessage(A_i, input);$
9:     **else**
10:      $aspect \leftarrow getRequestAspectForEvent(A_i, input);$
11:    **end if**
12:    $input \leftarrow executeMethod(aspect, A_i.getAdvice(), input);$
13: **end if**
14: **end while**
15: $output \leftarrow input;$

---

aspect or the corresponding advice to invoke. In lines from 4 to 14, the weaving
of the aspects included in A is performed. The first step is to check if the input
holds the restriction included in the *AspectDescription* (line 6). In this case, we
need to know the role that the aspect plays in the agent architecture. If the
aspect encapsulates the coordination of the agent using a coordination protocol
(*Role.COORDINATION* in line 7), then the input is handled as a message and
on the contrary is handled as an event. At runtime, aspects can be active or
not, so in the methods in line 8 and 10, aspects are selected if are active or
instantiated in the case they are not. It is different to instantiate an aspect for a
message and for an event. In the case of messages we can have multiple aspects
of the same coordination protocol active that corresponds with different conversation of the agent. So we have to select/instantiate the aspect for the specific
conversation. In the other case, there is a single instance of the corresponding
aspect described in *AspectDescription*. When the aspect is selected, the advice
is executed (line 12) and the output is assigned (line 15).

2.4   The Monitoring Function

The monitoring function gathers information from the external world and the
internal agent configuration and updates the *SystemContext* with it. The interface with the real world is modeled as a set of *Facet* elements, that encapsulates
the sensing of a specific resource. There are facets that are passive and needs
to be explicitly inquired, while others are active, and provide their measures by
events. Facets decouple the sensed resource from the sensing function and allows
to have multiple monitoring aspects specialized for a specific context. For example, in the *VisitorAgent*, which is aware of its battery level and consumption,

a single facet element provides battery-related measures, and two monitoring aspects gather measures about current battery level and the battery life from it.

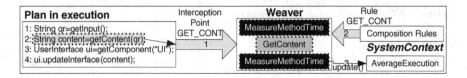

Fig. 2. Aspect weaving process example for response time monitoring in *VisitorAgent*

For an agent that is running in a lightweight device there are a number of issues that can be monitored: (i) a resource of the system; (ii) the response time of a function, this comes from the time required to execute an operation; and (iii) the quality of context information.

The behavior of a *Monitor* aspect consists of periodically collecting data from a source of information. These aspects are configured at runtime to monitor a given *Facet* element. So, each monitor aspect follows certain settings for measurement, which determines, for instance, the frequency of getting a new sample. These settings can be reconfigured at runtime in order to save resources.

In order to collect the measure data which is provided by means of events, the monitoring is based in *ContextAware* aspects, that encapsulate the context dependant behavior of the agent. These aspects are usually affected by the interception point *THRW_EVNT* and the advice *handleEvent* described in Section 2.3. This kind of monitoring allows the agent to be aware of the state of the other agents in the system (using heart beat monitors). In the case of the *SecurityAgent* that must be aware of the presence of people in the museum, it can receive alive signals from *GuideAgents*.

The monitoring of the response time of a system requires the modification of the source code introducing not desirable delays when this information is not necessary. AO enables this kind of monitoring and provides a mechanism to disable it to avoid delays even at runtime. As stated in Section 2.3, the weaving mechanism of our agent is extensible and allows new interception points to be added to the agent. An example of this is the case of the *VisitorAgent* that downloads information about the objects of the exposition. The downloading process can be measured if we extend the agent with a new interception point and method (*GET_CONT* and *getContent* respectively). The visitor uses a mobile phone to scan a QR code attached to an object, this generates a goal that causes the execution of the plan depicted in Figure 2. This plan uses as an input the QR code and retrieves the content using the method *getContent* of the *VisitorAgent*. The call of this function start the aspect weaving process, that follows the composition rule depicted in the center of Figure 2. In order to measure the time for getting the content, the aspect *MeasureMethodTime* is applied around (i.e. before and after) the aspect *GetContent*. After the aspect composition process, the plan has the content and the *SystemContext* is updated with the execution time of this method. Note that if we change the composition rule for this interception point removing the *MeasureMethodTime* aspect, we disable the time measurement function and avoid the delay introduced by it.

3 Discussion

The self-management of lightweight devices for the IoT is a very complex computing area, since many AI or formal techniques are unaffordable for these devices. The first issue to discuss is how to reason about all possible and even unexpected context changes, with limited resources. It is not realistic to provide solutions that consider all possibilities, due to the combinatorial explosion of the state space. So, we opt to define a limited set of observable elements and the elements that can be modified as part of a reconfiguration are also limited. Moreover, thanks to AO it is possible to perform reconfiguration actions very efficiently, as these actions are localized in certain elements, and the impact on the agent functioning is reduced. So, we consider that our approach is scalable regarding the list of context changes considered.

The correctness of the reconfiguration plans, is another key issue in self-management. With limited resources it is not affordable to validate and test each reconfiguration plan in all probable states at runtime. One possibility is to test the plan before executing, in terms of: (1) resource consumed by the plan execution; (2) the remaining energy after the plan is executed; (3) the quality of service. If the results are not good, then the plan is not executed and the corresponding goal is removed. But, this is merely a simulation, which cannot capture unexpected events. So, another possibility is to apply a transactional approach, which tests the plan after its execution. With this approach we can also verify if the agent gets into an unstable state as a consequence of the plan's execution, in which case a rollback mechanism is applied to take the system back to the previous stable state. But, this is not a trivial task since we need: (1) to undo a plan considering that some actions cannot be undone; (2) to store the complete agent previous state; (3) to detect what behavior is considered as an unstable state; (5) to identify which action caused the malfunction.

As we have said in previous sections, self-* are crosscutting, and improving one self-* can negatively impact on another self-*. For example, removing a security aspect improves the self-optimization of energy, but penalizes the self-protection. So, we are working on the incorporation of a suitable mechanism for dealing with conflictive system level goals [13], but we are still studying their feasibility for lightweight devices.

4 Conclusions

In this paper we have presented an AO solution for self-management of BDI-like agents for the IoT. Our approach, by exploiting aspects, gains in flexibility and modularity with respect to other agent-oriented frameworks. The use of AO mechanisms, allows us to address typical self-management functions in a non-intrusive manner. The proposed agent architecture addresses: (i) the explicit separation of the system context in a specific knowledge base; (ii) the definition of a configurable set of monitoring aspects in charge of monitoring system resources. We have used AO to improve the modularization of the agents' architecture, which makes: (i) the self-configuration of the agent internal components easier, and also (ii) the resultant agent architectural configuration is more resource-efficient, since only the minimum components are instantiated.

In previous work we have presented the general idea of this architecture and we have validated the self-management function using different tests [12] for agents running in sensors and Android lightweight devices, the presented work focus on the aspect composition process and how the AO can benefit the implementation of the self-management attributes.

Acknowledgments. This work has been supported by the Spanish Ministry Project RAP TIN2008-01942 and the regional project FamWare P09-TIC-5231.

References

1. Atzori, L., Iera, A., Morabito, G.: The internet of things: A survey. Computer Networks 54(15), 2787–2805 (2010)
2. Ayala, I., Amor, M., Fuentes, L.: Self-management of ambient intelligence systems: a pure agent-based approach. In: AAMAS 2012, pp. 1427–1428. IFAAMAS (June 2012)
3. Huebscher, M., McCann, J.: A survey of autonomic computing—degrees, models, and applications. ACM Computing Surveys (CSUR) 40(3), 7 (2008)
4. Marsh, D., Tynan, R., O'Kane, D., P O'Hare, G.: Autonomic wireless sensor networks. Engineering Applications of Artificial Intelligence 17(7), 741–748 (2004)
5. Chun, I., Park, J., Lee, H., Kim, W., Park, S., Lee, E.: An agent-based self-adaptation architecture for implementing smart devices in smart space. Telecommunication Systems, 1–12 (2011)
6. Amor, M., Fuentes, L.: Malaca: A component and aspect-oriented agent architecture. Information and Software Technology 51(6), 1052–1065 (2009)
7. Garcia, A.F., de Lucena, C.J.P., Cowan, D.D.: Agents in object-oriented software engineering. Software: Practice and Experience 34(5), 489–521 (2004)
8. Engel, M., Freisleben, B.: Supporting autonomic computing functionality via dynamic operating system kernel aspects. In: AOSD 2005, pp. 51–62. ACM (2005)
9. Chan, H., Chieu, T.: An approach to monitor application states for self-managing (autonomic) systems. In: OOPSLA 2003, pp. 312–313. ACM (2003)
10. Janik, A., Zielinski, K.: Aaop-based dynamically reconfigurable monitoring system. Information and Software Technology 52(4), 380–396 (2010)
11. Dobson, S., Sterritt, R., Nixon, P., Hinchey, M.: Fulfilling the vision of autonomic computing. Computer 43(1), 35–41 (2010)
12. Ayala, I., Amor, M., Fuentes, L.: Self-configuring agents for ambient assisted living applications. Personal and Ubiquitous Computing, 1–11 (2012)
13. Pokahr, A., Braubach, L., Lamersdorf, W.: A goal deliberation strategy for bdi agent systems. Multiagent System Technologies, 82–93 (2005)

Distributed Learning of Best Response Behaviors in Concurrent Iterated Many-Object Negotiations

Jan Ole Berndt and Otthein Herzog

Center for Computing and Communication Technologies (TZI), Universität Bremen, Germany
{joberndt,herzog}@tzi.de

Abstract. Iterated negotiations are a well-established method for coordinating distributed activities in multiagent systems. However, if several of these take place concurrently, the participants' activities can mutually influence each other. In order to cope with the problem of interrelated interaction outcomes in partially observable environments, we apply distributed reinforcement learning to concurrent many-object negotiations. To this end, we discuss iterated negotiations from the perspective of repeated games, specify the agents' learning behavior, and introduce decentral decision-making criteria for terminating a negotiation. Furthermore, we empirically evaluate the approach in a multiagent resource allocation scenario. The results show that our method enables the agents to successfully learn mutual best response behaviors which approximate Nash equilibrium allocations. Additionally, the learning constrains the required interaction effort for attaining these results.

1 Introduction

Iterated negotiations are a well-established means for coordinating distributed activities in multiagent systems. Autonomous agents can negotiate on allocations of resources, delegations of tasks, as well as commissions of services. This enables them to identify appropriate partners which complement their own capabilities in order to meet their individual objectives [5,15].

Nevertheless, a problem occurs if several of these interactions take place concurrently. In this situation, the participants' activities can mutually influence each other. That is, the outcome of each negotiation depends on those being performed simultaneously. This is particularly the case in many-object negotiations which require the agents to compromise about their desired agreements. In order to enable efficient and robust multiagent coordination, the agents have to take these interdependencies into account when selecting and evaluating their respective actions in iterated negotiations. That is, they must adapt their behavior to the activities of others.

In a competitive setting, a game theoretical equilibrium [11] denotes a combination of each individual agent's best response to the others' behaviors. However, acting in a partially observable environment, the agents are unable to explicitly compute such an equilibrium. Therefore, we propose to approximate it by means of agents adapting their activities to each other. To this end, we apply distributed reinforcement learning to agent decision-making in iterated multiagent negotiations. Using this technique, each agent learns a best response behavior to the others' activities without the necessity to

I.J. Timm and C. Guttmann (Eds.): MATES 2012, LNAI 7598, pp. 15–29, 2012.

directly observe them. This results in an equilibrium of mutual best responses to implicitly emerge from the agents' concurrent learning efforts.

We structure this paper as follows. Section 2 elaborates on concurrent iterated many-object negotiations and discusses their challenges as well as existing approaches to address them. Subsequently, Section 3 presents the main contribution of this paper which is twofold. First, we model concurrent negotiations as repeated games and propose multiagent learning for coordinating them; second, we introduce decentral decision-making criteria for terminating these negotiations. Section 4 empirically evaluates this approach in a distributed resource allocation scenario. Finally, Section 5 concludes on the achievements of this paper and outlines directions for future research.

2   Iterated Multiagent Negotiations

Iterated multiagent negotiations denote a process of distributed search for an agreement among two or more participants [8]. This process consists of the *negotiation objects*, an *interaction protocol*, the participating *agents*, and their *decision-making* mechanisms. The negotiation objects determine the search space of potential agreements. In the process, the agents exchange proposals which their counterparts can either accept or reject. While the protocol defines the possible sequences of messages, an agent selects its actions among those possibilities by means of its decision-making mechanism. If the agents find a mutually acceptable agreement according to their individual preferences, the search returns this solution as its result. Otherwise, it terminates without success.

In the following, we further elaborate on these aspects of multiagent negotiations. In particular, Section 2.1 examines negotiation objects and protocols. This provides the foundations for discussing the challenges of agent decision-making as well as existing approaches to cope with these challenges in Section 2.2.

2.1   Negotiation Objects and Protocols

The negotiation objects define the topic on which the participating agents attempt to reach agreement [8]. They cover the target of a negotiation such as the desired service fulfillment or resource allocation. Moreover, they denote the cardinality of these items: Either single or multiple ones. In the latter case, the agents negotiate on possible combinations of the target products or services. In these many-object negotiations, they must identify a mutually acceptable compromise out of the range of those combinations. In the following, we concentrate on many-object negotiations as they subsume the special case of single-object ones as well as meeting the requirements of a wide range of application domains [1].

To structure the negotiation process, there are two basic protocol types for exchanging proposals [8]. In *auction type* negotiations, one or more agents exclusively propose potential agreements while the others only accept or reject them. An example for this is the Dutch auction in which the auctioneer repeatedly decreases the proposed price until one or more buyers accept the current offer. Contrastingly, in negotiations of the *bargaining type* the agents bilaterally exchange offers and counter-offers. Hence, they mutually attempt to steer the search in their individually favored direction. On the one

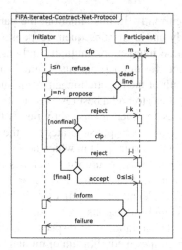

Fig. 1. The FIPA Iterated Contract Net interaction protocol (adapted from [6])

hand, this increases the speed of reaching an agreement; on the other hand, it requires all participants to be capable of both evaluating and generating meaningful proposals [5]. In this paper we mainly focus on negotiations of the auction type. Nevertheless, in Section 3.3 we also suggest to adapt our approach to bargaining type interactions.

A well-known protocol for iterated auction type negotiations is the FIPA Iterated Contract Net [6] as depicted in Figure 1. It is particularly suitable for situations in which a consumer agent attempts to find the best partner among the potential providers of a required service or product. In many-object negotiations, this can also be a set of agents if no single participant is able to fulfill the initiator's demands on its own. However, this approach requires the initiator to address all potential participants from the beginning on as there is no way to include additional agents during the process. If the initial selection is insufficient to fulfill the initiator's requirements, the whole negotiation will fail.

In large multiagent systems, including all possible participants induces a lot of interaction effort [15]. To overcome this issue, we slightly modify the original FIPA protocol. Instead of narrowing the set of participants to a subset of the initial receivers in each iteration, we allow for including alternative ones while keeping their overall number constant. That is, the initiator selects a fixed number m of participants and replaces those $m - k$ which propose none or only unacceptable agreements (*refuse/reject*) with alternative candidates. Thus, it refills the set of receivers for the next iteration's *call for proposals (cfp)* with x new ones to a size of $k + x = m$. This keeps the number of participating agents (and therewith the interaction effort) reasonably low.

2.2 Agent Decision-Making: Challenges and Related Work

If there is exclusively one single initiator agent at any time, its decision-making in the aforementioned protocol is simple. It only requires to keep track of the participants' offers to identify the currently best agreement, *accept* it when no further improvements occur, and *reject* all other proposals. However, this is not the case if several of these interactions take place concurrently. In this situation, the participants receive several *cfp* messages simultaneously and their subsequent responses depend on all of these messages. Consequently, these interactions mutually influence each other's outcome as the initiator agents compete for the participants' limited capacities. In order to still achieve the best possible result of the negotiation, an agent must take the actions of all others into account. That is, it has to find a best response to its counterparts' behaviors.

Determining best responses to other agents' activities is the subject of game theory [19]. If all agents pursue a best response strategy to the behaviors of the others, these strategies form a Nash equilibrium [11] in which no single agent can benefit from changing its current behavior. A Nash equilibrium denotes the agents' best possible activities in such a strictly competitive setting. Moreover, by approximating best responses to the others' behaviors, an agent maximizes its individual payoff, even if they fail to establish a corresponding best response in return. Therefore, each agent should select its actions in an iterated negotiation with respect to its counterparts' behaviors.

Existing methods for computing an equilibrium of mutual best responses often evaluate the structure of the game and suffer from a high computational complexity [12]. Nevertheless, each agent only has to identify its own best strategy. Consequently, it requires a decision-making method for finding its most beneficial activities, given the actions of the others. A well-known technique for this is the *minimax* rule [18] of 2-player decision-making and its generalization for *n*-player settings [10]. By assuming the others to pursue their most beneficial courses of actions, this rule selects the best response to those behaviors. As a result, an equilibrium emerges from the agents' mutually dependent action selections.

However, in concurrent negotiations, the *minimax* approach requires an agent to be aware of the other participating agents, their possible actions as well as their preferences (i.e., their scoring functions for the interaction's outcome). For competitive distributed negotiations, disclosing these trade secrets is inappropriate [5]. Consequently, the agents act in a partially observable environment as they must coordinate their negotiation behaviors while preserving the privacy of information. To achieve the latter, *combinatorial auctions* [4] provide a means for computing the best allocation of goods or services in a mediated interaction process. In these auctions, the participants express their preferences as bids on combinations of offered items. While such a bid represents the result of an agent's valuation of an offer, it hides the agent's private method for attaining that assessment. Moreover, combinatorial auctions are particularly suitable for many objects as the participants can express bids on arbitrary combinations. Nonetheless, the winner determination is a centralized process which creates a computational bottleneck [13]. This is undesirable in distributed systems.

To overcome this problem, we propose to enable the agents to learn best responses to each other's actions from observations of their personal performance. Deriving beliefs about successful behavior from the outcome of past interactions has been shown to enable the approximation of market equilibria in repeated trading activities [7]. That is, buyers and sellers determine mutually acceptable prices for the traded items by estimating the probabilities of reaching an agreement for potential price offers. Nevertheless, this requires the presence of a common currency to express those prices. In order to allow for best responses according to generic utility assessments, we rather apply *reinforcement learning* [17] to multiagent negotiations. This technique enables the agents to individually identify their most beneficial actions by observing the outcome of their own activities and adapting their behavior. To accomplish this, an agent receives a reward when performing an action from which it learns an estimation of the expected reward for potential future actions. Subsequently, it can select the next action based on this estimation. Multiagent reinforcement learning [2] has been applied successfully to approximate best response behaviors in distributed coordination tasks [3,1]. Therefore, it is a promising approach for determining an agent's most beneficial strategy in concurrent iterated negotiations.

3 Multiagent Learning in Iterated Negotiations

In the following, we apply multiagent reinforcement learning to concurrent iterated many-object negotiations. Section 3.1 interprets them as repeated games and provides a formal notation for the agents' decision-making environments and behaviors. Subsequently, Section 3.2 applies a stateless version of the *Q-learning* approach to agent decision-making in the aforementioned Iterated Contract Net. Finally, Section 3.3 discusses criteria for determining acceptable offers to terminate such a negotiation.

3.1 Iterated Multiagent Negotiations as Repeated Games

In order to facilitate a better understanding of the interdependencies of concurrent agent activities in iterated negotiations, we formalize them using the terminology of game theory and reinforcement learning. From this point of view, a single iteration of a multiagent negotiation is a *static (stateless) game*. In such a game, each of the agents simultaneously executes one action and receives a reward depending on all of these actions. Its formal definition is as follows [2].

Definition 1 (Static Game). *A static game is a triple* $\langle N, \mathcal{A}, R \rangle$. *$N$ is a set of agents being indexed $1, \ldots, n$. Each agent $i \in N$ has a finite set of atomic actions $\mathcal{A}_i$. Thus, $\mathcal{A} = (\mathcal{A}_1, \ldots, \mathcal{A}_n)$. $R = (R_1, \ldots, R_n)$ is the collection of individual reward functions for each agent i. Each $R_i : 2^{\mathcal{A}_1} \times \ldots \times 2^{\mathcal{A}_n} \to \mathbb{R}$ returns i's immediate reward for the simultaneous execution of sets of agent actions $A_1, \ldots, A_n$ with $A_j \subseteq \mathcal{A}_j, \forall j \in N$.*

In a concurrently executed Contract Net, the set of agents N consists of the initiators of the simultaneous negotiations. Each of them selects a set of participants to send them its *calls for proposals* specifying the negotiation objects. Thus, agent i's individual actions $\mathcal{A}_i$ contain all of these possible messages in conjunction with their respective receivers. As we consider many-object negotiations, the agent selects a set $A_i \subseteq \mathcal{A}_i$ of messages which contains a *cfp* for each single item. Instead of distributing the rewards directly, the participants subsequently respond with some *proposals* or *refuse* messages. A participant's responses depend on the entirety of messages it received in the current iteration. Each initiator can rate its individually received responses by calculating their respective payoff (i.e., the negotiation's expected outcome if it accepts the received offers). Thus, an agent obtains the conditional reward for its actions, even though it is unable to observe the actions of the others. Iterating this one-shot negotiation several times results in a *stage game* [2]. This repeated game describes the agents' decision-making environment during concurrent iterated negotiations. Only in its final iteration, an agent bindingly *accepts* or *rejects* its received offers. Until then, it can use the stage game to learn the most beneficial actions for that last static game.

In order to accomplish this learning, the agents repeatedly observe the payoff of their respective activities which enables them to reason about their expected reward in further iterations. In particular, a rational agent has the objective to maximize its personal payoff. Hence, it attempts to adopt a behavior which is a *best response* to the other agents' actions. In game theoretical terms, a deterministic best response strategy returns a combination of actions which maximizes an agent's payoff, given the actions of all others [2].

Definition 2 (Best Response). *A best response of agent $i \in N$ to the other agents' sets of actions $A_1, \ldots, A_{i-1}, A_{i+1}, \ldots, A_n$ is a collection of actions $A_i^* \subseteq \mathcal{A}_i$, such that $R_i(A_1, \ldots, A_i^*, \ldots, A_n) \geq R_i(A_1, \ldots, A_i, \ldots, A_n)$, $\forall A_i \subseteq \mathcal{A}_i$.*

In a competitive environment, each agent strives to maximize its individual payoff on its own. Therefore, all agents mutually attempt to find a best response to each other's activities. Such a situation, in which no single agent can beneficially deviate from its current behavior, forms a *Nash equilibrium* [11]. For deterministic agent strategies, this is defined as follows.

Definition 3 (Nash Equilibrium). *A Nash equilibrium is a vector $\left(A_1^*, \ldots, A_n^*\right)$, such that $\forall i \in N$, each action set A_i^* is a best response to the others.*

A Nash equilibrium does not ensure that the agents maximize their common payoff in the form of a social welfare optimum.[1] Nonetheless, it denotes each agent's best possible actions relative to the others' activities if all agents attempt to maximize their individual payoff. The objective of each agent in concurrent iterated negotiations is to identify such best response actions in order to select them in their decision-making. However, the agents are unable to directly determine whether their concurrent activities form a Nash equilibrium as there is no entity which can observe all of these behaviors. Instead, they must derive the best responses solely from their individual payoffs for the performed actions. If every agent succeeds in this endeavor, a Nash equilibrium emerges from their distributed efforts.

3.2   Distributed Reinforcement Learning for Iterated Negotiations

In order to enable an agent to determine its best response behavior without observing the others' actions, we apply *reinforcement learning (RL)* [17] to its decision-making in iterated multiagent negotiations. In a stage game, this technique allows for the agent to learn from its experiences to increase its future performance.

A well-understood RL algorithm for the case of one single learning agent is *Q-learning* [20]. In its stateless form, this algorithm estimates expected rewards (action

---

[1] A famous example for this is the prisoner's dilemma in which the equilibrium point is the only strategy combination not belonging to the Pareto frontier.

payoffs) as *Q-values* $Q(a)$ for each possible action a [3]. The agent uses the following update rule to refine its estimation when observing a reward $R(a)$ for action a.

$$Q(a) \leftarrow Q(a) + \lambda \cdot (R(a) - Q(a)) \tag{1}$$

If each action is sampled infinitely often, the agent's Q-values converge to the unobservable true values Q^* for every learning rate $0 < \lambda \leq 1$ [20,3]. This enables the learning agent to select its activities according to their expected payoff values. Hence, as the values converge, it can identify its individually optimal action.

However, the convergence property of single agent Q-learning does not hold for a distributed setting in which several agents simultaneously adapt their behaviors to each other. This results in non-stationary rewards as they depend on the combination of all concurrently executed actions. Therefore, the following two additional conditions become necessary to ensure the emergence of mutual best response behaviors [3,1].

1. At any time, every possible action of an agent must have a non-zero probability of being selected.
2. An agent's action selection strategy must be asymptotically exploitive.

Condition 1 ensures the infinite sampling of all agent actions for $t \rightarrow \infty$. Furthermore, it prevents the agents from executing strictly correlated explorations. That is, no combination of agent actions becomes impossible to occur. This is an extension of the infinite sampling requirement for single agent Q-learning: In a multiagent setting, each combination of actions must be executed infinitely often due to the payoff's dependence on all concurrently triggered other actions. Condition 2 requires the agents to pursue a *decaying* exploration strategy. This decreases the probability of concurrent exploration activities over time. Hence, the agents become less likely to disturb each other and their Q-values can settle. Although a formal proof of this behavior is still missing, the empirical evidence in [3] and [1] strongly supports this assumption.

In order to apply this technique to iterated negotiations, we construct the initiator agent's behavior as depicted in Figure 2. This behavior extends the message passing activities as specified in the FIPA Iterated Contract Net protocol definition [6] with an initialization step as well as the following repeatedly executed activities.

1. *Selecting* the receivers and contents for the next *calls for proposals*.
2. *Learning* from the observed responses.
3. *Deciding* on whether to terminate or continue the negotiation.

When entering a negotiation, each learning agent $i \in N$ initializes its *Q-Base* Q_i in which it stores the expected payoffs $Q_i(a_i)$ for all its possible atomic actions $a_i \in \mathcal{A}_i$. Its individual actions $\mathcal{A}_i$ consist of all *cfp* messages, given by their possible contents and receivers. The message contents depend on the agent's preferences toward the negotiation object and the receivers correspond to the possible providers of that object.

Subsequently, the agent enters the iterated part of the negotiation. To select the next action, it considers all meaningful message combinations $A_i \subseteq \mathcal{A}_i$ and looks up the stored Q-values $Q_i(a_i)$ of their components $a_i \in A_i$. Maintaining a Q-base for the atomic actions instead of their combinations keeps the required storage space small when using

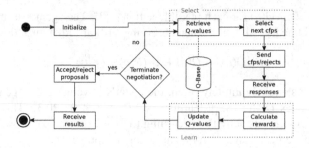

Fig. 2. Behavior of a learning initiator agent in the Iterated Contract Net

a lookup table [1]. Nevertheless, this requires the corresponding rewards $R_i(a_i)$ to be mutually independent. This is because the agent must aggregate its Q-values to identify the expectedly most beneficial message combinations $max\mathcal{A}_i \subseteq 2^{\mathcal{A}_i}$.

$$max\mathcal{A}_i = \arg\max_{A_i \subseteq \mathcal{A}_i} \left(\sum_{a_i \in A_i} Q_i(a_i) \right) \tag{2}$$

Choosing an action set from $max\mathcal{A}_i$ corresponds to a greedy strategy which maximizes the agent's expected payoff based on its experiences so far. However, in order to find out whether there is an even better option, the agent also has to explore alternative ones. To this end, we propose to use an ε-greedy strategy. That is, in iteration t of the negotiation, the agent selects its next actions $A_{i,t}$ from $max\mathcal{A}_i$ with a probability of $1 - \varepsilon$ (with $0 < \varepsilon \leq 1$). If there is more than one best option, it chooses randomly among them. Alternatively, with a probability of ε, the agent selects $A_{i,t}$ at random out of all suitable action sets in $2^{\mathcal{A}_i}$. Moreover, to ensure the aforementioned asymptotically exploitive selection with non-zero probabilities, it employs a *decaying* ε-greedy strategy. This requires a sequence ε_n with $\lim_{t \to \infty} \varepsilon_t = 0$ and $\forall t < \infty : \varepsilon_t > 0$. An example meeting these requirements is the *harmonic sequence*[2] with $\varepsilon_t = \frac{1}{t}, \forall t > 0$. This sequence leads to high exploration rates in the beginning of the negotiation which decrease over time. Once an agent has identified a highly rated combination of actions, it increasingly tends to stick to those actions as time proceeds.

After selecting the next actions, sending the chosen messages, and collecting the respective responses, the agent proceeds with the learning part of its behavior. To assess the usefulness of the selected actions $A_{i,t}$, it evaluates the response messages $result(a_{i,t})$, $\forall a_{i,t} \in A_{i,t}$ by means of a utility measure $U_i : \{result(a_i) \,|\, \forall a_i \in \mathcal{A}_i\} \to [0, 1]$. It uses the result of this calculation as the action's immediate reward $R_i(a_{i,t})$.

$$R_i(a_{i,t}) = U_i(result(a_{i,t})) \tag{3}$$

As the response messages depend on the concurrent actions of all agents participating in the negotiation, their utility implicitly reflects these actions as well. Therefore, it is sufficient for each learning agent to evaluate only the observable responses instead of

---

[2] That is, the sequence constituting the *harmonic series* which is defined as $\sum_{n=1}^{\infty} \frac{1}{n}$.

receiving a conditional reward for all simultaneous activities. In order to learn from this observation, the agent subsequently applies the standard update rule as in Equation 1 to modify its stored Q-value $Q_i(a_{i,t})$ for all performed actions $a_{i,t} \in A_{i,t}$. In the succeeding iteration, the refined entries in the Q-Base serve as the new Q-values for these actions.

According to the aforementioned convergence property of the Q-learning rule, an infinite number of these iterations will lead to each agent learning the best response to the others' activities. Hence, a Nash equilibrium will emerge from these distributed learning processes in concurrent negotiations. Nonetheless, an infinite negotiation never comes to a final result. To avoid this, each agent must decide after an iteration either to accept its received response messages as the result and terminate the negotiation or to continue it in the attempt to reach a better outcome. That is, while learning the best behavior for the repeated interaction process, it must eventually apply its findings to one single iteration to bring about a result of the negotiation. To facilitate this decision-making, the following section discusses individual tactics for terminating iterated negotiations.

3.3   Termination Criteria for Iterated Negotiations

A learning agent as specified in the preceding section is unable to determine whether it has already developed a best response behavior or not. This is because it would have to know all other agents' possible actions as well as their actual selections, the participants' respective responses, and the agents' utility measures for evaluating these responses. However, disclosing this information is inappropriate for competitive negotiations (cf. Section 2.2). As an alternative, negotiation *tactics* enable reaching individually acceptable agreements without requiring additional information. These tactics model an agent's bidding behavior in bargaining type negotiations consisting of offers and counter-offers. They can depend on the amount of *time* or other *resources* being available as well as on the observable bidding *behavior* of the negotiation opponents [5]. Such a tactic provides a function which approaches the agent's private *reservation value* in the course of the negotiation. This value denotes the minimal offer it is willing to accept. Thus, unless the agents come to a better agreement at some time during the negotiation, the reservation value denotes its last offer on which it insists until the end of the negotiation. If at some point in time neither agent concedes any further, the negotiation terminates without success.

In contrast to bargaining negotiations, in auction type mechanisms like the Iterated Contract Net it is unnecessary to generate counter-offers. Instead, the initiator agents only require a decision function which indicates whether or not one or more received *proposals* are acceptable. To this end, an agent must consider the payoff of the current offers. These values are already available from the reinforcement learning algorithm (Equation 3). Thus, we define agent i's decision function in dependence of its utility measure U_i for evaluating the perceived results of its actions. Analogously to the bargaining tactics, the agent has a *reservation level* of utilities U_{res}. This is the minimum utility it will accept for the *last offers* of the negotiation. If the reservation level turns out to be unreachable, it will terminate the negotiation without coming to an agreement.

However, in order to maximize its payoff, the agent must explore alternative actions in the course of the negotiation. Therefore, it should abstain from choosing the first option exceeding its reservation level as the final one. Only if it fails to achieve a better

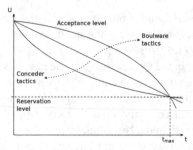

Fig. 3. Termination criteria based on acceptance and reservation utility levels

result, the agent should accept the current offer. To this end, we introduce an agent's *acceptance level* of utilities U_{acc} which denotes the minimum aggregated utility for the *current offers* to be acceptable. Varying over time during a negotiation, the acceptance level resembles an agent's tactic in bargaining: It consists of a function describing the agent's behavior of conceding to its reservation level. To enable the agent to benefit from its learning ability, this function starts from a sufficiently high value and decreases monotonically over time. As a result, the agent rejects all but the best offers in the early iterations. Nevertheless, if the offers' utility repeatedly fails to exceed the acceptance level, it becomes increasingly inclined to compromise about that utility.

Following from these considerations, an agent successfully terminates a negotiation in iteration t if the received offers' aggregated utility exceeds the current acceptance level: $U_{acc,t} < \sum_{a_{i,t} \in A_{i,t}} U_i(result(a_{i,t}))$. Furthermore, it terminates the process without success if the acceptance level falls below the reservation level: $U_{acc,t} < U_{res}$. In the first case, the agents come to an acceptable agreement. In the second case, they failed to reach an agreement under the least acceptable conditions. Figure 3 depicts these termination criteria for a range of acceptance level functions. Analogously to the concession behaviors in bargaining negotiations, these functions tend toward either the well-known *Boulware* or the *Conceder* tactics [5]. While the former attempts to reach a highly valued agreement as long as possible, the latter quickly approaches the reservation level.

In order to implement these tactics, we modify the polynomial time dependent function presented in [5] according to the aforementioned considerations. In the resulting function, the acceptance level $U_{acc,t}$ in iteration t ranges between the initial value $U_{acc,0}$ and the reservation level U_{res} as long as t adheres to a given deadline t_{max}. Moreover, the acceptance level is strictly monotonically decreasing if $U_{acc,0} > U_{res}$ and t_{max} is constant.

$$U_{acc,t} = U_{acc,0} - (U_{acc,0} - U_{res}) \cdot \left(\frac{t}{t_{max}} \right)^{\beta} \qquad (4)$$

According to this equation, the negotiation is guaranteed to terminate for all $t_{max} < \infty$. The parameter β controls the agent's concession behavior: While it pursues a Boulware tactic if $\beta > 1$, each $\beta < 1$ leads to a Conceder behavior. The intensity of these tactics increases the more β deviates from 1 (with $\beta = 1$ denoting the *neutral* linear tactic).

By means of Equation 4, an agent controls its negotiation behavior. Setting t_{max} to a fixed point in time allows for modeling situations in which the agents must finish their negotiation before some deadline exceeds. Moreover, this approach is also suitable to model resource and behavior dependent tactics. In the former case, t_{max} depends on a heuristic assessment of the availability of resources (e.g., the number of relevant service providers). If the agent updates its assessment during the negotiation, this will result in a dynamically shifting deadline, depending on its perceived pressure to come to an agreement [5]. Similarly, the agent can also adapt t_{max} to the behavior of the negotiation's participants and the progress of its learning (e.g., by delaying its concession while the received offers improve). Nevertheless, the dynamic approaches bear the risk of generating non-monotonic tactics. In bargaining, such tactics allow for bids to both approach as well as depart from an agent's reservation value. While these can be beneficial [21], they are often undesirable as they make a negotiation's outcome unpredictable and delay the process of reaching an agreement [14]. Thus, an agent designer must be careful when applying them.

In conjunction with the reinforcement learning technique, these termination criteria enable agents in concurrent multiagent negotiations to adjust their behaviors according to each other's distributed activities. While the learning approach leads to best responses of an agent to the unobservable behaviors of others, the termination criteria control the negotiation's duration. Moreover, deriving from negotiation tactics in bargaining, the latter even offer the possibility to transfer this approach to bilateral negotiations. As the acceptance level denotes the minimum utility for an agreement, an agent can invert its utility measure to generate counter-proposals to the perceived offers. If a common currency is used, this is easy to accomplish by mapping the learned values to price offers [7]. However, we leave the generalization of this adaptation as well as the analysis of its requirements and implications to future research.

4   Evaluation

In order to evaluate the proposed learning approach in iterated multiagent negotiations, we apply it to a many-object resource allocation problem using the simulation system PlaSMA [16]. Our scenario is an abstraction from a kind of problems occurring frequently in real-world applications like production scheduling and logistics [1]. In this scenario, n resource consumer agents concurrently negotiate with $m = n \cdot k$ resource providers as depicted in Figure 4. Each provider has one resource unit and each consumer requires k units. Thus, every bijection between the set of consumers and any partition of the set of providers into n subsets of size k forms an optimal allocation. In this case, each consumer allocates its required amount of resources without interfering with the others. Consequently, these mutual best responses in the scenario constitute its Nash equilibria which are also Pareto optimal and vice versa.

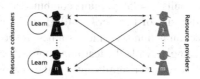

Fig. 4. Many-object resource allocation scenario with n consumers and $m = n \cdot k$ providers

To approximate a mutual best response allocation, the consumers act as initiators of a concurrent iterated negotiation. In each iteration, a consumer selects k providers for a *call for proposals*. If a provider still has its resource unit, it sends an offer for the allocation; otherwise it sends a *refusal*. In the case of a provider receiving two or more allocation attempts, it randomly selects one consumer for its offer and *refuses* all other *cfps*. The initiators evaluate these responses by means of the following utility function.

$$\forall a_{i,t} \in A_{i,t} : U_i(result(a_{i,t})) = \frac{1}{k} \cdot \begin{cases} 1 & \text{if } result(a_{i,t}) \text{ is a } propose \text{ message} \\ 0 & \text{otherwise} \end{cases} \tag{5}$$

Our evaluation assesses the capability of the proposed approach to approximate an allocation with the aforementioned properties and the required interaction effort for accomplishing this. To this end, we test it in a scenario with 50 homogeneously parameterized consumer agents with varying numbers k of negotiated objects per agent and different acceptance tactics β. For their learning, they use a learning rate of $\lambda = 0.4$ and an exploration rate of $\varepsilon_t = \frac{1}{(t+1)^{0.3}}$ for each iteration $t \geq 0$. For each agent $i \in N$ and every atomic action $a_i \in \mathcal{A}_i$, the initial Q-values are set to $Q_i(a_i) = 0$. This leads to a purely explorative behavior in the beginning of the negotiation and in case of repeated *refusals*. This initialization and randomized action selection avoids a premature over-estimation of potential agreements in the case of colliding allocation attempts. Nonetheless, as soon as an agent observes a (partially) successful combination of actions, it utilizes the ε-greedy strategy to exploit its experience. Thus, the agent increasingly tends to stick to those actions which have been beneficial in past iterations.

For terminating the negotiation, the agents employ a time dependent criterion as specified in Equation 4. They use an initial acceptance level of $U_{acc,0} = 1$, a reservation level of $U_{res} = 0.25$, and a deadline of $t_{max} = 800$ iterations. Furthermore, to assess the respective impact of learning and termination on the overall result, we compare their combined performance with that of a non-learning benchmark approach. Instead of keeping track of an agent's experience, the latter randomly selects k resource providers in each iteration while using the same acceptance tactic as a learning agent. Each experiment consists of 500 simulation runs.

Figure 5 depicts the average utility of a negotiation's results over all agents for varying k and β together with the respective standard deviation. A utility of one for all agents denotes an optimal allocation which is also a Nash equilibrium of mutual best response actions. The results for a constant $\beta = 1$ show that for small numbers of negotiated objects the acceptance behavior alone is sufficient to approximate the equilibrium (utility: 0.985 ± 0.006). However, for larger k, it fails to maintain this performance (0.667 ± 0.004 for $k = 40$). This is due to the rapidly increasing number of meaningful agent action sets $A_i \in \binom{\mathcal{A}_i}{k}$, consisting of all k-sized combinations of allocation requests (with $|\mathcal{A}_i| = n \cdot k$). For $n = 50$ and $k = 2$, this results in 4950 possible combined actions whereas an agent's space of action sets exceeds a size of 10^{83} for $k = 40$. Hence, it is almost impossible for an agent to randomly select an action set which is a best response to all other agents' actions for large k. Contrastingly, while the learning approach suffers from this combinatorial explosion as well, it shows a significantly better performance (0.997 ± 0.004 for $k = 2$ and 0.937 ± 0.004 for $k = 40$). Because of the agents' ability to learn expected payoffs for atomic actions $a_i \in \mathcal{A}_i$ they can avoid exploring all these combined actions.

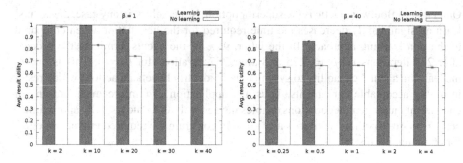

Fig. 5. Average utility of the negotiation's result for varying k (left) and β (right)

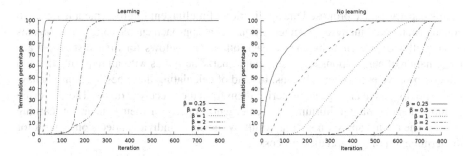

Fig. 6. Percentage of agents which already terminated the negotiation before iteration t

In fact, they can stick to successful atomic actions and aggregate them to beneficial sets of allocation attempts which drastically decreases their number of actions to explore.

Nevertheless, in order to learn which actions are most advantageous, an agent requires enough time to identify them and to explore possible alternatives. Therefore, its acceptance tactic influences its performance to a great extent as it controls how long the agent is willing to wait for finding an action with a highly rated outcome. Consequently, the results for $k = 40$ with a varying β (Figure 5, right) show a better performance of learning agents which follow a Boulware tactic (0.993 ± 0.005 for $\beta = 4$) than of those with a Conceder behavior (0.778 ± 0.008 for $\beta = 0.25$). In contrast to that, the pursued tactic is largely irrelevant for the non-learning agents because of their difficulty to explore any high payoff action sets.

However, the performance gain of the Boulware tactics comes at the cost of an increased interaction effort. As Figure 6 depicts, the agents terminate the negotiation much faster for Conceder tactics than for Boulware ones in the aforementioned experiment with $k = 40$. While 95% of the learning agents come to an acceptable agreement after 27 iterations for $\beta = 0.25$, the same amount of agents requires 377 iterations for $\beta = 4$. Thus, the agents trade the quality of their individual agreements off against the effort to achieve them. The acceptance tactics allow for controlling the balance of these opposing aspects. That is, an agent fares best with a Conceder behavior if it weights the interaction effort and the time to reach an agreement higher than its quality.

Otherwise, a Boulware tactic is the superior option. Nonetheless, in any case, the agents' learning significantly decreases the time required for the negotiation when compared to the non-learning approach. In the latter, 95% of the agents terminate the process after 239 iterations for $\beta = 0.25$ and after 757 iterations for $\beta = 4$. This is due to the learning agents' capability to systematically identify beneficial actions which result in highly acceptable agreements. Thus, the application of reinforcement learning in concurrent multiagent negotiations enables the agents both to successfully approximate best responses to others' activities as well as to constrain the required interaction effort for attaining this result.

5   Conclusions and Outlook

In this paper we have proposed the application of multiagent reinforcement learning to concurrent iterated many-object negotiations. That approach enables negotiating agents to mutually adapt their behaviors to each other. This allows for their distributed approximation of best responses to their counterparts' activities without requiring them to directly observe each other's actions. Instead of calculating these best response behaviors explicitly, the learning agents derive them from their received offers. Therefore, the resulting behavioral equilibrium is an emergent property of their concurrent learning efforts. The agents approximate this result by means of individual decision criteria for the termination of a negotiation process.

For the empirical evaluation of this approach, we have applied it to a multiagent resource allocation scenario. The results show that the learning agents come to a close approximation of mutual best responses even in settings with a high number of action alternatives. They achieve the best results when using Boulware termination strategies which attempt to maximize their individual payoff as long as possible. On the one hand, while allowing for the learning process to converge, this tactic implies an increased interaction effort. On the other hand, the application of reinforcement learning drastically decreases this effort by itself. Therefore, the approach enables the agents both to successfully approximate best responses to each other's behaviors as well as to constrain the required effort for attaining these results.

Nevertheless, there are still questions open for future research. While we have briefly mentioned the possibility to transfer our method to bargaining type negotiations, its actual implementation and evaluation will be subject to future work. Moreover, additional analyses of our existing approach will facilitate a better understanding of its components and their interaction. In particular, to guarantee the convergence of the reinforcement learning part to mutual best responses, a further analytical assessment is necessary. Recently, an adaptation of distributed Q-learning has been shown to converge to Nash equilibria in standard competitive settings with two agents [9]. A similar analysis may provide deeper insights into the convergence properties of the mechanism used in this paper. Additionally, further empirical evaluations will focus on different scenarios with heterogeneously parameterized populations to assess the capabilities and limitations of distributed learning in concurrent iterated negotiations.

References

1. Berndt, J.O., Herzog, O.: Distributed Reinforcement Learning for Optimizing Resource Allocation in Autonomous Logistics Processes. In: Kreowski, H.-J., Scholz-Reiter, B., Thoben, K.-D. (eds.) LDIC 2012, Bremen (2012)
2. Buşoniu, L., Babuška, R., De Schutter, B.: Multi-agent Reinforcement Learning: An Overview. In: Srinivasan, D., Jain, L.C. (eds.) Innovations in Multi-Agent Systems and Applications - 1. SCI, vol. 310, pp. 183–221. Springer, Heidelberg (2010)
3. Claus, C., Boutilier, C.: The Dynamics of Reinforcement Learning in Cooperative Multiagent Systems. In: AAAI 1998, Madison, pp. 746–752 (1998)
4. Cramton, P., Shoham, Y., Steinberg, R. (eds.): Combinatorial Auctions. The MIT Press, Cambridge (2006)
5. Faratin, P., Sierra, C., Jennings, N.R.: Negotiation decision functions for autonomous agents. Robot. Auton. Syst. 24(3-4), 159–182 (1998)
6. Foundation for Intelligent Physical Agents: FIPA Iterated Contract Net Interaction Protocol Specification, Standard (2002); document No. SC00030H
7. Gjerstad, S., Dickhaut, J.: Price Formation in Double Auctions. Game. Econ. Behav. 22(1), 1–29 (1998)
8. Jennings, N.R., Faratin, P., Lomuscio, A.R., Parsons, S., Wooldridge, M.J., Sierra, C.: Automated Negotiation: Prospects, Methods and Challenges. Group Decis. Negot. 10, 199–215 (2001)
9. Kaisers, M., Tuyls, K.: Frequency Adjusted Multiagent Q-learning. In: van der Hoek, W., Kaminka, G.A., Lespérance, Y., Luck, M., Sen, S. (eds.) AAMAS 2010, pp. 309–315. IFAAMAS, Toronto (2010)
10. Luckhart, C., Irani, K.B.: An Algorithmic Solution of N-Person Games. In: AAAI 1986, vol. 1, pp. 158–162. Morgan Kaufmann, Philadelphia (1986)
11. Nash, J.: Non-cooperative Games. Ann. Math. 54(2), 286–295 (1950)
12. Porter, R., Nudelman, E., Shoham, Y.: Simple search methods for finding a Nash equilibrium. Game. Econ. Behav. 63(2), 642–662 (2008)
13. Ramezani, S., Endriss, U.: Nash Social Welfare in Multiagent Resource Allocation. In: David, E., Gerding, E., Sarne, D., Shehory, O. (eds.) Agent-Mediated Electronic Commerce, pp. 117–131. Springer, Heidelberg (2010)
14. Richter, J., Klusch, M., Kowalczyk, R.: Monotonic Mixing of Decision Strategies for Agent-Based Bargaining. In: Klügl, F., Ossowski, S. (eds.) MATES 2011. LNCS, vol. 6973, pp. 113–124. Springer, Heidelberg (2011)
15. Schuldt, A., Berndt, J.O., Herzog, O.: The Interaction Effort in Autonomous Logistics Processes: Potential and Limitations for Cooperation. In: Hülsmann, M., Scholz-Reiter, B., Windt, K. (eds.) Autonomous Cooperation and Control in Logistics, pp. 77–90. Springer, Berlin (2011)
16. Schuldt, A., Gehrke, J.D., Werner, S.: Designing a Simulation Middleware for FIPA Multiagent Systems. In: Jain, L., Gini, M., Faltings, B.B., Terano, T., Zhang, C., Cercone, N., Cao, L. (eds.) WI-IAT 2008, pp. 109–113. IEEE Computer Society Press, Sydney (2008)
17. Sutton, R.S., Barto, A.G.: Reinforcement Learning: An Introduction. The MIT Press, Cambridge (1998)
18. v. Neumann, J.: Zur Theorie der Gesellschaftsspiele. Math. Ann. 100, 295–320 (1928)
19. v. Neumann, J., Morgenstern, O.: Theory of Games and Economic Behavior. Princeton University Press, Princeton (1944)
20. Watkins, C.J.C.H., Dayan, P.: Q-learning. Mach. Learn. 8(3-4), 279–292 (1992)
21. Winoto, P., McCalla, G.I., Vassileva, J.: Non-Monotonic-Offers Bargaining Protocol. Auton. Agent. Multi-Ag. 11, 45–67 (2005)

Gaining a Better Quality Depending on More Exploration in PSO

Tjorben Bogon, Meike Endres, and Ingo J. Timm

Business Information Systems 1
University of Trier
{bogon,s4meendr,ingo.timm}@uni-trier.de

Abstract. We present a potential extension for particle swarm optimization (PSO) to gain better optimization quality on the basis of our agent-based approach of steering metaheuristics during runtime [1]. PSO as population-based metaheuristic is structured in epochs: in each step and for each particle, the point in the search space and the velocity of the particles are computed due to current local and global best and prior velocity. During this optimization process the PSO explores the search space only sporadically. If the swarm "finds" a local minimum the particles' velocity slows down and the probability to "escape" from this point reduces significantly. In our approach we show how to speed up the swarm to unvisited areas in the search space and explore more regions without losing the best found point and the quality of the result. We introduce a new extension of the PSO for gaining a higher quality of the found solution, which can be steered and influenced by an agent.

1 Introduction

Finding a global optimum is a key challenge in the research field of metaheuristics. In an infinite continuous search space there is no chance to visit all possible points in finite time. Metaheuristics are methods which try to find the best point by combining knowledge about the environment with knowledge of the visited points in the past. One problem with all metaheuristics is to bridge the gap between exploration (to get an overview of the underlying fitness function) and exploitation (to focus on a promising area, and searching for the best point) [5]. How to bridge this gap is an important issue, which is approached by setting up parameters of the metaheuristic. In PSO, e.g., the influence of the parameter to slow down the velocity of the particle faster could be increased.

In our framework we are aiming at controlling PSO by agents. As a first step we im plemented and evaluated that this can be steered during runtime [1]. This framework based on an agent-based architecture to steer and observe metaheuristics during runtime. The underlying idea is to observe the behaviour of a metaheuristic and let the agent react deliberately to this optimization to gain a better optimization process. This paper presents an additional component for this framework: focussing on the gap between exploration and exploitation in a continuous infinite search space by randomly distributing points into the

I.J. Timm and C. Guttmann (Eds.): MATES 2012, LNAI 7598, pp. 30–39, 2012.
© Springer-Verlag Berlin Heidelberg 2012

search space and letting the swarm explore the area around these points without losing the previously found best point.

By using the standard PSO behaviour to explore the specific areas surrounding a random point, our approach includes the exploration of the path between the curent center of the swarm and the random point. We create an additional parameter set, which lets the agent steer and interact with the swarm without losing his behavior specified by the normal PSO parameter. To measure the increased exploration rate, we replace the search space with a grid for a better comparison between the new and the old PSO.

This work is structured as follows: section 2 describes our architecture for agent-based steering of metaheuristics. In section 3, we discuss the current state of the art in exploration of Particle Swarm Optimization, followed by our approach of the extended search space exploration in section 4. We discuss our approach and evaluate it in section 5. Finally, we discuss our results and give a short overview about our next steps and future work in section 6.

2   Agent-Based Steering Of Metaheuristics

In this section we briefly introduce the agent-based architecture (see figure 1a) [1]. The idea behind this architecture is that the agent observes every step and epoch of the metaheuristic and gets a summary of the actual state by the *observer* (see figure 1b).

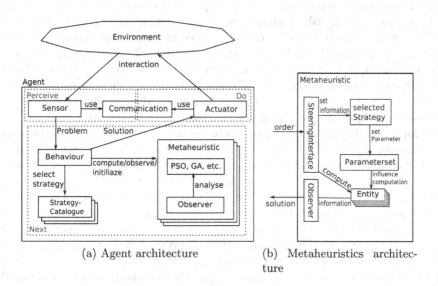

(a) Agent architecture

(b) Metaheuristics architecture

Fig. 1. The architecture of the agent-based steering of metaheuristics

Based on this information, the agent computes the next steps and – if required – influences the parameters of the metaheuristics, or integrates new knowledge (observed from the real environment) into the metaheuristic. For example, if the agent observes that the swarm of particles is slowing down and exploits an area he could influence this process by speeding up the swarm for increasing the exploration rate, if he has enough optimization epochs left. An additional advantage is that the agent could store the best visited points and integrate this knowledge as a new "strategy" into the metaheuristic. Through the *steering interface* different strategies are set to influence the behaviour of the PSO. For example, a strategy is to set new parameters or to integrate new information of a best point or area in the search space. The *steering interface* also allows the agent to start, to stop, and to compute the optimization stepwise. The *observer* collects all information about the running optimization process and infers knowledge about the actual state. This state gives an overview of the actual best point and the particles' parameter (velocity, area center, convex hull, etc.). A detailed description of this agent-based structure is specified in [1].

3   Exploration in Particle Swarm Optimization

Before we discuss exploration in Particle Swarm Optimization we briefly introduce the PSO for a better understanding of the algorithm.

3.1   Particle Swarm Optimization

Particle Swarm Optimization (PSO) is inspired by the social behavior of flocks of birds and shoals of fish. A number of simple entities, the particles, are placed in the domain of definition of some function or problem. The fitness (the value of the objective function) of each particle is evaluated at its current location. The movement of each particle is determined by its own fitness and the fitness of particles in its neighborhood [7]. The results of one decade of research and improvements in the field of PSO are recently summarized in [3], also recommending standards for comparing different PSO methods. Our definition is based on [3]. We aim at continuous optimization problems in a search space S defined over the finite set of continuous decision variables $X_1, X_2, \ldots, X_n$. Given the set Ω of conditions to the decision variables and the objective function $f : S \to \mathbb{R}$ (also called fitness function) the goal is to determine an element $s^* \in S$ that satisfies Ω and for which $f(s^*) \leq f(s)$, $\forall s \in S$ holds. $f(s^*)$ is called a global optimum.

Given a fitness function f and a search space S the standard PSO initializes a set of particles, the swarm. In a D-dimensional search space S each particle P_i consists of three D-dimensional vectors: its position $\vec{x}_i = (x_{i1}, x_{i2}, \ldots, x_{iD})$, the best position the particle visited in the past $\vec{p}_i = (p_{i1}, p_{i2}, \ldots, p_{iD})$ (particle best) and a velocity $\vec{v}_i = (v_{i1}, v_{i2}, \ldots, v_{iD})$. Usually the position is initialized uniformly distributed over S and the velocity is also uniformly distributed depending on the size of S. The movement of each particle takes place in discrete steps using an update function. In order to calculate the update of a particle we need a supplementary vector $\vec{g} = (g_1, g_2, \ldots, g_D)$ (global best), the best position of a particle in its neighborhood. The update function, called inertia weight, consists of two parts. The new velocity of a particle P_i is calculated for each dimension $d = 1, 2, \ldots, D$:

$$v_{id}^{new} = w \cdot v_{id} + c_1 \epsilon_{1d} \left(p_{id} - x_{id} \right) + c_2 \epsilon_{2d} \left(g_d - x_{id} \right). \tag{1}$$

As a next step, the position is updated: $x_{id}^{new} = x_{id} + v_{id}^{new}$. The new velocity depends on the global best (g_d), particle best (p_{id}) and the old velocity (v_{id}) which is weighted by the inertia weight w. The parameters c_1 and c_2 provide the possibility to determine how strong a particle is attracted by the global and the particle best. The random vectors $\vec{\epsilon}_1$ and $\vec{\epsilon}_2$ are uniformly distributed over $[0, 1)^D$ and produce the random movements of the swarm.

3.2   Exploration in PSO

Balancing exploration and exploitation is known as the key challenge for any population-based metaheurisitics [6]. El-Ghazali Talbi [11] describes a continuum reaching from random search representing extrem diversification (exploration) to local search representing strong intensification (exploitation). Population-based Metaheuristics, like PSO or evolutionary computing, are located more to the explorative side. In consequence, balancing exploration and exploitation is important to perform an adequate optimization process. If a good area is found, the metaheuristic has to search intensively in this area by disregarding the diversification. Different approaches are tested like an entropy-driven approach in evolutionary computing by Liu et all. [9].

Brits et al. introduce Niche PSO [4], where it is possible to find more than one global optimum by building subgroups (species) which act on the specific area trying to find a better point in the search space. This leads to a better exploration, but also a loss of the focus to a specific area because of the minor number of particles in the sub swarms.

An additional problem in PSO is the premature convergence of a swarm. This happens if a good point is found too early and the swarm cannot explore any further, because of the attraction of this *gbest*. Li et al. [8] developed a novel self-adaptive PSO (SAPSO) with a self-adjusting inertia weight parameter for every particle.

In previous work we focused on extracting, using, and distributing knowledge. In [10] we introduced parallel search with different cooperative swarms to find a better optimum in efficient time on more than one computer. The underlying idea, is based on more exploration and exchange of knowledge between the swarms. Furthermore, in [2]we analysed automatic parameter configuration which should lead to a better detection of a global optimum. Our research demontrates that the steering of the exploration rate highly depends on the configuration of the PSO. Additionally, feasibility of balancing exploration and velocity has been showned, here.

4   Extended Exploration

The fundamental idea of exploring the underlying fitness landscape, is to remember the areas which no particle has explored before. Obviously, it is impossible to store any points of an infinite search space, we select a point to represent the surrounding area. These points (we will call them random points) are points which are more or less attractive to the swarm based on how often the particles visited the area around this random point. Computed by a basic rule system the swarm switches between standard PSO behaviour and random point exploration state. In random point exploration state, the *gbest* is replaced by the random point. If during this state a better point than the prior *gbest* is found, it is not aplied until the swarm behaviour has been switched back to standard PSO state. Focusing on the random point takes place for a small number of epochs, only. By exploring the area around the random point and the way the swarm "flies" through the space depending on the attraction of this random point, the particles explore areas which they normally do not visit and explore in this optimization run. The problem is to find a good match between the rearranged focus of the swarm and the exploitation of the best found place.

The first idea is to check in every epoch, if the swarm should exploit or explore other regions in the search space depending on its state.

1. *normal pso state (or exploitation state):*
   In this state the swarm performs the normal optimization technique. Nothing is changed and we use the best found *gbest*-position as the *social factor* in the update-formula. In this state no extra parameter influences the optimization process and the swarm focuses automatically, if a new better *gbest* is found.
2. *random point exploration state:*
   The random point exploration is the new developed state of our PSO behaviour. In this state, we change the attraction of *gbest* with a random point attraction of an area, which is not visited by the swarm in the past epochs. The standard PSO technique is not changed, only the attraction of the *gbest* is set to a special point in the search space. This behaviour implies that the swarm speeds up and "flies" in the direction of the new area with sporadic controlling of points on the way to this random point.

Deciding when the swarm has to change its internal state in the current epoch depends on several different factors: [1] If the *gbest* does not change for a few epochs, it is necessary to explore another area for better places. [2] How long the swarm should focus on the random point. [3] If the *gbest* is changed all the time it might be important to look at other areas too, because of a hilly plateau where the swarm is stuck and only local minima are in this areas. To let the swarm focus on other points it is important to set a factor which describes the relationship between the exploring and focusing state. With a combination of these factors it is possible to steer the exploration rate.

As we described, a new steering behaviour for PSO is developed based on three parameters and the distribution of random points in the search space.

4.1   Random Points

To spread the random points in the bordered multi-dimensional search space we decide not to lay a regular grid pattern over the search space. The reason why we choose to create randomly generated points is that we do not know details about the fitness landscape. If we choose a regular grid we could lose information about an important place (for example in a layer with only one peak, only one random point would own this peak). We could lose this important place too, if we randomly spread the points over the search space but it has the same solution quality as a regular grid and in addition we have the option to use these random points in non-bordered search space. Random points can be initiated with respect to other random points and hold a minimal Euclidian distance between them.

Every random point counts the particles visiting the area around it. This allocation is computed by the Euclidian distance from the actual particle point to all random points choosing the nearest random point as hit. Every point a particle during the optimization reached is assigned to the random point with the shortest distance. Over the epochs, all random points get a raising counter and with this assignment it is possible to see which random point has never been hit and which is the farthest point from the center of the swarm. During the optimization process we decide to switch the focus of the optimization to the worst random point to get a better exploration. The worst random point is the farthest point which has the lowest hit rate.

In our evaluation in section 5 we discuss how many random points are necessary and if more random points lead to smaller areas around the point, or if the quality of the optimization will be raised.

4.2   Exploration vs. Exploitation

As described in section 4 we defined three parameters to steer the exploration and exploitation rate. These parameters set different behaviours and influence the gap between exploration and exploitation. All of them are combined together and let the swarm either be in the exploration state or in the standard exploitation state. After computing an epoch the decision of switching to another state is made by evaluating the actual state of the swarm behaviour based on the following three parameters.

1. *"Percent of epochs to explore factor"(POETE):*
   This parameter defines how many epochs are used to explore the random points, which were least visited. The percentage is set with respect to the whole epochs. If the parameter set to a high value, the particles will have more time to explore and the coverage of the search space will be higher. It is important to choose this value carefully, because of the risk that the fitness function is not optimized well when the exploration is too high. If the swarm is too long in the exploration state it will switch back to the normal PSO state.

2. *"Factor of Explore to focus"(FETF):*
This parameter determines how long a swarm is in the normal state and when it changes back to the normal state. With this value, the user can specify which factor the swarm should exploit longer in comparison to the exploration epochs. If a high value is chosen the swarm behaviour is likely the normal behaviour and only a few exploration states are computed.
3. *"Percent of* gbest *changes factor"(POGBC):*
This parameter determines the point when the swarm switches to the normal PSO state. If the value of the change of the *gbest* in the normal PSO state has reached the value of this parameter, the swarm changes to the exploitation state. This parameter assures that the swarm does not focus on a point, where the potential of optimization is stuck in a local minima. If the swarm has reached this value early on, there is a high potential to get a better value through exploitation.

5   Evaluation

In this section, our approach is evaluated to estimate its contribution for an improved optimization process of PSO. This better quality is not only a better or equal result as with the standard PSO, but furthermore a better exploration of the search space. To evaluate this approach, we discuss the underlying fitness function and how to measure the exploration.

5.1   Experimental Setup

The underlying fitness function are three of the recommended functions for PSO evaluation by Bratton and Kennedy [3]. We choose the Generalized Rosenbrock, the Generalized Rastrigin and the Ackley as our test function set. The Generalized Rosenbrock is a simple function with a linear falling landscape into one direction. Ackley has one central optimum and a few local minima where the PSO can get stuck in. The Rastrigin function is the hardest function, because of the very hilly and cliffy landscape. With these three functions, we test typical function landscapes to perform a benchmark between standard PSO (introduced in [3]) and the proposed approach. We use the same search space configuration like [3].

Abstracted Search Space. To get a measurement for the exploration of the swarm we compute an abstraction of the search space by a grid that is laid on it. This is necessary because of the infinite size of the search space and to get a countable possibility for the visited areas of the swarm. Each dimension of the function is fragmented in 1000 equal parts. An iterator logs if an area is visited. As a result, we can record how many different areas are visited by the particles. Through this, we know the frequency and the coverage of the search space. The number of the visits is limited by the number of epochs multiplied with the swarm size. The product of the epochs and the swarm size determines the maximum number of different visited fragments. In our approach it is important that we visit more areas than the standard PSO to solve a better and higher exploration.

5.2   Parameter Settings

With our experiment we want to analyse if the proposed approach reaches higher coverage of the search space as the normal PSO, with equal or even better fitness values. For this purpose we computed the fitness and the coverage of the search space for the three test functions over 6000 epochs and a swarm size of 50 particles (as recommended by [3]).

In the first test session, the identification of a parameter set is in focus which supports a "good" balance of exploration and exploitation on the the fitness functions. Within the experiments, the parameters are completely permutated as follows: POETE (stepsize 0.1, intervall: 0.6, 1.4), POGBC (stepsize 0.1, intervall: 0.5, 1.0), and FETF (stepsize 0.5, intervall: 1.0, 5.0). We take the mean value out of 100 runs initialized with the same seed value for each constellation and compare it with the mean value of 100 runs standard PSO.

The following figure 2 describes the results of this first test for the second function (Generalized Rastrigin) and draws a comparison between the values of the normal PSO (the flat layer in the figure) and the PSO with our new parameters (the hilly landscape). The third function computes similar results from a kind of visualisation which results from the hilly landscape of these two functions. For a better understanding we demonstrate only two parameters on the axis, the 3rd parameter is set to 1.3 (POETE). In figure 2a, you can see that our PSO constantly reaches a better fitness value than the normal PSO within our range. At the same time the coverage of the search space is also constantly higher which you recognize in figure 2b. The better fitness value is based on the higher exploration rate. The swarm explores more of the search space and the chance to find better places and escape from local minima is much higher with our exploration parameter.

On the linear falling function like the *Generalized Rosenbrock*, in our test more exploration leads to a lesser focus on the found points. The normal PSO performs the best optimization on these easy function. In this test case, we gain a better coverage of the search space but did not find a better result than the normal PSO. On the other hand, for the hilly function where it is hard to perform a good optimization without getting stuck on a local minimum, our PSO performed as expected a much better optimization behaviour and we get a better result. As a result of these tests we generate a standard parameter set, which leads to a good behaviour on all functions. Like the normal parameter sets of metaheuristics, every function has its own unified best parameter set but the standard set behaviour is adequate for all functions. As best parameter set we compute POETE = 1.3, FETF = 3.0 and POGBC = 0.8.

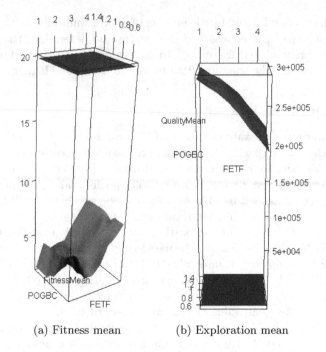

(a) Fitness mean   (b) Exploration mean

Fig. 2. Example of the permutation results for test function 2

5.3 Random Points

As described, in our second test we want to test how many random points are a reasonable number to set and if the number of random points influence the exploration behaviour. For this reason we chose our best found parameter set and tested different quantities of random points. As we search for the best quantity of random points where the fitness is minimal and the quality of search space coverage is high we identify the quantity of 100 as the best value. More random points leads to a lesser quality of the result. At this point we have the lowest value for the fitness and a high value for the coverage. We also recognize that with higher amount of random points the coverage rises and the fitness decreases. The negative side is, that with a higher amount of points, the complexity of evaluation increases and the calculation takes longer. In this setting, we keep 100 amount of random points as a good compromise of runtime complexity and optimization performance.

6   Discussion and Future Work

In this paper we show – without changing the PSO technique – how to explore new areas and get a higher exploration rates. Additionally, we test and build a standard parameter set which provides a high quality on different types of fitness landscapes. As we have seen the new parameter set lets increases the swarm exploration in contrast to the standard PSO. In our experiments, the results showed the same or higher quality as the standard PSO on hilly and difficult function landscapes. On linear functions the modified PSO performance is decreased as expected. We achieve this result by distributing random points over the search space and show that 100 points are sufficient with respect to the computing time to gain a good exploration result.

In our future work, we want to analyse how different patterns of distributing random points influence the results and how the PSO parameter influence our new parameter sets.

References

1. Bogon, T., Lattner, A.D., Lorion, Y., Timm, I.J.: An Agent-based Approach for Dynamic Combination and Adaptation of Metaheuristics. In: Schumann, M., Kolbe, L.M., Breitner, M.H., Frerichs, A. (eds.) Multikonferenz Wirtschaftsinformatik 2010, February 23-25, pp. 2345–2357. Univ.-Verl. Göttingen and Niedersächsische Staats-und Universitätsbibliothek, Göttingen and Göttingen (2010)
2. Bogon, T., Poursanidis, G., Lattner, A.D., Timm, I.J.: Automatic Parameter Configuration of Particle Swarm Optimization by Classification of Function Features. In: Dorigo, M., Birattari, M., Di Caro, G.A., Doursat, R., Engelbrecht, A.P., Floreano, D., Gambardella, L.M., Groß, R., Şahin, E., Sayama, H., Stützle, T. (eds.) ANTS 2010. LNCS, vol. 6234, pp. 554–555. Springer, Heidelberg (2010)
3. Bratton, D., Kennedy, J.: Defining a standard for particle swarm optimization. In: Swarm Intelligence Symposium, pp. 120–127 (2007)
4. Brits, R., Engelbrecht, A., Van Den Bergh, F.: Locating multiple optima using particle swarm optimization. Applied Mathematics and Computation 189(2), 1859–1883 (2007)
5. Eiben, A.E., Schippers, C.A.: On evolutionary exploration and exploitation. Fundam. Inf. 35(1-4), 35–50 (1998)
6. Gerdes, I., Klawonn, F., Kruse, R.: Evolutionäre Algorithmen: Genetische Algorithmen - Strategien und Optimierungsverfahren - Beispielanwendungen; [mit Online-Service zum Buch], 1st edn. Vieweg, Wiesbaden (2004),
   http://www.worldcat.org/oclc/76440323
7. Kennedy, J., Eberhart, R.: Particle swarm optimization. In: Proceedings of the 1995 IEEE International Conference on Neural Network, Perth, Australia, pp. 1942–1948 (1995)
8. Li, X., Fu, H., Zhang, C.: A Self-Adaptive Particle Swarm Optimization Algorithm. In: International Conference on Computer Science and Software Engineering, vol. 5, pp. 186–189 (2008),
   http://doi.ieeecomputersociety.org/10.1109/CSSE.2008.142
9. Liu, S.H., Mernik, M., Bryant, B.R.: To explore or to exploit: An entropy-driven approach for evolutionary algorithms. International Journal of Knowledge-Based and Intelligent Engineering Systems 13(3), 185–206 (2009),
   http://dx.doi.org/10.3233/KES-2009-0184
10. Lorion, Y., Bogon, T., Timm, I.J., Drobnik, O.: An Agent Based Parallel Particle Swarm Optimization - APPSO. In: Swarm Intelligence Symposium IEEE (SIS 2009), Piscataway (NJ) USA, pp. 52–59 (March 2009)
11. Talbi, E.G.: Metaheuristics: From design to implementation. Wiley, Hoboken (2009), http://www.gbv.de/dms/ilmenau/toc/598135170.PDF

Evolutionary Dynamics of Ant Colony Optimization

Haitham Bou Ammar, Karl Tuyls, and Michael Kaisers

Maastricht University, P.O. Box 616, 6200 MD Maastricht, The Netherlands

Abstract. Swarm intelligence has been successfully applied in various domains, e.g., path planning, resource allocation and data mining. Despite its wide use, a theoretical framework in which the behavior of swarm intelligence can be formally understood is still lacking. This article starts by formally deriving the evolutionary dynamics of ant colony optimization, an important swarm intelligence algorithm. We then continue to formally link these to reinforcement learning. Specifically, we show that the attained evolutionary dynamics are equivalent to the dynamics of Q-learning. Both algorithms are equivalent to a dynamical system known as the replicator dynamics in the domain of evolutionary game theory. In conclusion, the process of improvement described by the replicator dynamics appears to be a fundamental principle which drives processes in swarm intelligence, evolution, and learning.

1 Introduction

Artificial intelligence (AI) is a wide spread field. The applications of AI range from designing intelligent systems that are capable of dealing with un-anticipated changes in the environment to modeling interactions in biological and sociological populations. The success of learned behavior for any particular task greatly depends on the way the agent was designed and whether it suits that specific domain. In constructing artificial intelligence agents, designers have to choose from a wide range of available AI frameworks such as: swarm intelligence, reinforcement learning, and evolutionary game theory. The best choice depends on the application the agent is trying to tackle. For example, swarm intelligence is well suited for domains that require a robust behavior of the population of agents (i.e., if one agent fails the system still has to achieve its required goal). The merits of swarm intelligence have been exploited in applications like path planning, resource allocation and data mining [5,13,23,27]. On the other hand, reinforcement learning algorithms best fit agents that individually need to maximize a possibly delayed feedback signal from the environment. As an illustration, reinforcement learning can best fit agents that need to master chess playing [19], play soccer robotics and control [14,18] et cetera.

Both swarm intelligence and reinforcement learning have been explored empirically with considerable success, see for example [19,16,3,10]. Reinforcement learning has been thoroughly discussed in single-agent environments, for which proofs of convergence have been given, e.g., Q-learning [26]. In multi-agent settings, theoretical analysis poses additional challenges such as a non Markovian environment from the agent's point of view. Theoretical guarantees have been difficult to achieve, but [1,21] laid the

I.J. Timm and C. Guttmann (Eds.): MATES 2012, LNAI 7598, pp. 40–52, 2012.

foundation for a new approach, linking multi-agent reinforcement learning with evolutionary game theory. Recently, this link has been used to provide convergence guarantees for multi-agent Q-learning [11,12]. In swarm intelligence, there has been much less progress in formalizing the dynamics of the domain or linking them to other learning techniques.

In this paper we provide a formal derivation of Ant Colony Optimization (ACO), a well known swarm intelligence algorithm. Interestingly, this mathematical derivation reveals that swarm intelligence and reinforcement learning are intrinsically equivalent, both following the replicator dynamics from evolutionary game theory. This is in line with the conceptual equivalence conjectured in [??]. More specifically, this related work has established conceptual and empirical evidence for the similarity of ACO and a network of Learning Automata. This network of learning automata is formally related to the replicator dynamics [1] that form the basis of the formal equivalence established in this article. Here, it becomes clear that whether swarm intelligence, or reinforcement learning was involved in a specific learning task, there seems to be a common process that drives the improvement of the agents behavior, namely the replicator dynamics.

The remainder of the paper is organized as follows: Section 2 introduces concepts from swarm intelligence, reinforcement learning and evolutionary game theory that are the basis of the upcoming analysis. We proceed to introduce our mathematical formalization of swarm intelligence in Section 3. Section 4, builds on the attained derivation to formally link swarm intelligence and reinforcement learning. Section 5 presents related work. Section 6 concludes and reflects upon various future research directions.

2   Background

This section introduces the main concepts from swarm intelligence, reinforcement learning, and evolutionary game theory that this article is based on. Specifically, ACO and the update rule are first discussed. Then Q-learning, a specific reinforcement learning algorithm, as well as the replicator dynamics are presented.

2.1   Ant Colony Optimization (ACO)

Ant Colony Optimization, which is widely used in swarm intelligence, is a class of algorithms that takes inspiration from the foraging behavior of certain ant species. These ants deposit pheromones to indicate favorable routes that should be followed by other ants in the colony. ACO exploits similar biologically inspired behaviors in order to solve optimization problems. Since the ACO's introduction, there has been several variations to the original optimization algorithm. Here we limit our focus to Ant Systems (AS), the original ACO algorithm [2,4]. The main characteristic of AS is that all the pheromone levels are updated by all ants that have built a solution at the current iteration.

Typically in ACO the problem is defined by a graph $G = (V, E)$, with V being the set vertices, encoding states of the environment, and E representing the edges of the graph, representing state transitions. An example of such a graphical model is shown in Figure 1, whereby each of the edges admits a certain pheromone level $\tau_{i,j}$. The ants in such a scenario start at the initial vertex i and collectively find the shortest path to

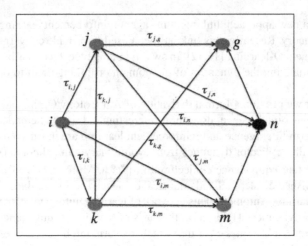

Fig. 1. Graph illustration of a domain in which Ant Colony Optimization can find the shortest path from i to g

the goal vertex g. The learning behavior for such a system is better explained through Algorithm 1. Learning starts by initializing the pheromone levels at each of the edges either randomly or uniformly. The ants transition from a certain node on the graph to another using a stochastic transition probability derived from the pheromones:

$$p_{i,j} = \frac{\tau_{i,j}^{\alpha} \eta_{i,j}^{\beta}}{\sum_c \tau_{i,c}^{\alpha} \eta_{i,c}^{\beta}} \tag{1}$$

where α and β are parameters that present the tradeoff between the pheromone levels $\tau_{i,j}$ and the heuristic information $\eta_{i,j}$[1]. Typically, $\eta_{i,j}$ is defined as inversely proportional to the distance between the nodes i and j.

Algorithm 1. Ant Colony Optimization Metaheuristic

1: Initialize the pheromone levels $\tau_{i,j} \leftarrow \tau_0 \; \forall (i,j) \in E$
2: Choose the starting vertex on the graph $v_{start} = i \in V$
3: **for** iteration $t = 1, 2 \ldots$ **do**
4:     **for** ant $m = 1, 2, \ldots$ **do**
5:         $v_{pos} = v_{start}$ and $u = \{\}$
6:         **while** $\exists$ feasible continuation (v_{pos}, j) of u **do**
7:             Select j according to $p_{i,j}$, where
8:             $p_{i,j} = \begin{cases} 0 & \text{if (i,j) infeasible} \\ \frac{\tau_{i,j}^{\alpha} \eta_{i,j}^{\beta}}{\sum_c \tau_{i,c}^{\alpha} \eta_{i,c}^{\beta}} & \text{otherwise} \end{cases}$
9:             $u = u \oplus (v_{pos}, j)$ and $v_{pos} = j$
10:     Update the pheromone trails $\tau_{i,j}$ using Equation 2.

---

[1] It is worth noting that $\eta_{i,j}$ plays a role similar to reward shaping in reinforcement learning.

Assuming there exists a feasible path to the goal, or more formally assuming that the graph is an ergodic set if the goal state is removed, then all ants will be absorbed in that goal state given sufficient time. After reaching the goal state the pheromone trail of that path is updated according to the following Equation [3] :

$$\tau_{i,j}(t+1) = (1-\rho)\tau_{i,j}(t) + \sum_{m=1}^{M} \delta_{i,j}(t,m), \tag{2}$$

where $\tau_{i,j}$ represents the pheromone level at the edge (i,j), ρ denotes the pheromone evaporation rate, M is the number of ants and $\delta_{i,j}(t,m) = Q\frac{n_{i,j}}{L}$ with Q being a constant, $n_{i,j}$ being the number of times edge (i,j) has been visited[2] by the mth ant and L being the total length of the mth ant's trajectory[3]. It may be convenient to choose $Q = \frac{1}{M}$ to maintain a bounded sum for an arbitrary number of ants.

2.2   Q-Learning

Q-learning [26] is a reinforcement learning algorithm that is designed to maximize a discounted sum of future rewards encountered by an agent interacting with an environment. Originally, Q-learning was used in a single-agent learning setting, where the learning process is markovian, i.e., the current state and action are considered to be sufficient statistics to determine the successor state and the reward.

By definition, the Q-learner repeatedly interacts with its environment, performing an action i at time t, and receiving reward $r_i(t)$ in return. It maintains an estimation $Q_i(t)$ of the expected discounted reward for each action i. This estimation is iteratively updated according to the following equation, known as the Q-learning update rule, where α denotes the learning rate and γ is the discount factor:

$$Q_i(t+1) \leftarrow Q_i(t) + \alpha \left(r_i(t) + \gamma \max_j Q_j(t) - Q_i(t) \right) \tag{3}$$

2.3   Evolutionary Game Theory

Evolutionary game theory takes a rather descriptive perspective, replacing hyper-rationality from classical game theory by the concept of natural selection from biology [17]. It studies the population development of individuals belonging to one of several species. The two central concepts of evolutionary game theory are the replicator dynamics and evolutionary stable strategies [20]. The replicator dynamics presented in the next subsection describe the evolutionary change in the population. They are a set of differential equations that are derived from biological operators such as selection, mutation and cross-over. The evolutionary stable strategies describe the possible

---

[2] Note that in some related work a visited edge may only be updated once [3]. In contrast, our model corresponds to an ant that dispenses a fixed pheromone amount per step, and may thus update a link for every time it has been visited.

[3] Please note that the number of trajectories and the number of ants are the same under the presented assumptions.

asymptotic behavior of the population. However, their examination is beyond the scope of this article. For a detailed discussion, we refer the interested reader to [9].

Consider a population comprised of several species, where each species i makes up a fraction x_i of the population $x = (x_1, x_2, \ldots, x_n)$. The replicator dynamics represent a set of differential equations that formally describe the population's change over time. A population comprises a set of individuals, where the species that an individual can belong to relate to pure actions available to a learner. The Darwinian fitness f_i of each species i can be interpreted as the expectation of the utility function $r_i(t)$ that assigns a reward to the performed action. The distribution of the individuals on the different strategies can be described by a probability vector that is equivalent to a policy for one player, i.e., there is one population in every agents *mind*. The evolutionary pressure by natural selection can be modeled by the replicator equations. They assume this population to evolve such that successful strategies with higher payoffs than average grow while less successful ones decay. The general form relates the time derivative $\dot{x}$ to the relative fitness of species i.

$$\dot{x}_i = x_i \left[f_i(x) - \sum_k x_k f_k(x) \right], \text{where } f_i = E\left[r_i(t)|x\right] \qquad (4)$$

In two-player asymmetric games, the fitness functions can be computed from the payoff bi-matrix (A, B), where e_i is the ith unit vector:

$$\dot{x}_i = x_i \left[e_i Ay - xAy\right]$$
$$\dot{y}_j = y_j \left[xBe_j - xBy\right] \qquad (5)$$

where x_i, y_i are the probabilities of a player picking action i and j respectively, x, y are the action probability vectors for each of the players and A, B are matrices representing the payoff, e.g., $f_i(x) = E\left[r_i(t)|y\right] = e_i Ay$ for the first player. Equation 5 clearly quantifies the selection scheme of a strategy i as being the difference between the attained payoff of that same strategy, i.e., $(Ay)_i$ compared to the average payoff over all other strategies $x^T Ay$.

These dynamics are formally connected to reinforcement learning [1,21,22]. For the ease of readability we leave this derivation for later sections. Namely, we present these equations in Section 4 once deriving the relation between ACO and reinforcement learning.

3   Mathematical Derivation

In this section we will provide the mathematical derivations involved in determining the theoretical link between swarm intelligence and evolutionary game theory.

3.1   Assumptions and General Framework

We examine the theoretical behavior of the Ant Colony Optimization (ACO) algorithm given an infinite number of ants. In order to bound the pheromone level, we assume that each ant dispenses an amount which is anti-proportional to the number of ants (i.e., $Q = \frac{1}{M}$). Note that the total trajectory length L equals $\sum_{b,c} n_{b,c}$. Under these mild assumptions, each pheromone update iteration can be described as follows:

$$\tau_{i,j}(t+1) \leftarrow (1-\rho)\tau_{i,j}(t) + \lim_{M\to\infty} \sum_{m=1}^{M} \frac{1}{M} \frac{n_{i,j}}{\sum_{b,c} n_{b,c}}, \qquad (6)$$

where $n_{i,j}$ and $n_{b,c}$ present the number of visits to the edges (i,j) and (b,c) respectively. The limit is used to denote that we are interested in the behavior of such a system as the number of ants grows to infinity.

ACO Replicator Dynamics Here we will derive the replicator dynamics of ACO and reflect upon the technicalities involved.

We commence by examining the variation in the transition probability for an ant being at a certain state i and moving to a state j. Taking the derivative of Equation 1 we get :

$$
\begin{aligned}
\dot{p}_{i,j} &= \left(\frac{\tau_{i,j}^{\alpha} \eta^{\beta}}{\sum_c \tau_{i,c}^{\alpha} \eta_{i,c}^{\beta}} \right)' \\
&= \frac{\alpha \tau_{i,j}^{\alpha-1} \dot{\tau}_{i,j} \eta_{i,j}^{\beta}}{\sum_c \tau_{i,c}^{\alpha} \eta_{i,c}^{\beta}} - \frac{\tau_{i,j}^{\alpha} \eta_{i,j}^{\beta} \sum_c \alpha \tau_{i,c}^{\alpha-1} \dot{\tau}_{i,c} \eta_{i,c}^{\beta}}{\left(\sum_c \tau_{i,c}^{\alpha} \eta_{i,c}^{\beta} \right)^2} \\
&= \alpha p_{i,j} \frac{\dot{\tau}_{i,j}}{\tau_{i,j}} - \alpha p_{i,j} \sum_c \frac{\dot{\tau}_{i,c}}{\tau_{i,c}} p_{i,c} \\
&= \alpha p_{i,j} \left(\frac{\dot{\tau}_{i,j}}{\tau_{i,j}} - \sum_c \frac{\dot{\tau}_{i,c}}{\tau_{i,c}} p_{i,c} \right) \qquad (7)
\end{aligned}
$$

Equation 7 clearly resembles the general replicator dynamics given in Equation 4 when written in the following form, where $\Theta_{i,j} = \frac{\dot{\tau}_{i,j}}{\tau_{i,j}}$:

$$\dot{p}_{i,j} = \alpha p_{i,j} \left(\Theta_{i,j} - \sum_k p_{i,k} \Theta_{i,k} \right) \qquad (8)$$

The attained model of ACO in Equation 8, quantifies the change in the probability of choosing an action j in a given state i and therefore, represents a generalization of the stateless replicator dynamics from Equation 4 to multiple-state games. This discussion is further detailed in Section 4. Equation 8 also clearly represents the change in the transition probabilities as a function of the level of the pheromone updates.

3.2 Rate of Change in the Pheromone Level

Next we will determine the rate of change in the pheromone level which is vital for solving Equation 8. Consider again the update rule given in Equation 6. Using the central limit theorem this is re-written in the following format:

$$\tau_{i,j}(t+1) = (1-\rho)\tau_{i,j}(t) + \mathbb{E}\left(\frac{n_{i,j}}{\sum_{b,c} n_{b,c}}\right)$$

$$\Delta\tau_{i,j}(t) = -\rho\tau_{i,j}(t) + \mathbb{E}\left(\frac{n_{i,j}}{\sum_{b,c} n_{b,c}}\right)$$

$$\frac{\Delta\tau_{i,j}(t)}{\tau_{i,j}(t)} = -\rho + \frac{\mathbb{E}\left(\frac{n_{i,j}}{\sum_{b,c} n_{b,c}}\right)}{\tau_{i,j}(t)} \tag{9}$$

Considering infinitesimal time changes, Equation 9 can be written as :

$$\frac{\dot{\tau}_{i,j}(t)}{\tau_{i,j}(t)} = -\rho + \frac{\mathbb{E}\left(\frac{n_{i,j}}{\sum_{b,c} n_{b,c}}\right)}{\tau_{i,j}(t)} \tag{10}$$

Next we will provide a formal method to determine the expectation of Equation 10. This formalization is based on the Markov Chain theory that will be introduced.

Markov Chain Theory. A Markov Chain (MC) is a discrete time random process that satisfies the Markov property. An MC typically involves a sequence of random variables that evolve through time according to a stochastic transition probability. In our current formalization we are more interested in an *Absorbing Markov Chain* (AMC). An AMC is a variation of the former to include an Absorbing state. In other words, the system has a state that once reach can never be left, therefore called absorbing.

In an AMC with t transient states and r absorbing state the probability matrix could be written in the canonical format of Equation 11,

$$\mathbf{P} = \left[\begin{array}{c|c} \mathbf{Q} & \mathbf{R} \\ \hline \mathbf{0} & \mathbf{I} \end{array}\right], \tag{11}$$

where $\mathbf{Q} \in \mathbb{R}^{t\times t}$ is the transient state probability matrix, $\mathbf{R} \in \mathbb{R}^{t\times r}$ is the absorbing transition probability matrix, $\mathbf{0} \in \mathbb{R}^{r\times t}$ zero matrix, and $\mathbf{I} \in \mathbb{R}^{r\times r}$ identity matrix.

The expected number of visits to a transient state is determined using, $\mathbf{N} = \sum_{k=0}^{\infty} \mathbf{Q}^k = (\mathbf{I} - \mathbf{Q})^{-1}$, while the expected transient probabilities of visiting all the transient states is given by $\mathbf{H} = (\mathbf{N} - \mathbf{I})\mathbf{D}^{-1}$, where $\mathbf{D} \in \mathbb{R}^{t\times t}$ is a diagonal matrix having the same diagonal entries as $\mathbf{N}$. The probability of an absorbing transition to occur is given by $\mathbf{B} = \mathbf{NR}$ with $\mathbf{B} \in \mathbb{R}^{t\times r}$.

Equation 12 represents the expectation using the AMC theory. We have divided a trajectory into three essential parts: (1) a transition from an initial state to a certain state i, (2) a transition between two transient states (i, j) and (3) a transition probability from a transient state to the goal or end state. These three parts present the possible combinations of an ant to start at a certain initial state and reach the required destination.

Using the AMC chain theory and the trajectory division idea, we can re-write in expectation. Many terms appear with powers related to $a, b, \alpha,$ and β, with a being the number of visits to a certain link (i, j), b represents the length of a trajectory, $(\mathbf{Q}^b\mathbf{R})_{end}$

signifies the probability of a transient state to be absorbed, $\mathbf{Q}_{1,i}^{\alpha}$ is the expected probability to transient from an initial to an ith state, $\mathbf{Q}_{j,i}^{\beta_1} \ldots \mathbf{Q}_{j,i}^{\beta_n}$ are all the expected probabilities of looping between states (i,j), and $\psi = b - a - \alpha - \sum_{i<j} \beta_i$, representing the remaining division to get absorbed.

$$
\mathbb{E}\left(\frac{n_{i,j}}{\sum_{b,c} n_{b,c}}\right) = \sum_{b=1}^{\infty} \sum_{a=0}^{b} \frac{a}{b}
$$
$$
\left[(\mathbf{Q}^b \mathbf{R})_{end} \sum_{\alpha=0}^{b-a} \sum_{\beta_j \in \{1,\ldots,n\}}^{\psi} \mathbf{Q}_{1,i}^{\alpha} \mathbf{Q}_{i,j}^{a} \mathbf{Q}_{j,i}^{\beta_1} \ldots \mathbf{Q}_{j,i}^{\beta_n} \mathbf{Q}_{j,end}^{b-a-\alpha-\sum_i \beta_i} \right] \tag{12}
$$

The attained results could now be substituted back in Equation 8, with $\Theta_{i,j}$ being:

$$
\Theta_{i,j} = -\rho + \frac{\sum_{b=1}^{\infty} \sum_{a=0}^{b} \frac{a}{b} \left[\chi \sum_{\alpha=0}^{b-a} \sum_{\beta_j \in \{1,\ldots,n\}}^{\psi} \boldsymbol{\Gamma} \boldsymbol{\Xi} \boldsymbol{\Lambda} \right]}{\tau_{i,j}} \tag{13}
$$

with $\chi = (\mathbf{Q}^b \mathbf{R})_{end}$, $\boldsymbol{\Xi} = \mathbf{Q}_{j,i}^{\beta_1} \ldots \mathbf{Q}_{j,i}^{\beta_n}$, $\boldsymbol{\Gamma} = \mathbf{Q}_{1,i}^{\alpha} \mathbf{Q}_{i,j}^{a}$, and $\boldsymbol{\Lambda} = \mathbf{Q}_{j,end}^{b-a-\alpha-\sum_i \beta_i}$. Substituting these in Equation 8 we get the full ACO model as :

$$
\frac{\dot{p}_{i,j}}{p_{i,j}} = -\alpha\rho + \alpha \frac{\sum_{b=1}^{\infty} \sum_{a=0}^{b} \frac{a}{b} \left[\chi \sum_{\alpha=0}^{b-a} \sum_{\beta_j \in \{1,\ldots,n\}}^{\psi} \boldsymbol{\Gamma} \boldsymbol{\Xi} \boldsymbol{\Lambda} \right]}{\tau_{i,j}}
$$
$$
- \alpha \sum_l p_{i,l} \left(\rho + \frac{\sum_{b=1}^{\infty} \sum_{a=0}^{b} \frac{a}{b} \left[\chi_l \sum_{\alpha=0}^{b-a} \sum_{\beta_j \in \{1,\ldots,n\}}^{\psi} \boldsymbol{\Gamma}_l \boldsymbol{\Xi}_l \boldsymbol{\Lambda}_l \right]}{\tau_{i,l}} \right) \tag{14}
$$

where the subscript l denotes each of the matrices depending on the required edge.

4 Relation to Reinforcement Learning

In this section we will draw the connection between the attained model of ACO and reinforcement learning. Namely, we start by presenting the dynamics of Q-learning and then linking them to the attained ACO equations.

4.1 Q-Learning Dynamics

In [21], the authors extend the work of [1] to derive the dynamics of Q-learning. Consider the policy of two players to be represented as probability vectors $x = (x_1, \ldots, x_k)$ and $y = (y_1, \ldots, y_z)$, where x_i indicates the probability for player one to choose an action i, k presents the kth allowed action for player one, y_j manifests the probability of the second player to pick action j, and z is the zth allowed action for player two.

Based on these definitions the dynamics of Q-learning in a two-player stateless matrix game are derived as,

$$\dot{x}_i = x_i \alpha \left(\tau^{-1} \dot{Q}_i - \sum_k \dot{Q}_k x_k \right)$$

$$\dot{y}_j = y_j \alpha \left(\tau^{-1} \dot{Q}_j - \sum_z \dot{Q}_z x_z \right) \quad (15)$$

Taking the update rule of Equation 3 into account, the dynamics of Q-learning could be written as,

$$\dot{x}_i = x_i \alpha \left(\tau^{-1} [e_i Ay - xAy] - \log x_i + \sum_k x_k \log x_k \right) \quad (16)$$

$$\dot{y}_j = y_j \alpha \left(\tau^{-1} [xBe_j - xBy] - \log y_j + \sum_z y_z \log z_z \right)$$

with x,y the policies of each player, α the learning rate, τ temperature parameter, A, B the payoff matrices, and e_i the ith unit vector. The most interesting part of this results is that the previous equations contain a selection part that is equivalent to the replicator dynamics and a mutation part. For more details interested readers are referred to [21].

With these equations the dynamics of Q-learning in two player stateless games could be better understood and analyzed. As we will discuss later in the document, our formulation of ACO and its relation to reinforcement learning requires an extension of the above equations to multi-state games. Some work on the generalization of the replicator dynamics to multiple-states in [8] had been achieved. But for a better understanding of the replicator dynamics of ACO we require a more general framework that explains the dynamics of more coupled states. This has not been achieved yet, but we hope that our ACO formulation could give a better insight on the analysis of complex forms multi-state games and present a rigorous starting point for more complex tasks.

4.2   Ant Colonies as Reinforcement Learning Agents

In analyzing this relation it is important to note that here we look at the dynamical model of ACO from a slightly different perspective where $p_{i,j}$ now denotes the probability of an agent to choose an action j at a certain state i. This view is intuitively equivalent to the previous where $p_{i,j}$ was manifesting the probability for an ant to visit an edge (i, j).

The dynamical model in Equation 8 clearly resembles close connections to the replicator equations of Q-learning in Equation 15. Both models have similar time derivatives representing the change in the probability of choosing a certain action by a player. On one hand, in reinforcement learning this probability, x_i in Equation 15, depends on the difference between the Q values for choosing the action i compared to that of picking all the others, i.e., $\dot{Q}_i - \sum_k \dot{Q}_k x_k$. On the other hand, in ACO the probability of choosing an action j in a state i, $p_{i,j}$ in Equation 8, depends on both the change in the pheromone level for $\dot{\tau}_{i,j}$ and on the original pheromone level $\tau_{i,j}$, i.e., $\frac{\tau_{i,j}}{\tau_{i,j}} - \sum_c \frac{\tau_{i,c}}{\tau_{i,c}} p_{i,c}$. The above observation reflects that the solution to the probability of a certain action in ACO lies in a higher dimensional space than that of the pheromone space and resembles additional complexities to Q-learning.

Another important observation is to been seen from a *state-locality* point of view. If each state was viewed as an agent by its own, then at this locality each agent, equivalently a state, admits its own replicator dynamics that are described in Equation 8. In such a setting the relation between swarm intelligence and reinforcement learning becomes apparent and clear. Using this *state-locality* view, Equation 8 could be re-written in the following format for each state-agent (i, j):

$$\dot{p}_i = \alpha p_i \left(\Theta_i - \sum_l p_l \Theta_l \right) \tag{17}$$

Here the dynamics of ACO clearly resemble those of Q-learning whereby Θ_i plays the same role as that of $\dot{Q}_i$ in Equation 15. At this stage, it is worth noting two important characteristics of the attained model: (1) The pheromone levels in ACO play the same role to the Q values, i.e., the expected total payoff in a reinforcement learning agent and (2) The variation of the action selection probabilities in ACO resemble more complexities compared to normal form Q-learning.[4] It is important to mention, that although the swarm intelligence and reinforcement learning seem to admit similar local behaviors the analysis of the dynamics of ACO is more complex from the global point of view as these states-agents are dynamically coupled.

A high-level pictorial view of this observation is shown in Figure 2. Under the state-agent equivalence view each state resembles its own replicator equations. The switching dynamics between each of the state-agent in ACO are beyond the scope of this paper and are left for further studying in the future work. A good starting point here is the work of [25], whereby the authors provided the switching dynamics for piece-wise linear systems. It is worth noting though, that this work still needs to be extended to suit the ACO model, as piece-wise linear behavioral models are not a suitable assumption in this case.

5   Related Work

Ant Colony Optimization has been shown to work empirically in various domains. Theoretically there have been various successes in providing convergence proofs for the ACO algorithms, see [3,6] for a thorough discussion. In the realm of modeling the dynamics of ACO less research has been done so far. For example [15] model the dynamical properties of the ACO algorithm using a deterministic model that assumes an average expected behavior of the ants. The model is best suited for a specific class of permutation problems. Another attempt to formalize the dynamics of ACO was provided in [7]. Gutjahr provides an analytical analysis of the finite-time dynamics of ACO

---

[4] Although this is not investigated in this paper, we speculate that ACO relates to Q-learning with eligibility traces which will be studied in deeper details in our future work.

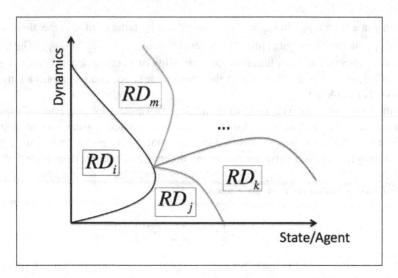

Fig. 2. A high level pictorial illustration of the dynamics of ACO at a local state level where RD_i denoted the replicator dynamics for a certain state-agent i. From the state-agent equivalent view, each state, is described by its own replicator differential equations dynamics.

based on a fitness-proportional pheromone update rule on arbitrary construction graphs. In [24], the authors attempt to formalize the dynamics of ACO based on an average reward Markov Decision Process model. It uses a very simple pheromone update rule ignoring the heuristics used in normal ACO.

The presented paper differs from these works by deriving a more general framework that describes the dynamical behavior of ACO which is applicable to a wider range of problems utilizing the full pheromone update rule. We further present, for the first time to the best of our knowledge, a formal link between swarm intelligence, evolutionary game theory and reinforcement learning.

6   Conclusions and Future Work

The contributions of this paper are twofold: (1) We presented a formal model of the dynamics of one of the most famous swarm intelligence algorithms, namely the replicator equations of ant colony optimization. (2) We provide a formal link between three well known learning schemes: swarm intelligence, evolutionary game theory and reinforcement learning. Although the update rules for the behavioral improvement of swarm intelligence and reinforcement learning appear to be very different, formally there is a common underlying process for improvement which is driven by the replicator dynamics.

The contributions of this paper range beyond the scope of linking the three different learning domains together and might serve as a rigorous starting point to the extension of the replicator dynamics beyond two-player stateless games to multi-players multi-state games which is considered to be one of the hardest problems in evolutionary game theory.

The established link provides several opportunities for future work. First, the ant colony optimization replicator dynamics (ACO-RD) provide a model that can be used to analyze the convergence behavior of the stochastic algorithm with tools from dynamical systems. In addition, they can be extended to obtain error bounds on the performance of the stochastic algorithm. Second, these ACO-RD are inherently multi-state, and we expect similarities to the dynamics of learning algorithms such as Q-learning with eligibility traces and bee-inspired swarm intelligence algorithms, to which this theoretical foundation may extend.

References

1. Börgers, T., Sarin, R.: Learning through reinforcement and replicator dynamics. Journal of Economic Theory 77(1), 1–14 (1997)
2. Dorigo, M., Colorni, A., Maniezzo, V.: Positive feedback as a search strategy. Technical Report 91-016, Dipartimento di Elettronica, Politecnico di Milano, Milan, Italy (1991)
3. Dorigo, M., Birattari, M., Sttzle, T.: Ant colony optimization – artificial ants as a computational intelligence technique. IEEE Comput. Intell. Mag. 1, 28–39 (2006)
4. Dorigo, M., Maniezzo, V., Colorni, A.: The ant system: Optimization by a colony of cooperating agents. IEEE Transactions on Systems, Man, and Cybernetics-Part B 26(1), 29–41 (1996)
5. Grosan, C., Abraham, A., Chis, M.: Swarm intelligence in data mining. In: Swarm Intelligence in Data Mining, pp. 1–20 (2006)
6. Gutjahr, W.J.: A graph-based ant system and its convergence. Future Gener. Comput. Syst. 16, 873–888 (2000)
7. Gutjahr, W.J.: On the finite-time dynamics of ant colony optimization. Methodology and Computing in Applied Probability 8(1), 105–133 (2006)
8. Hennes, D., Tuyls, K., Rauterberg, M.: State-coupled replicator dynamics. In: Proceedings of The 8th International Conference on Autonomous Agents and Multiagent Systems - Volume 2, AAMAS 2009, pp. 789–796. International Foundation for Autonomous Agents and Multiagent Systems, Richland (2009)
9. Sigmund, K.: Evolutionary Games and Population Dynamics. Cambridge University Press, Cambridge (1998)
10. Kaisers, M., Tuyls, K.: Frequency adjusted multi-agent Q-learning, pp. 309–316. International Foundation for Autonomous Agents and Multiagent Systems (2010)
11. Kaisers, M., Tuyls, K.: FAQ-Learning in Matrix Games: Demonstrating Convergence near Nash Equilibria, and Bifurcation of Attractors in the Battle of Sexes. In: Workshop on Interactive Decision Theory and Game Theory (IDTGT 2011). Assoc. for the Advancement of Artif. Intel. (AAAI) (2011)
12. Kianercy, A., Galstyan, A.: Dynamics of softmax q-learning in two-player two-action games. CoRR, abs/1109.1528 (2011)
13. Liu, D., Wang, B.: Biological swarm intelligence based opportunistic resource allocation for wireless ad hoc networks. Wireless Personal Communications (2011)
14. Mahadevan, S., Connell, J., Sammut, C., Sutton, R., Temporal Phd: Automatic programming of behavior-based robots using reinforcement learning (1991)
15. Merkle, D., Middendorf, M.: Modeling the dynamics of ant colony optimization. Evol. Comput. 10, 235–262 (2002)
16. Peters, J., Schaal, S.: Reinforcement learning of motor skills with policy gradients (2008)
17. Smith, J.M.: Evolution and the Theory of Games. Cambridge University Press, Cambridge (1982)

18. Stone, P., Balch, T., Kraetzschmar, G.K. (eds.): RoboCup 2000. LNCS (LNAI), vol. 2019. Springer, Heidelberg (2001)
19. Sutton, R.S., Barto, A.G.: Reinforcement Learning: An Introduction. MIT Press (1998)
20. Taylor, P.D., Jonker, L.B.: Evolutionary stable strategies and game dynamics. Mathematical Biosciences 40(1-2), 145–156 (1978)
21. Tuyls, K., Hoen, P.J., Vanschoenwinkel, B.: An evolutionary dynamical analysis of multi-agent learning in iterated games. The Journal of Autonomous Agents and Multi-Agent Systems, JAAMAS 12(1), 115–153 (2006)
22. Tuyls, K., Parsons, S.: What evolutionary game theory tells us about multiagent learning. Artificial Intelligence 171(7), 406–416 (2007)
23. Vigorito, C.M.: Distributed path planning for mobile robots using a swarm of interacting reinforcement learners. In: Proceedings of the 6th International Joint Conference on Autonomous Agents and Multiagent Systems, AAMAS 2007, pp. 120:1–120:8. ACM, New York (2007)
24. Vrancx, P., Verbeeck, K., Nowé, A.: Networks of Learning Automata and Limiting Games. In: Tuyls, K., Nowe, A., Guessoum, Z., Kudenko, D. (eds.) ALAMAS 2005, ALAMAS 2006, and ALAMAS 2007. LNCS (LNAI), vol. 4865, pp. 224–238. Springer, Heidelberg (2008)
25. Vrancx, P., Tuyls, K., Westra, R.L.: Switching dynamics of multi-agent learning. In: AAMAS (1), pp. 307–313 (2008)
26. Watkins, C.J.C.H., Dayan, P.: Technical note q-learning. Machine Learning 8, 279–292 (1992)
27. Zhou, J., Dai, G., He, D.-Q., Ma, J., Cai, X.-Y.: Swarm intelligence: Ant-based robot path planning. In: Proceedings of the Fifth International Conference on Information Assurance and Security, IAS 2009, Xi An, China, August 18-20, pp. 459–463. IEEE Computer Society (2009)

Human-Agent Teamwork in Cyber Operations: Supporting Co-evolution of Tasks and Artifacts with Luna

Larry Bunch[1], Jeffrey M. Bradshaw[1], Marco Carvalho[2], Tom Eskridge[1],
Paul J. Feltovich[1], James Lott[1], and Andrzej Uszok[1]

[1] Florida Institute for Human and Machine Cognition (IHMC), Pensacola, FL, USA
[2] Department of Computer Science, Florida Institute of Technology, Melbourne, FL, USA
{lbunch,jbradshaw,teskridge,pfeltovich,jlott,auszok}@ihmc.us
mcarvalho@fit.edu

Abstract. In this article, we outline the general concept of *coactive emergence*, an iterative process whereby joint sensemaking and decision-making activities are undertaken by analysts and software agents. Then we explain our rationale for the development of the Luna software agent framework. In particular, we focus on how we use capabilities for comprehensive policy-based governance to ensure that key requirements for security, declarative specification of task-work, and built-in support for joint activity within mixed teams of humans and agents are satisfied.

Keywords: Task-artifact cycle, coactive emergence, software agents, multi-agent systems, policy, Luna, KAoS, OWL, ontologies, cyber security.

1 Introduction

Despite the significant attention being given the critical problems of cyber operations, the ability to keep up with the increasing volume and sophistication of network attacks is seriously lagging. Throwing more computing horsepower at fundamentally-limited visualization and analytic approaches will not get us anywhere. Instead, we need to seriously rethink the way cyber operations tools and approaches have been conceived, developed, and deployed.

Though continuing research to improve technology is essential, the point of increasing such proficiencies is not merely to make automated tools more capable in and of themselves, but also to make analysts more capable through the use of such technologies. To achieve this objective, we must adopt a human-centered approach to technology development [1].

In a memorable encapsulation of themes relating to human-centered technology development, Ford, *et al.* [2] argued that the accumulated tools of human history could all profitably be regarded as orthoses—not in the sense that they compensate for the specific disabilities of any given individual, but rather because they enable us to overcome the biological limitations shared by all of us. With reading and writing anyone can transcend the finite capacity of human memory; with a power screwdriver

I.J. Timm and C. Guttmann (Eds.): MATES 2012, LNAI 7598, pp. 53–67, 2012.

anyone can drive the hardest screw; with a calculator, anyone can get the numbers right; with an aircraft anyone can fly to Paris; and with IBM's *Watson*, anyone can beat the world Jeopardy champion. Eyeglasses, a familiar instance of an "ocular orthosis," provide a particularly useful example of three basic principles:

- *Transparency.* Eyeglasses leverage and extend our ability to see, but in no way model our eyes: They don't look or act like them and wouldn't pass a Turing test for being an eye. Moreover, eyeglasses are designed in ways that help us forget we have them on—we don't want to "use" them, we want to see *through* them.
- *Unity.* Since our goal is not making smart eyeglasses but rather augmenting vision, the minimum unit of design includes the device, the person, and the environment. This mode of analysis necessarily blurs the line between humans and technology.
- *Fit.* Your eyeglasses won't fit me; neither will mine do you much good. Prostheses must fit the human and technological components together in ways that synergistically exploit their mutual strengths and mitigate their respective limitations. This implies a requirement for rich knowledge not only of technology, but also of how humans function.

Orthoses or prostheses are useful *only* to the extent that they "fit" — in fact, the "goodness of fit" will determine system performance more than any other specific characteristic. This is true whether one considers eyeglasses, wooden legs, or cognitive orthoses. One can identify two broad categories of fit — *species fit* and *individual fit*. In some cases, a particular aspect of human function can afford a consistent fit across most of a population of interest. In many other instances, however, an *individual fit* is desirable, and in these cases relevant differences among individuals must be accommodated [3]—and adjusted as needed.

Fig. 1. The Task-Artifact Cycle

The term "fit" is pertinent for an additional reason: it evokes the concept of evolution—specifically a *co-evolution* of the user *task* and the technology *artifact*. This concept of a co-evolution of tasks and artifacts is not new, but goes back two decades to an influential chapter by Carroll, *et al.* [4]. The task-artifact cycle includes two phases: the first involves the design and development of artifacts to help users perform their assigned tasks; the second concerns the way that the use of the artifacts defines new perceptions, possibilities, or constraints of use that change the way the task is performed (see fig. 1).

This never-ending cycle of co-evolution between mutually dependent tasks and artifacts is an inevitable challenge to software developers—though, on the bright side, it does provide job security. On the user side, however, it means that the capabilities of software will always lag behind current needs, particularly in domains such as cyber operations where the nature of threats is constantly changing.

In this article, we describe an agent-based approach to the support of co-evolution of tasks and artifacts to improve human performance while increasing transparency, unity, and fit. Though we will discuss cyber operations as an application example, we believe that the same principles and capabilities we outline here will be useful in many similar domains. Section 2 outlines the general concept of *coactive emergence* as an iterative process whereby joint sensemaking and decision-making activities are undertaken by analysts and software agents. Section 3 describes the background and motivation for our Luna agent framework, focusing primarily on its policy-based features that support the requirements for security, declarative specification of task-work, and built-in support for joint activity within mixed teams of humans and agents. Section 4 will give an overview of the KAoS policy services framework. Section 5 will briefly describe our objectives in the design of Luna agent framework, and selected highlights of its features. Section 6 will illustrate by example some of the ways in which policy governance is being exploited within Luna. Finally, section 7 will outline current areas of research and future directions.

2   Coactive Emergence

Coactive emergence describes an iterative process whereby secure system configurations, effective responses to threats, and useful interpretations of data are continuously developed through the interplay of joint sensemaking and decision-making activities undertaken by analysts and software agents [5]. The word "coactive" emphasizes the joint, simultaneous, and interdependent nature of such collaboration among analysts and agents. We will illustrate how this applies to cyber sensemaking (fig. 2):

1. Analysts gather evidence relating to their hypotheses through high-level declarative policies that direct and redirect the ongoing activities of agents.

2. Within the constraints of policy, agents manipulate system configurations to improve security and intepret the data, optionally enriching their interpretations through machine learning techniques. Because of their built-in abilities to work together dynamically to analyze and synthesize meaningful events from the raw data, agent interpretations can be more easily made to match the kinds of abstractions found in human interpretations more closely than in other approaches.

Fig. 2. The Coactive Emergence Cycle

3.   Agents aggregate and present their findings to analysts as part of integrated graphical displays, and analysts interact with these displays in order to explore and evaluate how agent findings bear on their hypotheses.

4. Based on refinements of their hypotheses and questions from these explorations and evaluations, analysts redirect agent activity as appropriate.

The process of "emergence" operates at two levels:

- First-order patterns emerge from agent and analyst interpretations of data that are shaped by problem-space constraints currently expressed within policies and tool configurations. For example, through the application of analyst-defined policy-based pattern recognition, agents may tag and display selected network data as instances of emergent threats. Likewise, a display of current agent results may lead analysts to recognize the possibility of additional emergent threat patterns that the agents may have missed.

- Second-order emergence arises from dynamic changes made by agents and analysts to the problem-space constraints. For example, analysts may add, delete, or change agent policies in order to refine their data interpretations or their responses to threats. Agents may also change their own policies through policy learning. When permitted, agents may also propagate learned policies to other agents.

3   Background and Motivation for the Luna Agent Framework

IHMC's innovations in research and development of software agent frameworks for multi-agent systems stretch back more than fifteen years (see, e.g., [6, 7, 8]). As a happy consequence of progress in the field since those early days, there now exists a range of interesting agent frameworks, serving different purposes, available from a variety of commercial sources and research institutions, that can be applied with confidence to many practical applications. For this reason, we had not expected that we would ever have to create a new agent system. However, contrary to expectation, we have recently developed a new agent framework called *Luna*, named for the founder of Pensacola, Tristán de Luna y Arellano (1519 – 1571). In this section of the paper, we attempt to explain the reason why.

The short answer is that when we were confronted with the need to apply software agent technology within the domain of cybersecurity operations, we found that no current platform adequately met our needs. Foremost among our requirements were the following three requirements, which we will discuss one by one.

In considering the *security requirements* of currently available software agent platforms, the key role of policy constraints that could govern behavior at every level of the agent system readily became apparent. In our previous experiences with agent systems, we had discovered that people sometimes were reluctant to deploy agents exhibiting significant autonomy because of concerns that the freedom and indeterminacy of such agents might allow them to do undesirable things [9]. We have found that the ability to use policy to impose constraints on agent behavior, in essence providing a guarantee to people that agent autonomy would always be exercised within specified bounds, gave people the assurance they needed to feel that highly capable agents could act in a trustworthy, predictable, and safe manner.

Second, with respect to the need for a platform supporting the interactive *formulation of common agent tasks by end users*, rather than by software developers, we believe that policy systems may also prove useful. In past experience with military, space, and intelligence applications, we have learned that many common tasks can be formulated as declarative obligation policies that require given actions to occur when triggered by a specified context. Further enhancing the usefulness of such capabilities to define agent taskwork is the potential for specifying abstract obligations (i.e., "goal" policies or "collective obligations") on an initially-unspecified population of agents in a fashion that is similar to how concrete obligations are imposed on specific classes and instances of agents.

Third, to satisfy the need for a platform that would provide built-in support for effective *coordination of joint activity within mixed teams of humans and agents*, we believe that a policy-based approach also provides a viable option. Based on our research and development experience in a variety of applications involving the coordination of human-agent-robot teamwork (HART), we believe that important aspects of teamwork such as observability, directability, interpredictability, learning, and multiplicity can be addressed by policy-based mechanisms [10, 11].

In the following section, we describe the KAoS policy services framework that provides the basis for the governance of the Luna platform and its agents.

4   The KAoS Policy Services Framework

Because agents are powerful, we use powerful policy management and enforcement frameworks to govern their actions. Whereas many special-purpose policy approaches are optimized only for specific kinds of tasks (e.g., access control) and support only the ability to permit or forbid an action, the ontology-based approach of KAoS enables semantically-rich specifications of virtually any kind of policy. It supports not only the ability to permit or forbid an action in a given context, but also to require that certain actions be performed when a dynamic, context-specific trigger is activated (e.g., start doing X, stop doing Y, reduce your bandwidth usage, log certain actions)— or to waive such an obligation dynamically if the situation warrants.

The KAoS Policy Services framework [12] was the first to offer an ontology-based approach (based on the W3C standard, OWL 2 (http://www.w3.org/TR/owl2-overview/) to policy representation and reasoning. It is currently the most successful and mature of all such efforts. Following collaborative efforts by the NSA-sponsored Digital Policy Management (DPM) Architecture Group and IHMC, the KAoS core ontology was adopted as the basis for future standards efforts in DPM [13].

KAoS has already been integrated into IHMC's Luna agent framework, as well as several other agent platforms and traditional service-oriented architectures. Preliminary work has been done on agent learning mechanisms that propagate learning with localized opportunistic mechanisms inspired by biological analogues. In addition, we plan to develop capabilities for KAoS to take advantage of localized agent learning results by allowing new policies to be constructed programmatically, with optional human oversight. This would allow learning results from groups of individual agents that are of high generality or urgency to be rapidly propagated to whole classes of other agents.

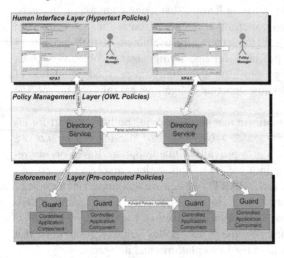

Fig. 3. Notional KAoS Policy Services Architecture

Two important requirements for the KAoS architecture are modularity and extensibility. These requirements are supported through a framework with well-defined interfaces that can be extended, if necessary, with the components required to support application-specific policies. The basic elements of the KAoS architecture are shown in . Within each of the layers, the end user may plug-in specialized extension components if needed. KAoS also contains capabilities for dealing with a variety of policy conflicts and for analyzing and testing policies.

KAoS ensures that the Luna agents respect all security and privacy policies, that they respond immediately to human redirection, and that they have the teamwork knowledge they need to work with analysts and other agents collaboratively. KAoS policies also ensure that the entire system adapts automatically to changes in context, environment, task reprioritization, or resources. New or modified policies can be made effective immediately.

5   The Luna Agent Framework

5.1   Overview of Luna Features

In our cybersecurity applications, Luna agents function both as interactive assistants to analysts and as continuously-running background aids to data processing and knowledge discovery. Luna agents achieve much of their power through built-in teamwork capabilities that, in conjunction with IHMC's KAoS policy services framework, allow them to be proactive, collaborative, observable, and directable. Luna also relies on KAoS for capabilities such as registration, discovery, self-description of actions and capabilities, communications transport, and messaging.

Figure 4 shows how KAoS integrates with Luna to provide services and to enforce policies. An OWL representation of Luna is maintained within the KAoS Distributed Directory Service. Through its interactions with the Luna host environment, KAoS

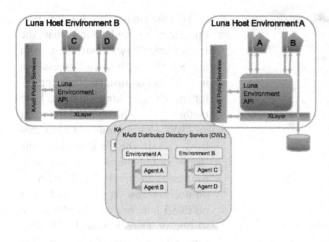

Fig. 4. Luna Conceptual Architecture

regulates the lifecycle of both the environment (e.g., start and stop Luna) and the agents (e.g., create, pause, resume, stop, and move agents). Policy can also regulate environment context for shared agent memory (e.g., getting and setting its properties), allowing efficient parallel processing of large data sets. An agent-based implementation of context mirroring across different Luna environments is provided. Through policy, the Luna host environment also governs agent progress appraisal—a subject to which we will return later.

Because Luna policy checking and enforcement is done by virtue of KAoS-based "method-call" messages to agents and other components, actions taken by an agent on its own (invoking its own methods) are not subject to policy. This design choice posed no problems for the use cases we envisioned.

In the future, KAoS will also integrate with VIA to provide a means of policy enforcement outside the Luna host enironment. VIA [14] is a next generation cross-layer communications substrate for tactical networks and information systems. VIA allows fine-grained enforcement of policy down to operating-system-level operations such as the opening of a socket and the monitoring and filtering of specific elements of agent messaging.

In order to support dynamic scalability, load balancing, adaptive resource management, and specific application needs, the Luna platform supports the policy-governed option of allowing the *state* of agents (vs. *code* of agents) to migrate between operating environments and hosts. The Luna environment maintains agent mailboxes with message forwarding when agents migrate. Luna state mobility will provide the foundation for future implementation of agent persistence (i.e., saving and loading agent state to a persistent store).

5.2 Automated Mapping between Java and OWL

Within the base class for Luna cyber agents are defined some common agent tasks that can be called through OWL descriptions. However, one of the most important innovations in Luna is the ability to add custom agent actions to the policy ontology, based on their Java equivalent. IHMC provides a Java2OWL tool to assist with this task.

Fig. 5. Java2OWL Tool

To understand this feature, it is important to understand that the framework allows translation from the KAoS 'method call' messages to OWL action instance descriptions for policy checking, and back to method calls. The ability to convert an OWL description to a Java method call is the feature that puts 'teeth' in obligations. A Luna environment can invoke such methods on itself or any set of agents hosted on that Luna, or pass the obligation to one or more remote Luna environments for execution. Combine this obligation invocation feature with the fact that obligations can be triggered by one set of actors and fulfilled by another set of actors (e.g., Luna obligated to do X when Agent does Y, All Agents obligated to do X when Luna does Y), and we have a foundation for the implementation of what are called in KAoS "collective obligations" [12]. These are obligations that specify *what* must be done by some group of agents without saying exactly *how* it should be done and *which* specific agent(s) should do it.

The Java2OWL tool (fig. 5) can be used to browse custom agent code, select methods to bring under policy control, and generate an OWL description for the selected method signatures. These methods are then available for policies as Actions performed by Agents of that type. The only prerequisite is that agent code must be available (on the classpath) when Luna starts.

Our ontology for method call requests is currently low-level, representing Java Methods and their parameters including the parameter data types and the order of the parameters in the method signature.

5.3   Selected Applications of Luna to Cyber Operations

Agents play a variety of roles in Sol, our cyber operations framework [15]. Among the most demanding is in multi-layer agent processing and tagging of live or retrospectively played-back NetFlow data representing worldwide Internet traffic. A high-level view of roles and relationships among agents relating to these functions is shown in figure 6.

Incoming UDP traffic goes to a NetFlow agent for parsing and transformation into Java objects (1). In principle, the same or different data could be routed to multiple NetFlow agents on the same or different hosts to share the processing load. The Net-Flow agent sends the data to any number of Tagger agents that work in parallel in real-time to tag the data (2). For example, Watchlist agents tag data that appears on

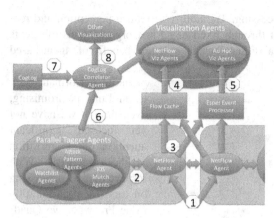

Fig. 6. Agent processing and tagging of NetFlow data

whitelists or blacklists while IDS Match agents tag data corresponding to intrusion detection alerts. Drawing on selected results from low-level tagging agents, Attack pattern agents may be defined to look for higher-level attack patterns. By this means, agent annotations do not merely highlight low-level indicators of threat patterns, but can directly identify the type of threat itself. For instance, instead of requiring the analyst to notice that a configuration of connecting lines (some of which may be obscured) indicates a distributed port scan, agents working on abstracted data semantics can directly indicate the source of the attack. As another example, if a message is anomalous because it is sending oversized packets to a port associated with an SQL database, higher-level agents can abstract that message and represent it as an instance of an SQL injection attack. A system of semaphores ensures that all the Tagger agents have completed their work before the NetFlow agent sends results to the Flow Cache (3). NetFlow Visualization agents enforce policies that mediate data being sent to analyst displays, ensuring, among other things, that data not authorized for viewing by particular users are automatically filtered out (4).

The Esper complex event processor [16] provides support for efficient ad hoc queries of many types that can be initiated and consumed by other visualization agents (e.g., Stripchart View agent) or by agents of other types for further processing (5). We are also considering the use of Esper for data stream handling further upstream in the agent analytic process.

CogLog Correlator agents ingest combined data from selected Tagger agents operating on real-time data (6) and historical data within the CogLog (7). The CogLog is a Semantic-Wiki-based tool prototype with which software agents and human analysts can maintain and use a log of findings pertinent to a given investigation, while also linking to other relevant information from prior cases. Unlike the real-time Tagger agents, the Correlator agent can perform deeper kinds of analytics in "out of band" mode. Among other things, this correlated information can help different analysts "connect the dots" between related investigative efforts. The Correlator agents may send additional data annotations to NetFlow Visualization agents and/or to agents supporting other visualizations (e.g., Connection Graph view) (8). Our Attack Pattern Learning Agents provide another example of an "out of band" agent type. These agents consume and process all NetFlows (rather than just subsets of tagged data produced by Tagger agents) in order to learn and propagate useful threat patterns.

In the future, exploration of larger questions of adversarial intent, attack strategies, and social connections among attackers could also proceed along similar lines of increasing abstraction in agent processing. The ability to reduce perception and reasoning requirements on the analyst through fixed or ad hoc organizations of agents processing visual and logical data dimensions is a major benefit of agent-based analytics.

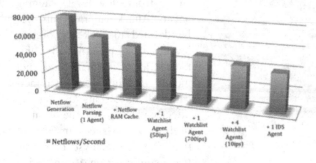

Initial performance data on Luna is promising, even though we have not yet focused significant attention on optimization of the framework. With respect to live processing on our test configuration (Mac Pro with two Quad-core Intel Xeon @ 2.26GHz with 16 GB RAM, 1000baseT Ether-

Fig. 7. Initial Luna performance data

net, Mac Pro RAID Level 0, 4x2TB), the IHMC network of ~100 nodes is the only one we have tested thus far. Performance at this small scale of less than 1000 flows/second is, of course, excellent.

With respect to retrospective performance in our current configuration, the maximum rate of our CyberLab NetFlow emulator playing back Internet 2 data is 80k flows/second (~14MB/second) and the maximum rate of Luna agent NetFlow parsing is 60k flows/second. Sample configurations that include the additional task of maintaining a cache of NetFlows in shared RAM result in rates of 52k flows/second (single watchlist agent with 50 ips on its list), 49k flows/second (a Watchlist agent added with 700 IPs on its list), 43k flows/second (four more Watchlist agents added with 10 IPs each on their lists), and 39k flows/second (an IDS Match agent added whose performance is constrained by file I/O).

We realize that these performance numbers fall short of requirements for some large-scale cyber applications. We are confident that an effort to optimize agent processing within and between agents would yield significant performance increases. More importantly, because of the distributed nature of the Luna architecture, we are in a good position to take advantage of whatever scale of computing and network resources might be available for a given application.

6   Luna Policy Examples

Luna is governed by policy statements that take either the form of authorization or obligation policies as follows:

- Actor is [*authorized* | *not authorized*] to perform Action requested by Actor with attributes…
- [*before* | *after*] Actor performs Action requested by Actor with attributes, Actor is [*obligated* | *not obligated*] to perform Action with attributes…

When Luna policies are defined, the underlined terms above (<u>Actor</u>, <u>Action</u>) are replaced in point-and-click fashion with more-specific concepts automatically drawn from the extensible ontologies maintained within KAoS. Actors in the policy statements above could be made to refer to one or more classes or instances of the Luna host environment, e.g.:

- Class: *All Luna environments*
- Extensionally defined collection of groups: *Luna in group 'NOC_A', 'NOC_B'*
- Intensionally defined collection of groups: *Luna with context property 'Alert Level' in ('Critical', 'High')*
- Extensionally defined collection of individuals: *LunaNOC_A_1, Luna-NOC_A_Shared*
- Intensionally defined collection of individuals: *Luna containing agent 'BotnetC2Correlator'*

Actors could also be made to refer to classes and instances of Luna agents, e.g.:

- Class: *All Agents*
- Intensionally defined Group: *Watchlist matching agents*
- Extensionally defined Group: *Agents in group NOC_A*
- Extensionally defined Group: *Agents running in Luna NOC_A_1*
- Specific Instances: *BotnetC3Correlator_Agent, ZeusWatchlistAgent*

To make these ideas more concrete, we now give two groups of examples: 1). Teamwork policies; 2). Network Operations Center scenario policies.

6.1   Teamwork Policy Examples

It is one thing to enable software agents to perform the taskwork needed to help human analysts with complex high-tempo tasks and quite another to equip them with the capabilities that allow them to become good team players. Our perspective on resilient human-agent teamwork comes from joint activity theory [17], a generalization of Herbert Clark's work in linguistics [18, p. 3]. Our theory describes the criteria for joint activity, outlines aspects of its "choreography," and highlights the major requirements for effective coordination in situations where the activities of parties are interdependent. For the purposes of this discussion, we focus primarily on examples of the sorts of policies we are designing to support human-agent teamwork, under the headings of *observability, directability, interpredictability, learning,* and *multiplicity*:

- *Observability*: An important aspect of observability is being able to know how agents are progressing on their current tasks, especially those in which their actions are interdependent (e.g., "I'm not going to be able to get you the information you need to get started on your task by the deadline to which we agreed previously.") To support this, we have implemented built-in mechanisms and policies for *progress appraisal* [19] in Luna.

- *Directability*: When agents need to be redirected due to changes in priorities, new knowledge, or failures, users can add and retract obligations on particular agents or classes of agents or Luna environments at runtime. This includes obligations relating to life-cycle control, such as pausing or resuming their operation.
- *Interpredictability*: One way in which the interpredictability of an agent can be assessed is through a combination of data on its current progress with its past history of work in similar contexts.
- *Learning*: The observability features of agents can be used to support capabilities for policy learning—i.e., creating new KAoS policies programmatically based on patterns that are consistent and important to tasks being undertaken by a whole class of agents. The process of learning itself may be subject to policies relating to the scope of adaptation permitted in a given context. It may also be subject to optional policy requirements for human oversight.
- *Multiplicity*: Multiplicity, the requirement for multiple perspectives on the same data, can be supported by policy-based enforcement of data consistency across these perspectives. For example, policies would ensure that changes in one view of the data would propagate correctly (and with the appropriate policy restrictions on what can be viewed) to other kinds and instances of views on that data.

Of the areas mentioned above, progress appraisal and agent (re-)directability through obligations are currently the most well-worked-out aspect of these five human-agent-teamwork-based considerations in Luna. As an illustration of how these considerations can be supported through policy, we describe our implementation of progress appraisal below.

Providing regular reports of agent progress is an integral feature of every Luna agent. The Luna environment handles all of the progress management including:

- Registration and deregistration of users and agents to receive progress reports from particular agents;
- Maintaining a timer to send agent progress reports periodically (e.g., every minute);
- Querying the agent periodically for its current progress, or providing an interface for agents to announce milestone-based progress events;
- Distributing the agent's progress reports to the interested parties.

The decision to have the Luna environment manage progress appraisal rather than relying on the agents themselves was a deliberate one. Some of the key advantages over agent self-managed progress appraisal include:

- Luna can provide progress in conditions where the agent cannot;
- Luna may pause an agent so that it would no longer capable of sending progress messages.
- The agent may be buggy or otherwise unresponsive, but Luna will still send progress to users (indicating that the agent is unresponsive);
- Policy control over the frequency and recipients of progress appraisal enables directing or redirecting progress appraisals from groups of agents to other agents for further analysis.

6.2   Network Operations Center Scenario Policy Examples

In the development of experimental scenarios for network operations center use of our framework, we considered requirements for access control, action authorization, information sharing, and coordination between local and remote sites. Below we give some illustrative examples of KAoS policy support in Luna for these issues.

Imagine a scenario involving two cooperating network operations centers (NOC) at different locations, NOC_A and NOC_B. Each NOC has its own policies, in addition to policies that are shared between them.

NOC_A has three Luna environments:

- *Luna_NOC_A_Monitoring*: Within this environment, monitoring administrators from NOC_A create and maintain agents to support shared visualizations.
- *Luna_NOC_A_Analysis*: Within this environment, analysts from NOC_A create agents to perform ad hoc analysis and investigation tasks.
- *Luna_NOC_A_Shared*: Within this environment, analysts from either NOC_A or NOC_B can create agents to perform ad hoc analysis and investigation tasks.
  NOC_B has one Luna environment:
- *Luna_NOC_B*: Within this environment, analysts from NOC_B create agents to perform monitoring, ad hoc analysis, and investigation tasks.

KAoS uses the concept of "domains" to define the scope of policies. In this case, the two NOCS will share a domain. In addition, each NOC will have its own domain, and, within NOC A, each NOC A Luna environment will be a subdomain to the NOC A domain. For the convenience of the administrator wanting to minimize the number of policies that need to be defined, the mode of a domain can be set to be "tyrannical" (where everything is forbidden that is not explicitly authorized) or "laissez-faire" (where everything is permitted that is not explicitly forbidden). Here are some examples of policies in the scenario, assuming a tyrannical domain.

Authorization Policy Examples. This positive authorization policy specifies that NOC Administrators can make any request of any Luna environment:

Any Luna is authorized to perform any Action

requested by a member of the NOC_Administrators Group

This positive authorization policy allows any user to make requests of any Luna environment belonging to the same group as that user.

Luna in any Group is authorized to perform any Action

requested by a member of the same Group

The positive authorization policy permits remote users from NOC_B to manage agents within the shared Luna environment, while the negative authorization policy prevents these users from lifecycle actions such as stopping the environment or changing its context properties:

LunaNOC_A_Shared is authorized to perform any Action

requested by a member of Group NOC_B

LunaNOC_A_Shared is not authorized to perform any environment lifecycle action

requested by a member of Group NOC_B

Obligation Policy Examples. This positive obligation policy requires any newly created Watchlist agent to send progress reports to the Watchlist Correlation agent:

After Any Luna performs create agent of type 'Watchlist Agent,' that Luna is obligated to add agent progress listener where:
  listener is 'Watchlist Correlation Agent'
  agent is the agent that was created

This positive obligation policy requires approval by NOC-Aadmin before any agents not specifically requested migrate into the NOC_A group:

Before Luna_NOC_A_Shared performs move agent where:
  destination in group NOC_A
  and not requested by 'NOC-AAdmin'
That Luna is obligated to obtain approval from 'NOC-AAdmin'

Obligation Policy Examples Combining Luna Agents and Environments. The Actors in an obligation policy may be a mix of Luna environments and agents. In this way, a Luna environment can respond to specified agent actions and vice versa.

For example, this positive obligation policy requires the Luna_NOC_A_Analysis environment to send a progress update every time a Botnet agent identifies a new botnet command-and-control address:

After BotnetAgent performs FoundC2
Luna_NOC_A_Analysis is obligated to perform SendAgentProgressUpdate

This positive obligation policy requires a class of agents that keep large data caches in RAM to clear their caches before being paused:

Before Luna performs PauseAgent where
Agent is of type CacheAgent
That Agent is obligated to perform DumpCache

7   Conclusions

This article has provided an overview of some of the unique features of the Luna agent framework. In particular, we have shown how Luna is specifically designed to allow developers and users to leverage different forms of policy-based governance in an endless variety of ways. Although our illustrations have been drawn from the application of Luna to cyber operations, we believe that its features will prove useful in the future for many additional problem domains.

References

1. Hoffman, R.R., Bradshaw, J.M., Ford, K.M.: Introduction. In: Hoffman, R.R. (ed.) Essays in Human-Centered Computing, 2001-2011, pp. 2001–2011. IEEE Press, New York City (2012)
2. Ford, K.M., Glymour, C., Hayes, P.: Cognitive prostheses. AI Magazine 18(3), 104 (1997)
3. Ford, K.M., Hayes, P.: On computational wings: Rethinking the goals of Artificial Intelligence. Scientific American. Special issue on "Exploring Intelligence 9(4), 78–83 (1998)

4. Carroll, J.M., Kellogg, W.A., Rosson, M.B.: The task-artifact cycle. In: Carroll, J.M. (ed.) Designing Interaction: Psychology at the Human-Computer Interface. Cambridge University Press, New York (1991)
5. Bradshaw, J.M.M., Carvalho, L., Bunch, T., Eskridge, P., Feltovich, C., Forsythe, R.R., Hoffman, M., Johnson, D.: Coactive emergence as a sensemaking strategy for cyber operations. ICST (Institute for Computer Science, Social Informatics, and Telecommunications Engineering) Transactions of Security and Safety. Special section on The Cognitive Science of Cyber Defense Analysis (in press, 2012)
6. Carvalho, M., Cowin, T.B., Suri, N.: MAST: A mobile agent based security tool. In: Proceedings of the Seventh World Multiconference on Systemics, Cybernetics, and Informatics, SCI 2003 (2003)
7. Bradshaw, J.M., Dutfield, S., Benoit, P., Woolley, J.D.: KAoS: Toward an industrial-strength generic agent architecture. In: Bradshaw, J.M. (ed.) Software Agents, pp. 375–418. AAAI Press/The MIT Press, Cambridge (1997)
8. Suri, N., Bradshaw, J.M., Breedy, M.R., Groth, P.T., Hill, G.A., Jeffers, R., Mitrovich, T.R., Pouliot, B.R., Smith, D.S.: NOMADS: Toward an environment for strong and safe agent mobility. In: Proceedings of Autonomous Agents 2000, Barcelona, Spain (2000)
9. Bradshaw, J.M., Beautement, P., Breedy, M.R., Bunch, L., Drakunov, S.V., Feltovich, P.J., Hoffman, R.R., Jeffers, R., Johnson, M., Kulkarni, S., Lott, J., Raj, A., Suri, N., Uszok, A.: Making agents acceptable to people. In: Zhong, N., Liu, J. (eds.) Intelligent Technologies for Information Analysis: Advances in Agents, Data Mining, and Statistical Learning, pp. 361–400. Springer, Berlin (2004)
10. Klein, G., Woods, D.D., Bradshaw, J.M., Hoffman, R.R., Feltovich, P.: Ten challenges for making automation a "team player" in joint human-agent activity. IEEE Intelligent Systems 19(6), 91–95 (2004)
11. Bradshaw, J.M., Feltovich, P., Johnson, M.: Human-Agent Interaction. In: Boy, G. (ed.) Handbook of Human-Machine Interaction, Ashgate, pp. 283–302 (2011)
12. Uszok, A., Bradshaw, J.M., Lott, J., Johnson, M., Breedy, M., Vignati, M., Whittaker, K., Jakubowski, K., Bowcock, J.: Toward a flexible ontology-based approach for network operations using the KAoS framework. In: Proceedings of MILCOM 2011, pp. 1108–1114. IEEE Press, New York City (2011)
13. Westerinen, A., et al.: Digital Policy Management Ontology Discussion. Presentation at the DPM Meeting, January 25 (2012)
14. Carvalho, M., Granados, A., Perez, C., Arguedas, M., Winkler, R., Kovach, J., Choy, S.: A Cross-Layer Communications Susbtrate for Tactical Environments. In: McDermott, P., Allender, L. (eds.) Collaborative Technologies Alliance, Advanced Decisions Architecture, ch. 5 (2009)
15. Bradshaw, J.M., Carvalho, M., Bunch, L., Eskridge, T., Feltovich, P., Johnson, M., Kidwell, D.: Sol: An Agent-Based Framework for Cyber Situation Awareness. Künstliche Intelligenz 26(2), 127–140 (2012)
16. EsperTech, http://esper.codehaus.org/ (accessed July 18, 2012)
17. Klein, G., Feltovich, P.J., Bradshaw, J.M., Woods, D.D.: Common ground and coordination in joint activity. In: Rouse, W.B., Boff, K.R. (eds.) Organizational Simulation, pp. 139–184. John Wiley, New York City (2004)
18. Clark, H.H.: Using Language. Cambridge University Press, Cambridge (1996)
19. Feltovich, P.J., Bradshaw, J.M., Clancey, W.J., Johnson, M., Bunch, L.: Progress Appraisal as a Challenging Element of Coordination in Human and Machine Joint Activity. In: Artikis, A., O'Hare, G.M.P., Stathis, K., Vouros, G.A. (eds.) ESAW 2007. LNCS (LNAI), vol. 4995, pp. 124–141. Springer, Heidelberg (2008)

A Novel Strategy for Efficient Negotiation in Complex Environments

Siqi Chen and Gerhard Weiss

Department of Knowledge Engineering, Maastricht University
Maastricht, The Netherlands
{siqi.chen,gerhard.weiss}@maastrichtuniversity.nl

Abstract. A complex and challenging bilateral negotiation environment for rational autonomous agents is where agents negotiate multi-issue contracts in unknown application domains against unknown opponents under real-time constraints. In this paper we present a novel negotiation strategy called **EMAR** for this kind of environment which is based on a combination of Empirical Mode Decomposition (EMD) and Autoregressive Moving Average (ARMA). **EMAR** enables a negotiating agent to adjust its target utility and concession rate adaptively in real-time according to the behavior of its opponent. The experimental results show that this new strategy outperforms the best agents from the latest Automated Negotiation Agents (ANAC) Competition in a wide range of application domains.

1 Introduction

Automated negotiation has a broad spectrum of potential applications in domains and fields such as task and service allocation, web and grid, electronic commerce and electronic markets, online information markets, and automated procurement. This potential has led to rapidly increasing research efforts on automated negotiation in recent years. The work described in this paper focuses on automated bilateral multi-issue negotiation (e.g., [16]). A key feature of this negotiation form is that two agents negotiate with the intention to agree on a profitable contract for a product or service, where the contract consists of multiple issues which are of conflictive importance for the negotiators. Examples of such issues are price and quality. More specifically, the paper concentrates on realistic scenarios for bilateral multi-issue negotiations which are particularly complex for the following four reasons. First, the negotiating agents do not know each other (i.e., they have not encountered before) and thus have no information about the preferences or strategies of their respective opponents. Second, the negotiators have no prior knowledge about the negotiation domain (e.g., about resource limitations) and thus have to cope with uncertainty about the domain. Third, we concentrate on negotiation with deadline and discount, that is, negotiation happens are under real-time constraints (the agents thus should take into consideration at each time point the remaining negotiation time) and the final utility decreases over time according to some discounting factor. And

I.J. Timm and C. Guttmann (Eds.): MATES 2012, LNAI 7598, pp. 68–82, 2012.

fourth, computational efficiency is important because agents may have very limited computing resources. Negotiation scenarios showing these characteristics are particularly challenging but common in reality.

This paper introduces a novel negotiation strategy called **EMAR** for those scenarios. **EMAR** integrates two key aspects of successful negotiation: efficient opponent modeling and adaptive concession making. Opponent modeling realized by **EMAR** aims at predicting the utilities of the opponent's future counter-offers through two standard mathematical techniques, namely, Empirical Mode Decomposition (EMD, e.g. [7]) and Autoregressive Moving Average (ARMA, e.g. [2]).[1] Adaptive concession making is achieved by dynamically adapting the concession rate (i.e., the degree at which an agent is willing to make concessions in its offers) on the basis of the utilities of future counter-offers which can be expected according to the acquired opponent model.

The remainder of this paper is structured as follows. Section 2 overviews important related work. Section 3 describes the standard negotiation environment used in the our research. Section 4 presents **EMAR** in detail. Section 5 offers a careful experimental analysis of **EMAR**. Section 6 identifies some important research lines induced by the described work and concludes the paper.

2   Related Work

An early influential work in the field of automated negotiation is [8]. This work raised awareness of issues related to concession making and tactical negotiation which are also relevant to the approach described here. Based on this early work and subsequent works it triggered, it had been realized that successful negotiation needs to be based in one way or another on opponent modeling. Various approaches today are available that aim at generating and utilizing opponent models in order to optimize an agent's negotiation behavior (see [11] for a useful overview). Available approaches can be classified into two groups. First, approaches that aim at learning the opponent's *preference profile*, including e.g. the opponent's reservation value (i.e., the minimum utility an agent wants to obtain) and issue/value ordering. An example of such an approach is [17], where Lin et al. use Bayesian learning to approximate the opponent preference profile; another example is [6] where kernel density estimation is used as an approximation technique. A critical drawback of preference modeling is that it tends to quickly become computationally intractable for domains having a large outcome space (especially if real-time constraints apply). Second, approaches that aim at learning the opponent's *negotiation strategy*. For instance, Saha et al. [20] make use of Chebychev polynomials to estimate the chance that the negotiation partner accepts an offer in repeated single-issue negotiations. Brzostowski et al. [3] investigate the prediction of future counter-offers online on the basis of the previous negotiation history by using differentials, thereby assuming that the opponent strategy is based on a mix of time- and behavior-dependent one.

---

[1] As the underlining shall indicate, the acronym **EMAR** is composed of "EM" and "AR".

Hou [13] employs non-linear regression to predict the opponent's tactic (though in single-issue negotiation), thereby supposing that the opponent uses a pure tactic as introduced in [8] and that the types of tactics are fixed. In [4] artificial neural networks (ANNs) are applied and explored in offline competition against human negotiators. Another interesting work in this area is [21]. There Williams et al. apply Gaussian processes to predict the future opponent concession before the deadline of negotiation is reached and to set the agent's "optimum" concession rate accordingly. This approach performed better than the best negotiating agents of ANAC 2010 and made the 3rd place in ANAC 2011 (ANAC is the International Automated Negotiation Agents Competition). (Our approach, **EMAR**, is experimentally evaluated against this and other agents, details are given in Section 5.) A disadvantage of available approaches exploiting learning of an opponent's negotiation strategy are the strong and often unrealistic assumptions on which they are based (as described above). In contrast, **EMAR** – which belongs to the "negotiation strategy learning" class – is designed to avoid such assumptions; in particular, it does not require any prior knowledge about the opponents and the negotiation domain.

3   Negotiation Environment

We adopt a basic bilateral multi-issue negotiation setting which is widely used in the agents field (e.g., [6,8,9]) and the negotiation protocol we use is based on a variant of the alternating offers protocol proposed in [18].[2] Let $I = \{a, b\}$ be a pair of negotiating agents, i represent a specific agent ($i \in I$), J be the set of issues under negotiation, and j be a particular issue ($j \in \{1, ..., n\}$ where n is the number of issues). The goal of a and b is to establish a contract for a product or service. Thereby a contract consists of a package of issues such as price, quality and quantity. Each agent has a lowest expectation for the outcome of a negotiation; this expectation is called reserved utility u_{res}. w_j^i ($j \in \{1, ..., n\}$) denotes the weighting preference which agent i assigns to issue j, where the weights of an agent are normalized (i.e., $\sum_{j=1}^{n}(w_j^i) = 1$ for each agent i). During negotiation agents a and b act in conflictive roles which are specified by their preference profiles. In order to reach an agreement they exchange offers O in each round to express their demands. Thereby an offer is a vector of values, with one value for each issue. The utility of an offer for agent i is obtained by the utility function defined as:

$$U^i(O) = \sum_{j=1}^{n}(w_j^i \cdot V_j^i(O_j))   \tag{1}$$

where w_j^i and O are as defined above and V_j^i is the evaluation function for i, mapping every possible value of issue j (i.e., O_j) to a real number.

Following Rubinstein's alternating bargaining model [19], each agent makes, in turn, an offer in form of a contract proposal. Negotiation is time-limited instead

---

[2] The description of the environment in this section is taken from our previous publication on automated negotiation, see [5].

of being restricted by a fixed number of exchanged offers; specifically, negotiators have a shared hard deadline by when they must have completed or withdraw the negotiation. The negotiation deadline of agents is denoted by t_{max}. In this form of real-time constraints, the number of remaining rounds are not known and the outcome of a negotiation depends crucially on the time sensitivity of the agents' negotiation strategies. This holds, in particular, for discounting domains, that is, domains in which the utility is discounted with time. As usual for discounting domains, we define a so-called discounting factor δ ($\delta \in [0, 1]$) and use this factor to calculate the discounted utility as follows:

$$D(U, t) = U \cdot \delta^t \qquad (2)$$

where U is the (original) utility and t is the standardized time. As an effect, the longer it takes for agents to come to an agreement the lower is the utility they can achieve.

After receiving an offer from the opponent, O_{opp}, an agent decides on acceptance and rejection according to its interpretation $I(t, O_{opp})$ of the current negotiation situation. For instance, this decision can be made in dependence on a certain threshold $Thres^i$: agent i accepts if $U^i(O_{opp}) \geq Thres^i$, and rejects otherwise. As another example, the decision can be based on utility differences. Negotiation continues until one of the negotiating agents accepts or withdraws due to timeout.[3]

4   EMAR

EMAR includes two core stages – opponent modeling and adaptive concession making – as described in detail in 4.1 and 4.2, respectively. A third important stage of our strategy, its response mechanism to counter-offers, is described in 4.3. An overview of EMAR is given in *Algorithm 1* (the individual steps are explained in the text).

4.1   Opponent Modeling

Opponent modeling realized by EMAR aims at predicting the future behavior of the negotiating opponents. It is mainly based on the combination of Empirical Mode Decomposition (EMD, [7,10,14]) and Autoregressive Moving Average (ARMA, [2]), which applies the "divide-and-conquer" principle to construct a reasonable forecasting methodology. More specifically, first EMD is employed to decompose the time series given by the utilities of past counter-offers into a finite number of components and then ARMA is applied to predict future values of these sub-components. EMD, which is based on the Hilbert-Huang transform (HHT), is a decomposition technique which relies on time-local characteristics

---

[3] If the agents know each other's utility functions, they can compute the Pareto-optimal contract [18]. However, in most applications a negotiator will not make this information available to its opponent.

Algorithm 1. The **EMAR** approach. Let t_c be the current time, δ the time discounting factor, and t_{max} the deadline of negotiation. O_{opp} is the latest offer of the opponent and O_{own} is a new offer to be proposed by **EMAR**. χ is the time series comprised of the maximum utilities over intervals. ξ is the lead time for prediction and ω is the estimated central tendency of χ. E is predicted received utility series. u_{res} is the reservation utility, specifying the lowest expectation to negotiation benefit, and e_{min} is the conservative estimation of opponent concession. R is the dynamic conservative expectation function. u' is the expected utility at time t_c.

```
1:  Require: R, δ, ξ, t_max
2:  while t_c <= t_max do
3:      O_opp ⇐ receiveMessage;
4:      recordBids(t_c, O_opp);
5:      if TimeToUpdate(t_c) then
6:          χ ⇐ preprocessData(t_c)
7:          (ω, E) ⇐ getForecast(χ, ξ);
8:          (u_res, e_min) ⇐ updateParas(ω, χ, t_c);
9:          R ⇐ (u_res, e_min);
10:     end if
11:     u' = getExpUtility(t_c, E, δ, R);
12:     if isAcceptable(u', O_opp, t_c, δ) then
13:         accept(O_opp);
14:     else
15:         O_own ⇐ constructOffer(u') ;
16:         proposeNewBid(O_own);
17:     end if
18: end while
```

of data and can deal with nonlinear and non-stationary time series in a adaptive manner. EMD has been widely applied as a powerful data analysis tool in a broad scope of fields such as finance, image processing, ocean engineering and solar studies.

A main advantage of EMD as the decomposition method is that it is very suitable for analyzing complicated data and is fully data driven (thus requiring no additional decomposition information) – this makes EMD adaptive and very efficient. Compared to traditional Fourier and wavelet decompositions, EMD has several distinct advantages [15,22]. First of all, fluctuations within a time series are automatically selected from the time series. Second, EMD can adaptively decompose a time series into several independent components called Intrinsic Mode Functions (IMFs). With the help of the IMFs a residue can be calculated which easily captures the main trend of the time series. Lastly, unlike wavelet decomposition, no filter base function (e.g. scaling and wavelet functions) need to be determined beforehand – which is particularly helpful when there is no prior knowledge about which filters work properly.

The IMFs satisfy the following conditions:

1. In the whole data set (time series), the number of extrema and the number of zero crossings must either equal or differ at most by one.

2. At any point, the mean value of the envelope defined by the local maxima and the envelope defined by the local minima is zero.

Any data series can be decomposed into IMFs according to the following sifting procedure (let $k \geq 1$, k indicates the iterative decomposition level):

1. Take signal r_{k-1} as input, with r_0 representing the original signal $\chi(t)$.
   (a) Identify all local extrema of the signal r_{k-1}.
   (b) Construct the upper envelop $Upp(r_{k-1})$ and the lower envelop $Low(r_{k-1})$ by interpolating via cubic spline the maximum and minimum values, respectively.
   (c) Approximate the local average based upon the envelop mean as
   $Mean(r_{k-1}) = \frac{Upp(r_{k-1}) + Low(r_{k-1})}{2}$
   (d) Compute the candidate implicit mode $h_{kn} = r_{k-1} - Mean(r_{k-1})$.
   (e) If h_{kn} is an IMF, then calculate r_k as $r_k = r_{k-1} - h_{kn}$. Otherwise replace r_{k-1} with h_{kn} and repeat sifting.
2. If r_k has an implicit oscillation mode, set r_k as input signal and repeat step 1.

This sifting process serves two purposes: to eliminate riding waves and to make the wave profiles symmetric.

The decomposition procedure can be repeated on all subsequent components r_j, and the result is

$$r_0 - c_1 = r_1, r_1 - c_2 = r_2, \ldots, r_{n-1} - c_n = r_n. \tag{3}$$

This procedure terminates when (1) the latest residue r_k becomes a monotonic function (from which no more IMFs can be extracted) or (2) the IMF component c_k or the residue becomes less than the predetermined value of substantial consequence. Overall, c_1 contains the signal at a fine-grained time scale and subsequent IMFs include information at increasingly longer time periods. Eventually, the data series $\chi(t)$ can be expressed by

$$\chi(t) = \sum_{i=1}^{n} c_i + r_n \tag{4}$$

where n is the total decomposition layer (i.e., the number of IMFs), c_i is the i-th IMF component and r_n is the final residue (which represents the main trend of the data series). With that, we are able to achieve a decomposition of the data into n empirical modes and one residue. The IMFs contained in each frequency band are independent and nearly orthogonal to each other (with all having zero means) and they change with variation of the data series $\chi(t)$, whilst the residue part captures the central tendency.

The process of opponent modeling corresponds to the lines 2 to 10 in *Algorithm 1*. When receiving a new bid from the negotiation opponent at the time t_c, the agent records the time stamp t_c and the utility $U(O_{opp})$ this bid offers to it according to its utility function. The maximum utilities in consecutive equal

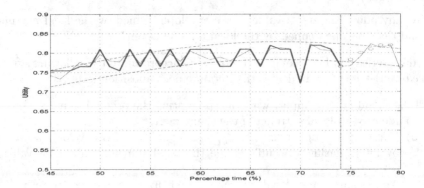

Fig. 1. Illustrating the prediction power of our model. The original time series χ, represented by the thick solid line, is received from negotiation with agent Agent_K2 in domain *Camera*. The prediction is depicted by the thin solid line, and the two dash lines show the estimated upper and lower bounds of χ. The vertical thick dash-dot line indicates the time point at which **EMAR** calculated the prediction, and the circles right to this line are the utilities actually received in the subsequent negotiation phase.

time intervals and the corresponding time stamps are used periodically as input for predicting the opponent's behavior (line 5 and 6). The reasons for *periodical* updating are similar to those mentioned in [21]. First, this reduces the computation complexity of **EMAR** so that the response speed is improved. Assume *all* observed counter-offers were taken as input, then it would be necessary deal with perhaps many thousands of data points at once. This computational load would have a clear negative impact on the quality of negotiation in a real-time setting. Second, the effect of noise can be reduced.This is important because in multi-issue negotiations a small change in utility of the opponent can result in a large utility change for the other agent – and this can easily result in a fatal misinterpretation of the opponent's behavior.

In the next stage, ARMA is used to extend all resulting components, and then ensemble them to predict opponent behaviors (shown in line 7). ARMA is a common analysis regression model which is widely used in many fields, with the formal expression as follows:

$$(1 + \sum_{i=1}^{p} \phi_i L^i)X_t = (1 + \sum_{i=1}^{q} \theta_i L^i)\epsilon_i \qquad (5)$$

where L is the lag operator, the ϕ_i are parameters for the p-order autoregressive term, the θ are parameters for the moving average term with q order, and ϵ is a parameter capturing white noise.

Equation 5 is applied with appropriate parameters for each component extracted by EMD (i.e. c_i and the residue) for the purpose of making accurate forecasting, and then **EMAR** ensembles them to predict the future counter-offers of the opponent. Fig. 1 exemplifies this methodology, depicting the prediction power of our model with a lead time of 6 intervals. Further details of usage are given in section 4.2.

4.2   Adaptive Concession Making

EMAR adjusts the concession on the basis of the generated opponent model. Thereby a dynamic conservative expectation $R(t)$ is used to avoid "irrational concession" caused by inaccurate or over-pessimistic predictions. This makes sense in the case of negotiation opponents that are "sophisticated and tough" and always avoid making any concession in bargaining: in this case the prediction results could lead to a misleading, very low expectation about the utility offered by the opponent and this, in turn, could result in an adverse concession behavior. Furthermore, using global prediction could make this situation even worse. (This phenomenon is also considered in 5.2.)

$R(t)$ guarantees the desired minimum utility at each step, yielding values which are a lower bound of the agent's expected utilities. For the purpose of adaptation to complex negotiation sessions, $R(t)$ requires two parameters e_{min} and u_{res}. They are both periodically updated depending on the forecast of the opponent concession (line 8). e_{min} is defined as the minimum expectation of the compromise suggested by the opponent. Specifically, e_{min} is set it to the maximum value from $\psi^{low}(t)$, which is the estimated lower bound of the extended χ given by the central trend. Formally:

$$\psi^{low}(t) = \omega(t) \cdot (1 - Stdev(r_{[0,t_l]})) \tag{6}$$

where ω is the extended main tendency of χ, $r_{[0,t_l]}$ is the ratio between ω over χ within $[0,t_l]$ and $Stdev$ is the standard deviation. Having obtained ψ^{low}, e_{min} can be defined as follows:

$$e_{min} = \begin{cases} \vartheta & if \ \vartheta > Max(\psi^{low}) \\ Max(\psi^{low}) & otherwise \end{cases} \tag{7}$$

where $Max(x)$ gives the maximum value of input vector x. Because counter-offers with utilities indicated by ψ^{low} have already been received or can be expected during the lead time with high probability, using the maximum value assures an increase of the agent's potential profit even without significant concession.

The variable u_{res} is the reservation utility specifying the lowest expectation about the eventual benefit from a specific negotiation session. Formally this is captured by:

$$u_{res} = \begin{cases} \vartheta & if \ \vartheta > Max(\psi^{low}_{0,t_l}) \\ \frac{1}{2}(Max(\psi^{low}_{0,t_l}) + \vartheta) & otherwise \end{cases} \tag{8}$$

Because the final negotiation outcome (failure or agreement) is more sensitive to u_{res} than e_{min}, **EMAR** adopts a cautious and conservative way to specify it, where only ψ^{low}_{0,t_l} is considered.

Based on the above specifications, $R(t)$ is defined as follows:

$$R(t) = e_{min} + \frac{e_{min} - u_{res}}{2}(1 - t^{5\delta}) + \cos(\frac{1 - \delta}{1.1}t^{\lambda})(1 - t^{1/\beta})(getMaxU(P)\cdot\delta^{\eta} - u_{res})$$

(9)

where β and λ are concession factors affecting the concession rate, $getMaxU(P)$ is the function specifying the maximum utility dependent on a given preference P, δ is the discounting factor, and η is the risk factor which reflects the agent's optimal expectation about the maximum utility it can achieve. $R(t)$ can be characterized as a "dynamic conservative expectation function which carefully suggests utilities".

The subsequent process is then to decide the target utility **EMAR** expects to achieve, represented by line 11. The ensemble of all predicted components provide useful information about the opponent behavior in the lead time. This is essential because the observation of ω (and its estimated bound ψ) only gives the ambiguous area where opponent would make a compromise (rather than how the compromise might look like). Let the predicted utility series be $E(t)$, given as follows:

$$E(t) = \sum_{i=1}^{n} f_i(c_i(t), \xi) + f_{n+1}(r_n(t), \xi)$$

(10)

where $f_i(x)$ is the corresponding prediction model for components c_i (the IMFs) and r_n (the residue). Assume that the future expectation we have obtained from $E(t)$ is optimistic (i.e., there exists an interval $\{T | T \neq \varnothing, T \subseteq [t_c, t_s]\}$), that is,

$$E(t) \geq R(t)), \quad t \in T$$

(11)

where t_s is the end point of the predicated series and $t_s \leq t_{max}$. In this case the time $\hat{t}$ at which the maximal expectation $\hat{u}$ is reached is set as follows:

$$\hat{t} = argmax_{t \in T} E(t) \quad .$$

(12)

Moreover, in this case $\hat{u}$ is defined as

$$\hat{u} = E(\hat{t}) \quad .$$

(13)

On the other hand, now assume that the estimated opponent concession is below the agent's expectations (according to $R(t)$), that is, there exists no such time interval T as in the "optimistic case". In this case it is necessary to define the probability of accepting the best possible utility that can be achieved under this pessimistic expectation. This probability is given by

$$\varphi = 1 - \frac{D(R, t_{\nu}) - D(E, t_{\nu})}{\rho \cdot \sqrt{1 - \delta}D(getMaxU(P)\delta^{\eta}, t_{\nu})}, \quad t_{\nu} \in [t_c, t_s]$$

(14)

where ρ indicates the acceptance tolerance for the pessimistic forecast and t_{ν} is given by

$$t_{\nu} = argmin_{t \in [t_c, t_s]}(|D(E, t) - D(R, t)|)$$

(15)

φ is compared to a random variable x with uniform distribution from the interval $[0,1]$, and the best possible outcome in the "pessimistic" scenario is chosen as the target utility if $\delta \geq x$. The rationale behind it is that if the agent rejects the "locally optimal" counter-offer (which is not too negative according to ρ), it probably loses the opportunity to reach a fairly good agreement. In the acceptance case, $\hat{u}$ and $\hat{t}$ are defined as $E(t_\nu)$ and t_ν, respectively. Otherwise, $\hat{u}$ is defined as -1, meaning it does not have an effect, and $R(t_c)$ is used to set the expected utility u'. When the agent expects to achieve a better outcome (see Equation 11), it chooses the optimal estimated utility $\hat{u}$ as its target utility (see Equations 12 and 13).

It is apparently not rational and smart to concede immediately to $\hat{u}$ when $u_l \geq \hat{u}$, and it is not appropriate for an agent to concede $\hat{u}$ without delay if $u_l < \hat{u}$ (especially because the predication may be not very accurate). To deal with this, **EMAR** simply concedes linearly. More precisely, the concession rate is dynamically adjusted in order to be able to "grasp" every chance to maximize profit. Overall, u' is calculated as follows:

$$u' = \begin{cases} R(t_c) & if \ \hat{u} = -1 \\ \hat{u} + (u_l - \hat{u})\frac{t_c - \hat{t}}{t_l - \hat{t}} & otherwise \end{cases} \qquad (16)$$

where u_l is the utility of last bid before **EMAR** performs prediction process at time t_l.

4.3   Response to Counter-Offers

This stage corresponds to lines 12 to 17 in Algorithm 1. When the expected utility u' has been determined, the agent needs to examine whether the utility of the counter-offer $U(O_{opp})$ is better than u' or whether it has already proposed this offer earlier in the negotiation process. If either of these two conditions is satisfied, the agent accepts this counter-offer and finishes the current negotiation session. Otherwise, the agent constructs a new offer which has an utility within some range around u'. There are two main reasons for this kind of construction. First, in multi-issue negotiations it is possible to generate a number of offers whose utilities are the same or very similar for the offering agent, but have very different utilities the opposing negotiator. (Note that in real-time constraints environment there are no limits for the number of negotiation rounds, which means that an agent in principle can construct a large amount of offers having a utility close to u' and, thus, has the opportunity to explore the utility space with the purpose of improving the acceptance chance of its offers.) Second, it is sometimes not possible to make an offer whose utility is exactly equivalent to u'. It is thus reasonable that an agent selects any offer whose utility is in the range $[(1 - 0.005)u', (1 + 0.005)u']$. If no such solution can be constructed, the agent makes its latest bid again in the next round. Moreover, with respect to negotiation efficiency, if u' drops below the value of the best counter offer in terms of its utility based on our own utility function, the agent chooses that best counter offer as its next offer. This makes much sense because this counter offer can well satisfy the expected utility of the opponent who then will be inclined to accept it.

5   Experimental Analysis

In order to evaluate the performance of **EMAR**, the General Environment for Negotiation with Intelligent multipurpose Usage Simulation (GENIUS) [12] is used as the testing platform. GENIUS is the standard platform for the annual International Automated Negotiating Agents Competition (ANAC) [1]. In this environment an agent can negotiate with other agents in a variety of domains, where every is defined by the utility function of each negotiating party. The performance of an agent (its negotiation strategy) can be evaluated via its utility achievements in negotiation tournaments which include a possibly large number of negotiation sessions for a variety of negotiation domains. Subsection 5.1 describes the overall experimental and Subsection 5.2 then presents the experimental results.

5.1   Environmental Setting

EMAR is compared against the best winners (i.e., the top five agents) of ANAC2011; these are HardHeaded, Gabhoninho, IAMhaggler2011, BRAMAgent and Agent_K2 (descending order in ANAC2011). Moreover, we use five standard domains created for ANAC. All but one of them – the *"Camera"* domain – were originally used in ANAC as non-discounting domains. Three of these domains were used in ANAC2010 and two were used in ANAC2011. This choice of domains from ANAC2010+2011 makes the overall setting balanced and fair and avoids any advantageous bias for **EMAR** (note that the creators of the 2011 winners knew the ANAC2010 domains and could optimize their agents accordingly). Agent_K2, for instance, would like to accept an offer early in the domain *Energy* designed for ANAC2011, which is completely meaningless for the agent as this proposal grants the maximum profit to the opponent while no benefit is given to itself. For convenience, we refer to the non-discounting domain *"Travel"* as U_1, *"Itex vs Cypress"* as U_2, *"England vs Zimbabwe"* as U_3, *"Amsterdam party"* as U_4, and *"Camera"* as U_5. The corresponding versions with time-dependent discounting are referred to as $D_1, D_2, \ldots, D_5$, respectively. The application domains we choose cover a wide range of domain characteristics with respect to four key aspects, as overviewed in Table 1.

Table 1. Overview of application domains

Domain features	U1(D1)	U2(D2)	U3(D3)	U4(D4)	U5(D5)
Domain issues	7	4	5	6	6
Domain size	188,160	180	576	3024	3600
Opposition	weak	strong	medium	medium	weak
Discounting factor	1(0.4)	1(0.5)	1(0.6)	1(0.7)	1(0.89)

We, for each domain, ran a tournament consisting of 6 agents (i.e., the five 2011 winners and our **EMAR** agent) 10 times to get results with high statistical confidence, where each agent negotiates against all other agents in different roles. (These roles are predefined in ANAC and correspond to conflictive "buyer" and "seller" roles.) The agents do not have any information about their opponents' strategies and they are prohibited to take advantage of knowledge they might have acquired in previous negotiation sessions about the behavior of their opponents. The duration of a negotiation session is 180 seconds.

The **EMAR** agent divides the overall duration of a session into 100 consecutive intervals of 1.8 seconds each. The lead time ξ is 6, the threshold θ is 0.6, the pair concession coefficients of (β, λ) is (0.04,3) and the risk factor η is 0.2, the tolerance coefficient ρ is 0.05. These values work well in practice, but we have not intended to tweak them to stay away the issues of over-fitting and unfair competition.

5.2   Experimental Results

We show the experimental results achieved by each agent in terms of raw score based on non-discounting domains in Fig. 2(a), and discounting domains in Fig. 2(b). As shown in figures, the agent using **EMAR** demonstrates excellent bargaining skills. More precisely, **EMAR** wins in eight domains with 17.4% above the mean score achieved in these domains by the five competing agents. Moreover, **EMAR** made the second place for the other two domains (i.e., U5 and D2), where the performance of **EMAR** for these domains is only marginally (namely, 0.82% and 2.34%) below the score achieved by the best performer. Most notably and impressive, **EMAR** outperforms the other agents in the most competitive domain, U2, by 35.2% (compared to the mean score achieved by the other agents) and in the domain with the largest outcome space, U1, by 15.8% (compared to mean score).

Table 2 shows the overall score of all agents in terms of raw and normalized results averaged over the ten domains. Normalization is done in the standard way, using the maximum and minimum utility obtained by all agents. According to the overall performance depicted in this table, **EMAR** is the best agent, with an average normalized score of 0.772. This is 14% above the second best agent – Hardheaded –, and 30.1% above the mean score of all five opponents. Moreover, the performance of **EMAR** is very stable – compared to the other agents it shows the smallest variance values. **EMAR** is followed by HardHeaded and Gahboninho; these two agents made the first and the second place in ANAC2011. Agent_K2, which is a refined version of the champion (named Agent_K) in ANAC2010, made the fourth place. To summarize, these results show that **EMAR** is pretty efficient and significantly outperforms in a variety of negotiation scenarios the state-of-the-art automated negotiators (resp. negotiation strategies) currently available.

An interesting observation is that there is the noticeable gap between **EMAR** and IAMhaggler2011. More specifically, this agent only reaches 68.5% of the performance of **EMAR** in terms of normalized utility. As described in [21], similar

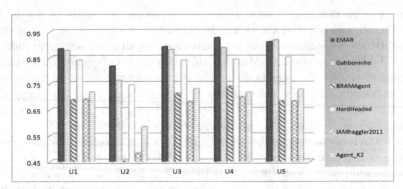

(a) Average raw scores of all agents in non-discounting domains

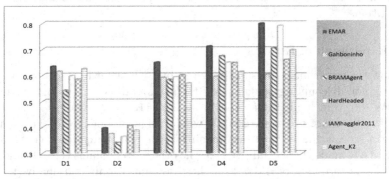

(b) Average raw scores of all agents in discounting domains

Fig. 2. Average raw scores of all agents in the ten domains. The vertical axis represents utility and horizontal axis represents domain.

to **EMAR** IAMhaggler2011 aims at predicting an opponent's future in order to be able to adjust its own behavior appropriately. Unlike **EMAR**, IAMhaggler (i) applies Gaussian process as prediction tool and (ii) adapts its concession rate on the basis of a global prediction view (i.e., on the basis of the whole preceding negotiation process). Our experimental studies suggest that a main reason for this performance gap lies in the global prediction view: this view seems to be vulnerable to "irrational concession making" induced by pessimistic predictions (see also 4.2). The phenomenon of irrational concession becomes increasingly apparent when IAMhaggler2011 bargains with "sophisticated and tough" opponents like HardHeaded, Gahboninho, and **EMAR**. For instance, when competing against these opponents in the most conflictive domain (U_2) then IAMhaggler2011 achieves only a mean utility of 0.313 while the three opponents achieve 0.903 on average. The situation furthermore is similar for other domains in our experiments.

Table 2. Overall performance of every agent, represented by mean and variance

Agent	Raw Score		Normalized Score	
	mean	variance	mean	variance
EMAR	**0.768**	**0.0011**	**0.772**	**0.0035**
HardHeaded	0.712	0.0012	0.677	0.0031
Gahboninho	0.711	0.0021	0.675	0.0058
Agent_K2	0.637	0.0022	0.559	0.0057
IAMhaggler2011	0.614	0.0026	0.528	0.0070
BRAMAgent	0.612	0.0091	0.526	0.0219

6 Conclusion

This work introduced an effective strategy for automated bilateral negotiation in complex scenarios (multi-issue, time-constrained, unknown opponents, no prior domain knowledge, computationally feasible, etc.). The strategy, **EMAR**, outperforms the five best agents of the International Automated Negotiation Agents Competition (ANAC) 2011. We think the exceptional results justify to invest further research efforts into this approach.

Research described in this paper opens several interesting research avenues. First, is the **EMAR** strategy robust and flexible enough if the opponent has an incentive to deviate? (Independent of **EMAR**, this question has not yet been treated sufficiently in the field of automated negotiation.) An idea we pursue at the moment is to address this question with the help of empirical game analysis. Second, are there opponent modeling techniques which are even more efficient than the one used by **EMAR**? Techniques that could be considered here are e.g. GMDH networks or artificial neural networks. And, last but not least, is it possible to extend opponent modeling of **EMAR**, which focuses on modeling the opponents' negotiation strategies, toward modeling the opponents' preferences as well? We believe such an extension could lead to a significant increase in negotiation power (not only for **EMAR** but in general), though at the cost of assuming the availability of certain domain knowledge.

References

1. Baarslag, T., Hindriks, K., Jonker, C., Kraus, S., Lin, R.: The First Automated Negotiating Agents Competition (ANAC 2010). In: Ito, T., Zhang, M., Robu, V., Fatima, S., Matsuo, T. (eds.) New Trends in Agent-Based Complex Automated Negotiations. SCI, vol. 383, pp. 113–135. Springer, Heidelberg (2012)
2. Box, G., Jenkins, G.M., Reinsel, G.C.: Time Series Analysis: Forecasting and Control, 3rd edn. Prentice-Hall (1994)
3. Brzostowski, J., Kowalczyk, R.: Predicting partner's behaviour in agent negotiation. In: Proceedings of the Fifth Int. Joint Conf. on Autonomous Agents and Multiagent Systems, AAMAS 2006, pp. 355–361. ACM, New York (2006)

4. Carbonneau, R., Kersten, G.E., Vahidov, R.: Predicting opponent's moves in electronic negotiations using neural networks. Expert Syst. Appl. 34, 1266–1273 (2008)
5. Chen, S., Weiss, G.: An Efficient and Adaptive Approach to Negotiation in Complex Environments. In: Proceedings of the 20th European Conference on Artificial Intelligence (ECAI 2012), Montpellier, France. IOS Press (2012)
6. Coehoorn, R.M., Jennings, N.R.: Learning on opponent's preferences to make effective multi-issue negotiation trade-offs. In: Proceedings of the 6th Int. Conf. on Electronic Commerce, ICEC 2004, pp. 59–68. ACM, New York (2004)
7. Hunag, N.E., Shen, Z., Long, S.R.: The empirical mode decomposition and the hilbert spectrum for nonlinear and nonstationary time series analysis. Proc. R. Soc. Lond. A, 903–995 (1998)
8. Faratin, P., Sierra, C., Jennings, N.R.: Negotiation decision functions for autonomous agents. Robotics and Autonomous Systems 24(4), 159–182 (1998)
9. Faratin, P., Sierra, C., Jennings, N.R.: Using similarity criteria to make issue trade-offs in automated negotiations. Artif. Intell. 142(2), 205–237 (2002)
10. Flandrin, P., Rilling, G., Gonçalvès, P., Basics, I.E.: Empirical mode decomposition as a filter bank. IEEE Signal Proc. Lett. 11, 112–114 (2004)
11. Hendrikx, M.: A survey of oppnent models in automated negotiation. Technical report, Delft University of Technology, The Netherlands (September 2011)
12. Hindriks, K., Jonker, C., Kraus, S., Lin, R., Tykhonov, D.: Genius: negotiation environment for heterogeneous agents. In: Proceedings of AAMAS 2009, pp. 1397–1398 (2009)
13. Hou, C.: Predicting agents tactics in automated negotiation. In: IEEE / WIC / ACM International Conference on Intelligent Agent Technology, pp. 127–133. IEEE Computer Society, Los Alamitos (2004)
14. Huang, N.E., Shen, S.S.P.: Hilbert-Huang transform and its applications. World Scientific (2005)
15. Huang, N.E., Wu, M.-L., Qu, W., Long, S.R., Shen, S.S.P.: Applications of hilbert-huang transform to non-stationary financial time series analysis. Appl. Stoch. Models Bus. Ind. 19(3), 245–268 (2003)
16. Lai, G., Li, C., Sycara, K., Giampapa, J.: Literature review on multi-attribute negotiations. Technical Report CMU-RI-TR-04-66, Robotics Institute, Pittsburgh, PA (December 2004)
17. Lin, R., Kraus, S., Wilkenfeld, J., Barry, J.: Negotiating with bounded rational agents in environments with incomplete information using an automated agent. Artif. Intell. 172, 823–851 (2008)
18. Raiffa, H.: The art and science of negotiation. Harvard University Press, Cambridge (1982)
19. Rubinstein, A.: Perfect equilibrium in a bargaining model. Econometrica 50(1), 97–109 (1982)
20. Saha, S., Biswas, A., Sen, S.: Modeling opponent decision in repeated one-shot negotiations. In: Proceedings of the Fourth International Joint Conference on Autonomous Agents and Multiagent Systems, AAMAS 2005, pp. 397–403. ACM, New York (2005)
21. Williams, C., Robu, V., Gerding, E., Jennings, N.: Using gaussian processes to optimise concession in complex negotiations against unknown opponents. In: Proceedings of the 22nd Internatioanl Joint Conference on Artificial Intelligence. AAAI Press (2011)
22. Yu, L., Wang, S., Lai, K.K.: Forecasting crude oil price with an emd-based neural network ensemble learning paradigm. Energy Economics 30(5), 2623–2635 (2008)

Selfish Road Users – Case Studies on Rule Breaking Agents for Traffic Simulation

Jörg Dallmeyer[1], Andreas D. Lattner[1], and Ingo J. Timm[2]

[1] Information Systems and Simulation, Institute of Computer Science
Goethe University Frankfurt, P.O. Box 11 19 32, 60054 Frankfurt, Germany
[2] Business Informatics I, University of Trier, D-54286 Trier, Germany

Abstract. Many studies in the context of traffic simulation investigate effects of new regulation strategies on travel times. However, in most cases it is assumed, that these regulations are followed by all actors. This work investigates the effects of non-compliance of simulated road user agents. In particular it is analyzed to what extent rule breaking agents have advantages on the cost of the remaining road users. For evaluation we take into account three different scenarios: Overtaking prohibition for trucks on motorways, bicycles pushing to the front at traffic lights and pedestrians crossing roads in aggressive manner. In all scenarios, the fraction of rule breaking agents is varied. Simulation results show that rule breaking does not always lead to disadvantages for the remaining road users.

Keywords: Traffic Simulation, Multiagent-Based Simulation (MABS), Non-Compliance.

1 Introduction

Traffic research established in the first half of the preceding century, mostly focusing on car movement on freeways (see, e.g., [13]). The investigation of compliance to rules and to what extent road users accept to wait, when not having the right of way has become a field of study as the traffic volume increased. Ashton investigates, for instance, the acceptance of gaps when cars need to wait at intersections and determined an influence of the direction of turning and the overall traffic situation [1].

In traffic research, non-compliance or rule breaking is often called *aggressiveness*. According to Laagland, a driving style is aggressive when it intentionally increases the probability for traffic accidents and is motivated by impatience, anger, hostility or the attempt to save time [24].

Referring to Sharkin, the causes for aggressions in traffic have to be separated into different categories: situation and environmental dependent aggressions, character of the driver, and demographic characteristics [29]. Unexpected high traffic volumes or jams increase the risk of becoming aggressive in traffic [31]. In studies it is reported that aggressions in traffic are not dependent on sex [15], but younger drivers (about 18 to 23 years old) tend to be more aggressive than older drivers [33].

I.J. Timm and C. Guttmann (Eds.): MATES 2012, LNAI 7598, pp. 83–95, 2012.
© Springer-Verlag Berlin Heidelberg 2012

The behavior of different road users changes due to influences of emotions and social norms. The behavior of bicyclists changes, when riding in a bunch [18]. Johnson et al. studied the non-compliance rates for red lights and found 3.0% up to 13.0% of bicycles ignoring red traffic lights, for different places of study [17].

Pedestrians safe up to 22% of crossing time, when ignoring red lights [32]. Whether a pedestrian crosses a road at the intended position or not depends on the additional time needed for crossing and its personality [16,21]. Brewer et al. investigated the gap acceptance behavior of pedestrians and found out, that pedestrians cross roads with an underestimation of the time gap in road traffic of 0.58s on average.

Aggressive behavior may be simulated in a microscopic traffic simulation system, like, e.g., MAINS^{2}IM which is used in this study. The agent technology provides powerful opportunities to model an arbitrary behavior and to investigate the influence of this behavior on the overall traffic situation in the simulation area. Agents are frequently used for traffic simulation. A survey is given in [20]. This work analyzes three case scenarios, each of it simulating one kind of aggressive behavior.

The overall research goal is two-fold. On the one hand, it is necessary to model such behavior in order to understand how it influences urban traffic. The first step on the way to an enhancement is always to understand, why the current situation is like it is and then to try influencing actions. On the other hand we model aspects of urban driving that occur in reality and thus aim at making MAINS^{2}IM more realistic.

The paper is structured as follows. The next section discusses related work. Section 3 briefly describes the simulation system MAINS^{2}IM, used for this work. A view on the used microscopic traffic models for cars, bicycles and pedestrians is provided in section 4, discussing the opportunity to model non-compliance to norms. Section 5 shows the conducted case studies. The work closes with conclusions and ideas for future investigations in section 6.

2   Related Work

Enabling agents to make the decision to violate rules has been regarded in different works. In this context, terms like norms, conventions, contracts, obligations, and sanctions have been used to formulate requested behavior and consequences if certain regulations are violated. Modeling a high degree of autonomy can thus leave the final decision to the agent if it is willing to accept consequences of non-compliant behavior. Boella and Lesmo [4] introduce an approach where obligations and norms can be modeled following Goffman's work in sociology. They show how this model can be integrated in BDI (Belief, Desire, Intention) architectures to explicitly model obligations and sanctions.

Dignum [10] proposes three levels of norms, namely the private level, the contract level, and the convention level. In the private level, built-in norms of agents are modeled which are also taken into account for pro-active behavior decision.

The contract level allows for modeling obligations and authorizations including consequences for violations. Referring to Dignum, this can be used for legal contracts as well as for informal agreements between agents. Regarding conventions, interpretation rules and prima facie norms can be modeled, representing laws or social norms.

In our society, many rules and norms exist. One example: When two pedestrians run the risk of colliding with each other, both try to sidestep in order to prevent from collision. Baek et al. use a simple cellular automaton model for movement of pedestrians and investigate, what happens, when a certain percentage of pedestrians does not comply to this norm [2]. The risk of jamming due to high traffic densities can be minimized, when a small amount of pedestrians is non-compliant [2].

Ehlert and Rothkrantz present a microscopic traffic simulation system with reactive driving agents [11] that focuses on modeling of human driving behavior for car traffic. The agents may violate traffic rules like velocity restrictions, using one-way roads only in the correct direction and driving on the right side of the road. Drivers, preferring higher velocities are modeled to have a higher probability to overtake slower vehicles. Unfortunately, the used car model is not described and evaluated. Nevertheless, the paper presents interesting ideas for modeling of aggressive behavior for urban traffic simulation systems.

Yuhara and Tajima discuss the need for multi agent-based traffic simulation systems in the context of road safety studies with focus on driver assistance systems [34]. The proposed decision making part of the driver agents considers individual settings for lane choices, gap acceptances, time delays and other values. The model takes account for probabilities to stop or go at red or yellow traffic lights and control actions taken for emergency collision avoidance. In other words, non-compliance is one of the topics of this work.

The simulation software Paramics uses a car following model with an included parameter for manipulation of driver characteristics with focus on aggressivity. However, the parameter only influences the safety distances, held by driver agents [30].

3   Simulation System

The case studies presented in this work are done with the traffic simulation system MAINS^{2}IM (MultimodAl INnercity SIMulation). The system uses cartographical material from *OpenStreetMap*[1] and automatically splits the data into several GIS^2-layers in the shapefile format for different types of geometry and logical grouping of information (e.g., landscape polygons, waterways, buildings, points, railways, routes and roads). Geographical operations and visualization are done with help of the *GeoTools*[3] library.

---

[1] http://www.openstreetmap.org
[2] Geographical Information System.
[3] http://www.geotools.org

A graph data structure is built from the layers and several analysis and correction steps detect important information, e.g., speed limitations, right-of-way, traffic lights, zebra crossings or roundabouts.

The simulation system is written in Java and can be used on a standard desktop PC. More detailed information can be found in [6,7] and on the corresponding website http://www.mainsim.eu.

Road users are modeled as simple reflex agents, representing driver-$road -$ $user$-entities (with $road - user \in \{car, bicycle, walker\}$). This enables to take account for individual driving capabilities like target velocity, probability of dallying or valuation of safety distances. All used road user models are microscopic models. The next section deals with the different types of road users and their inclusion in MAINS^{2}IM and discusses extensions of the models to allow for rule breaking in certain situations.

4   Traffic Models

The microscopic traffic models of MAINS^{2}IM include models for cars, bicycles and pedestrians. The following subsections provide a brief introduction to their functionalities.

4.1   Cars

The car model is a continuous version of the well known Nagel-Schreckenberg-Model (NSM) [27]. NSM has been shown to behave realistic in freeway scenarios with respect to flow-density relationships. It is a cellular automaton based approach with each simulation time step lasting $1s$ real-time. Each cell has a length of $7.5m$, leading to movements of $v \cdot 7.5m$.

Each simulated car performs the following steps in parallel. At first, try to accelerate ($v \leftarrow v + 1$), if $v < 5$. Determine the gap γ to the preceding car. Set $v \leftarrow \min (v, \gamma)$. Dally with probability τ. When dallying, set $v \leftarrow \max (0, v - 1)$.

Many extensions like, e.g., the consideration of brake lights [14], a slow-start rule [5] and rules for multi-lane traffic [22] have been developed. A shortcoming of NSM is its cell size, leading to only a few different velocities. Thus, the size of the cells has been reduced in [23].

MAINS^{2}IM uses a space continuous car model on basis of NSM (see, e.g., [6]) with modifications mentioned above. Each car has an individual value of τ. The model also reproduces realistic values for freeway traffic and is capable of the simulation of different amounts of acceleration and car length [6].

In urban traffic, bicycles and pedestrians need to be respected. Interaction with bicycles takes place when a relatively slow bicycle slows down a car. Assuming that a driver that has a low probability to dally τ will be likely to overtake, the car decides whether to overtake the bicycle with probability $1 - \tau$. Overtaking will be possible, if the width of the road is bigger than the sum of the widths of the car, the bicycle and a potential upcoming road user. Otherwise, a sufficient gap in traffic is needed to overtake and to move back to the right-hand side of the road, before colliding with upcoming traffic. Additionally, overtaking is not possible, when the maneuver would last more than $5s$ (horizon of planing) or a crossing would be passed during overtaking (risk of accident).

Interaction with pedestrians takes place when pedestrians use traffic lights or crosswalks or just cross roads without sufficient gaps in traffic. Pedestrians and bicycles are treated like other cars with regard to slowing down in order to keep the safety distance to them.

MAINS^{2}IM provides passenger cars, trucks and delivery vehicles. The differences between those classes are the values for width, length, acceleration and maximum velocity. Trucks have $\tau = 0$, assuming the use of cruise control mechanisms.

4.2 Bicycles

Bicycles are entities, mainly driving on roads. Thus, the model of behavior is strongly related to the car model. The differences are a slower values of τ, a fixed length of $2m$, a fixed width of $1m$ (including a side wise distance when a car overtakes a bicycle) and smaller values of acceleration, maximum velocity and safety distance.

Bicycles can be enabled to elbow their way through the city road map. In this case, road users in front will be overtaken, when they drive below a threshold velocity of $2m \cdot s^{-1}$. It is assumed that it is possible to overtake in every situation without respect to rules. This behavior mostly takes place at traffic lights.

The difference in routing between cars and bicycles is that cars prefer fast routes with respect to travel time. Bicycles perform short routes under preference of bicycle paths.

4.3 Pedestrians

The simulation of pedestrians is done with a twofold model, because pedestrians are able to move on edges and nodes in the graph. Edges are ways and pedestrians use sidewalks. Nodes are crossing points like, e.g., a crossing of two roads, a crosswalk or a traffic light. When pedestrians walk on sidewalks, it is assumed, that interaction between pedestrians will average over time and a pedestrian will basically be able to move with an individual average travel velocity for sidewalks.

A pedestrian can cross a road on an edge, when a sufficient gap in traffic is given. According to [28] it certifies, that the estimated crossing time (ECT) for a road with width w and a walking velocity of v

$$ECT = \frac{w}{v} + AF \tag{1}$$

is smaller than the given gap. The summand AF is called aggressiveness factor and influences the gap acceptance behavior of the pedestrians. The value of AF decreases, when a pedestrian needs to wait for crossing, because of insufficient gaps. Afterwards it recovers to its original value.

The other method to cross a road is the usage of nodes. Interaction with other pedestrians mainly occurs at those places, in reality. Thus, a microscopic pedestrian model is used to take account for this. A continuous version of the model presented in [3] is used.

Pedestrians also estimate gaps for crossing nodes of the simulation graph, except when crossing with right of way at crosswalks. Traffic lights are used, via literally pressing the button and then waiting for green time.

Detailed information about the model can be found in [8] and [25].

5 Case Studies

The case studies presented in this work focus on road users with non-compliant behavior. The experiments examine the corresponding effects and especially the questions:

- Is it advantageous for the non-compliant road users to break rules?
- What is the effect of this behavior for the remaining road users?

The first experiment takes place on a motorway, followed by two experiments in a city.

5.1 Motorway: Overtaking Prohibition for Trucks

The motorway for this simulation experiment is a synthetic graph consisting of a circle of 20km length. The road has no branch connections. The speed limit is set to $55\text{m} \cdot \text{s}^{-1}$, resulting in each car driving as fast as desired or rather as possible due to interactions with other cars. The motorway has two lanes, enabling for overtaking maneuvers. This assembly basically matches the motorways for evaluation of traffic models, extensively used in literature (see, e.g., [27,12,19,35]).

An amount of 250 cars (85% passenger cars, 15% trucks) drives on the motorway. Trucks are prohibited to overtake on the whole motorway. The truck agents do not always comply to this rule. 100 settings are generated. Each setting consists of 250 individual cars with randomly chosen starting position and car behavioral parameters. Each simulation run consists of a settlement phase of 900 simulation iterations and a measurement phase of 18,000 iterations (5 hours real-time). The velocities for the group of passenger cars, trucks and overall are denoted for each simulation iteration during the measurement phase. The results of a simulation run are the average values for those velocities. Because of the stochastic nature of the used car model, the average result of 5 simulation runs with identical setup (replications) is generated and taken as the result of the corresponding non-compliance rate.

The experiment starts with a non-compliance rate of 0%. Then, the non-compliance rate is incremented with a step size of 10% using the same setup. This is done until all rates till 100% are simulated. The whole procedure is

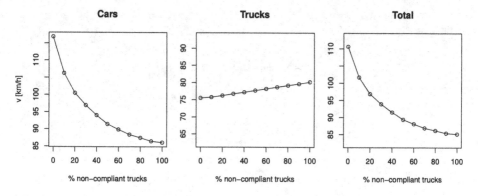

Fig. 1. Simulation results for the motorway experiment

repeated for 100 settings. The results shown in figure 1 are average values of the 100 settings.

The group of truck agents raises its average velocity around $4.66 \text{km} \cdot \text{h}^{-1}$ between the extreme settings, that every agent complies and that no agent complies to the overtaking prohibition for trucks. On the other hand, the passenger cars loose about $30.85 \text{km} \cdot \text{h}^{-1}$ when no truck agent complies to the rule. The small amount of 10% of the truck being non-complient reduces the passenger car velocities by about $10.63 \text{km} \cdot \text{h}^{-1}$.

The reduction in passenger car velocity results from overtaking trucks, that are very slow in comparison to passenger cars. The trucks profit from non-compliance, because the problem of getting stuck behind a slower truck is resolved. The overall average velocity graph shows, that the total average velocity of all road users decreases by about $25.46 \text{km} \cdot \text{h}^{-1}$. Thus, non-compliance of trucks is disadvantageous in this scenario.

5.2   Urban Scenario Design

The urban scenarios for this work are located in the city of Trier. Figure 2 shows an excerpt of the simulation area. The first experiment focuses on bicycles, followed by a second experiment on pedestrians.

The simulation in the city of Trier consists of 1,000 road users (50% passenger cars, 25% bicycles and 25% pedestrians). Source and destination points are chosen randomly. Two routing mechanisms are used: A bidirectional A* method and a probability-based routing mechanism that only considers starting positions and then builds a route on basis of turning probabilities after the method, discussed in [9]. What routing method to use is chosen randomly for each road user.

Beside the changed mixture and amount of road users, the different routing characteristics and the usage of real world cartographical material, the simulation procedure remains identical in relation to the preceding experiment.

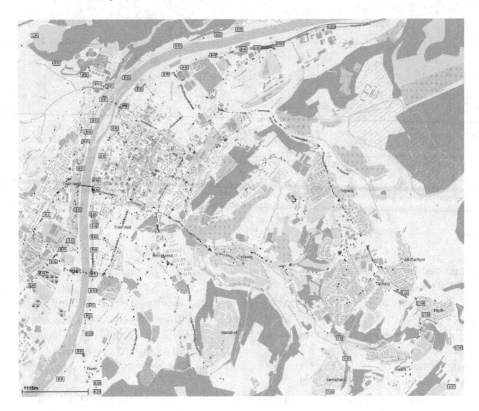

Fig. 2. Area of simulation. The graph consists of 4495 nodes and 5386 edges and has a total length of roads 485km.

5.3   Pushing Bicycles

The first urban experiment undertakes the influence of bicycles pushing to the front at traffic lights. It is assumed that pushing is not allowed. The non-compliant action is to enable bicycles to use the overtaking mechanism, described in section 4.2 and thus to push. The idea is that cars might need to overtake the same bicycle several times, because it pushes at each traffic light on its way. This should lead to a significant loss of time for the cars. The measurement examines travel times of simulated road users of the three different types. Figure 3 shows the simulation results.

Bicycle agents have an advantage, when pushing to the front, because they can still move on, when they should wait. The reduction of travel time for bicycles is 14.85s, when no bicycle complies to the rules. The influence of pushing is small ($\approx 1,75\%$ reduction of travel time), because most of the travel time is not spent pushing at red lights.

Pedestrians are not effected, at all, because they spend most of the time on sidewalks and the interactions with bicycles do not change due to pushing at traffic lights. The interesting result is, that cars are not restrained by

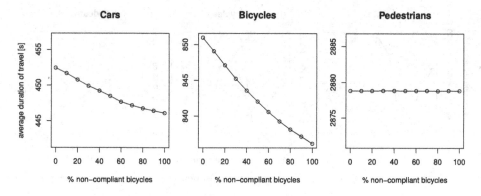

Fig. 3. Simulation results for non-compliant bicycles experiment

non-compliant bicycle agents in this simulation scenario. Quite the contrary, cars save about 6.33s ($\approx 1,40\%$) of their average travel time, when all bicycles push.

One reason for this could be, that cars and bicycles use different routing characteristics. Bicycles prefer short roads and cars favor fast roads. Thus bicycles often use smaller roads with less lanes and lower velocity restrictions, that are not frequently used by cars. This could result in bicycles not hindering cars when the traffic light switches to green, because of the use of different turning directions. The more bicycles push at a traffic light, the shorter the waiting queue. This effect may lead to a relatively faster downsizing of the queue, when the traffic light switches to green.

The overall result of this experiment is, that pushing bicycles may decrease their own travel times, as well as the overall travel times for cars and bicycles. Thus, pushing bicycles improve traffic flow in this scenario. Of course, this experiment does not focus on the potentially increasing probability of accidents.

5.4   Aggressive Pedestrians

This experiment studies aggressive behavior by pedestrians. An aggressive pedestrian has $AF = -3$, according to the formalism presented in section 4.3. This leads to a false estimation of gaps by 3s, resulting in pedestrians crossing roads with a time gap up 3s less the time needed to cross the road. Affected cars or bicycles need to brake in order to avoid an accident and wait until the pedestrian has left the road. At crossings (nodes in the graph), aggressive pedestrians disregard red traffic lights or road traffic. This leads to pedestrians that will not wait for other road users and just walk. The effect on road traffic is comparable to the adjusted AF.

The results are shown in figure 4. At first, it has to be noted that the whole range of simulation results, shown in the figure is about 0.31s difference from overall minimum to maximum value (both in the travel time graph for the simulated cars). This is a deviance of $\approx 0.07\%$. Thus, the main result of this

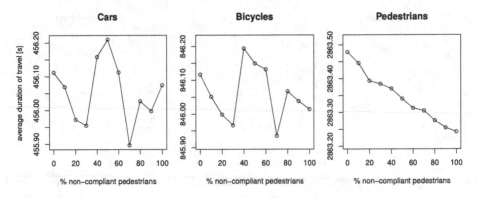

Fig. 4. Simulation results for non-compliant pedestrians experiment

experiment is that aggressive pedestrian behavior does not lead to notable changes in travel times for any of the simulated types of road users.

The graph of the average travel time of pedestrians shows a clear trend to a marginally lowering of travel time, the more pedestrians behave aggressive. The effect is very low, because most of the travel time, pedestrians walk on sidewalks and do not need to cross roads or change the side of the road.

The plots for car and bicycle travel times show no clear trend. Note, that two opposed effects take place, when pedestrian behave aggressive. On the one hand, pedestrians enter roads and force cars and bicycles to slow down. On the other hand, pedestrians stop using traffic lights, leading to a higher efficiency of traffic management at intersections.

6   Conclusions and Future Work

In this paper, we have presented three case studies on non-compliance to traffic rules. The scenarios have been performed with the microscopic agent-based traffic simulation for multi modal traffic MAINS^{2}IM.

The first scenario has investigated the influence of trucks that overtake on a two lane synthetic motorway, even though this action was prohibited for trucks. The influence on the remaining road users on the motorway is strongly negative.

A second scenario has taken place on a road map of the city of Trier. The effects of bicycles pushing to the front in waiting queues in front of red traffic lights are positive for the bicycles. Interestingly, the remaining road users did not suffer from that. Cars even slightly reduced their own travel times.

The third scenario has investigated aggressive pedestrian behavior with respect to changing the side of road. The simulation results do not exhibit considerable deviations in travel time for any of the simulated types of road users.

The scenarios in the city of Trier used realistic road maps, but did not use realistic compositions of traffic and origin-destination information. Thus, the results should not be taken as absolute values, but as indicators of tendencies. Further investigations need to transfer the experiments to calibrated city traffic.

The field of traffic agents that are non-compliant to traffic rules is interesting both for traffic simulation and for multi-agent research. Further investigations could deal with different scenarios. The following questions could be addressed:

In [26], a variable message sign is used that urges car agents to switch to the left lane when nearing to a junction of a motorway under certain traffic conditions. This fastens the process of entering the motorway and increases the overall velocity in the scenario. How robust is this idea if some car agents simply do not switch to the left lane?

Velocity restrictions in urban scenarios may lead to road safety and an overall enhancement in travel times. On freeways, traffic is homogenized by this way. Will the benefits be still achieved, if, for instance, only 80% of the car agents follow this rule?

Different road users accept different gaps in traffic for entering of roads. Very aggressive drivers may cause accidents, very defensive drivers may cause jams behind them. What amount of aggressiveness is efficient for the corresponding road users and for the remaining traffic?

To what extent does aggressive behavior affect the rate of accidents? Accidents may occur, when sufficient braking is not possible, because of an undersized braking distance or when a road user is simply inattentive, as already included in MAINS^{2}IM [26].

Target velocities differ from driver to driver. Consider a three lane motorway. The right lane is mostly used by trucks. The middle lane by slow passenger cars and the left lane for overtaking. The more slow passenger cars drive on the middle lane, the more cars need to overtake on the left lane. This should lead to a slowdown on the left lane. An interesting question is: How many very slow drivers may be tolerated on motorways?

Acknowledgments. This work was partly supported by the *MainCampus* scholarship of the *Stiftung Polytechnische Gesellschaft Frankfurt am Main*.

References

1. Ashton, W.D.: Gap-acceptance problems at a traffic intersection. Journal of the Royal Statistical Society. Series C (Applied Statistics) 20(2), 130–138 (1971), http://www.jstor.org/stable/2346461
2. Baek, S.K., Minnhagen, P., Bernhardsson, S., Choi, K., Kim, B.J.: Flow improvement caused by agents who ignore traffic rules. Physical Review E (Statistical, Nonlinear, and Soft Matter Physics) 80(1), 016111+ (2009), http://dx.doi.org/10.1103/PhysRevE.80.016111
3. Blue, V.J., Adler, J.L.: Cellular automata microsimulation for modeling bi-directional pedestrian walkways. Transportation Research Part B: Methodological 35(3), 293–312 (2001), http://www.sciencedirect.com/science/article/B6V99-41YG51Y-5/2/22693b4ec6fd5d3898831f17d2000bc6
4. Boella, G., Lesmo, L.: A game theoretic approach to norms and agents. Cognitive Science Quaterly 2(3/4), 492–512 (2002)

5. Clarridge, A., Salomaa, K.: A Cellular Automaton Model for Car Traffic with a Slow-to-Stop Rule. In: Maneth, S. (ed.) CIAA 2009. LNCS, vol. 5642, pp. 44–53. Springer, Heidelberg (2009), http://dx.doi.org/10.1007/978-3-642-02979-0_8
6. Dallmeyer, J., Lattner, A.D., Timm, I.J.: From GIS to Mixed Traffic Simulation in Urban Scenarios. In: Liu, J., Quaglia, F., Eidenbenz, S., Gilmore, S. (eds.) 4th International ICST Conference on Simulation Tools and Techniques, SIMUTools 2011, Barcelona, Spain, March 22-24, pp. 134–143. ICST (Institute for Computer Sciences, Social-Informatics and Telecommunications Engineering), Brüssel (2011) ISBN 978-1-936968-00-8
7. Dallmeyer, J., Lattner, A.D., Timm, I.J.: GIS-based Traffic Simulation using OSM. In: Cervone, G., Lin, J., Waters, N. (eds.) Data Mining for Geoinformatics: Methods and Applications. Springer (accepted, 2012)
8. Dallmeyer, J., Lattner, A.D., Timm, I.J.: Pedestrian Simulation for Urban Traffic Scenarios. In: Bruzzone, A.G. (ed.) Proceedings of the Summer Computer Simulation Conference 2012. 44rd Summer Simulation Multi-Conference (SummerSim 2012), pp. 414–421. Curran Associates, Inc. (2012)
9. Dallmeyer, J., Schumann, R., Lattner, A.D., Timm, I.J.: Don't Go with the Ant Flow: Ant-inspired Traffic Routing in Urban Environments. In: Seventh International Workshop on Agents in Traffic and Transportation (ATT 2012), Valencia, Spain (2012)
10. Dignum, F.: Autonomous agents with norms. Artificial Intelligence and Law 7, 69–79 (1999)
11. Ehlert, P.A.M., Rothkrantz, L.J.M.: Microscopic traffic simulation with reactive driving agents. ITSC 2001 2001 IEEE Intelligent Transportation Systems Proceedings Cat No01TH8585 40(5), 860–865 (2001), http://ieeexplore.ieee.org/lpdocs/epic03/wrapper.htm?arnumber=948773
12. Emmerich, H., Rank, E.: An improved cellular automaton model for traffic flow simulation. Physica A: Statistical and Theoretical Physics 234(3-4), 676–686 (1997), http://www.sciencedirect.com/science/article/B6TVG-3VSFH3D-1M/2/68da6d108491eafd93924e74226e428a
13. Greenshield, B.D.: A study of traffic capacity. Proceedings of the 14th Annual Meeting Highway Research Board 14 468, 448–477 (1935)
14. Hafstein, S.F., Pottmeier, A., Wahle, J., Schreckenberg, M.: Cellular Automaton Modeling of the Autobahn Traffic in North Rhine-Westphalia. In: Troch, I., Breitenecker, F. (eds.) Proc. of the 4th MATHMOD, pp. 1322–1331 (2003)
15. Hennessy, D.A., Wiesenthal, D.L.: Gender, driver aggression, and driver violence: An applied evaluation. Sex Roles 44, 661–676 (2001), http://dx.doi.org/10.1023/A:1012246213617, doi:10.1023/A:1012246213617
16. Jason, L.A., Liotta, R.: Pedestrian jaywalking under facilitating and nonfacilitating conditions. Journal of Applied Behavior Analysis 15(15), 469–473 (1982), http://www.pubmedcentral.gov/articlerender.fcgi?artid=1308291
17. Johnson, M., Newstead, S., Charlton, J., Oxley, J.: Riding through red lights: The rate, characteristics and risk factors of non-compliant urban commuter cyclists. Accident Analysis & Prevention 43(1), 323–328 (2011), http://dx.doi.org/10.1016/j.aap.2010.08.030
18. Johnson, M., Oxley, J., Cameron, M.: Cyclist bunch riding: A review of the literature. Tech. rep., Monash University Accident Research Centre (January 2009) iSBN: 0-7326-2355-3
19. Kerner, B.S., Klenov, S.L., Wolf, D.E.: Cellular automata approach to three-phase traffic theory. Journal of Physics A: Mathematical and General 35(47), 9971 (2002)

20. Kesting, A., Treiber, M., Helbing, D.: Agents for traffic simulation. Arxiv preprint arXiv08050300 physics.so, 325–356 (2008), http://arxiv.org/abs/0805.0300
21. King, M.J., Soole, D.W., Ghafourian, A.: Relative risk of illegal pedestrian behaviours. In: Australasian Road Safety Research, Policing and Education Conference, pp. 768–778 (2008), http://eprints.qut.edu.au/17630/
22. Knospe, W., Santen, L., Schadschneider, A., Schreckenberg, M.: A realistic two-lane traffic model for highway traffic. Journal of Physics A: Mathematical and General 35(15), 3369–3388 (2002)
23. Krauss, S., Wagner, P., Gawron, C.: Continuous limit of the Nagel-Schreckenberg model. Phys. Rev. E 54(4), 3707–3712 (1996)
24. Laagland, J.: How to model aggressive behavior in traffic simulation. In: Twente Student Conference on IT, Enschede 3 (2005)
25. Lattner, A.D., Dallmeyer, J., Paraskevopoulos, D., Timm, I.J.: Approximation of Pedestrian Effects in Urban Traffic Simulation by Distribution Fitting. In: Troitzsch, K.G., Möhring, M., Lotzmann, U. (eds.) Proceedings of the 26th EUROPEAN Conference on Modelling and Simulation, pp. 574–580 (2012) ISBN 978-0-9564944-4-3
26. Lattner, A.D., Dallmeyer, J., Timm, I.J.: Learning Dynamic Adaptation Strategies in Agent-Based Traffic Simulation Experiments. In: Klügl, F., Ossowski, S. (eds.) MATES 2011. LNCS, vol. 6973, pp. 77–88. Springer, Heidelberg (2011)
27. Nagel, K., Schreckenberg, M.: A cellular automaton model for freeway traffic. Journal de Physique I 2(12), 2221–2229 (1992)
28. Ottomanelli, M., Caggiani, L., Giuseppe, I., Sassanelli, D.: An Adaptive Neuro-Fuzzy Inference System for simulation of pedestrians behaviour at unsignalized roadway crossings. In: 14th Online World Conference on Soft Computing in Industrial Application 14 (2009)
29. Sharkin, B.S.: Road rage: Risk factors, assessment, and intervention strategies. Journal of Counseling and Development 82, 191–199 (2004)
30. Speirs, E., Braidwood, R.: Quadstone paramics v5.0 technical notes. Tech. rep., Quadstone Paramics Ltd. (2004)
31. Tasca, L.: A review of the literature on aggressive driving research. In: Aggressive Driving Issues Conference (2000)
32. Virkler, M.R.: Prediction and measurement of travel time along pedestrian routes. Transportation Research Record No. 1636, Bicycle and Pedestrian Research 1636, 37–42 (1998) iSSN: 0361-1981, http://dx.doi.org/10.3141/1636-06
33. Wiesenthal, D.L., Hennessy, D., Gibson, P.M.: The driving vengeance questionnaire (dvq): The development of a scale to measure deviant drivers' attitudes. Violence and Victims 15(2), 115–136 (2000)
34. Yuhara, N., Tajima, J.: Multi-driver agent-based traffic simulation systems for evaluating the effects of advanced driver assistance systems on road traffic accidents. Cognition, Technology & Work 8, 283–300 (2006), http://dx.doi.org/10.1007/s10111-006-0045-9, doi:10.1007/s10111-006-0045-9
35. Zhu, H.B., Lei, L., Dai, S.Q.: Two-lane traffic simulations with a blockage induced by an accident car. Physica A: Statistical Mechanics and its Applications 388(14), 2903–2910 (2009)

Modelling Emotional Trajectories of Individuals in an Online Chat*

Maros Galik[1] and Stefan Rank[2]

[1] Faculty of Mathematics, Physics and Informatics,
Comenius University Bratislava, Slovakia
`maros.galik@gmail.com`
[2] Austrian Research Institute for Artificial Intelligence (OFAI)
Vienna, Austria
`stefan.rank@ofai.at`

Abstract. Online communications involve an emotional component that influences the behaviour of internet users. Datasets on online communication allow for modelling emotional effects on individual and collective behaviour of users to make predictions about behaviour in online chat environments. One application of such models is decision-support for online bots that interact with users in real-time for studying the role of emotions in online communication, Affect Listeners, requiring short-term predictions about current participants. We describe an agent-based simulation of individuals' emotional interaction online based on automatic annotation of the affective content of exchanged messages. In particular, we focus on using this model to derive a default model, a 'personality', for new users joining an environment based on already observed users.

Keywords: agent-based simulation, cyberemotions, conversational systems, affective control architectures.

1 Introduction

Online communities are a young phenomenon that started to grow substantially with the common use of the internet among the general population[1]. The communication medium serves as a way to fulfill a typical human need, to form groups - to socialize, as shown by the success of online *boards*, *forums* or *chats*.

Communication online differs substantially from face-to-face interaction. Online, users often communicate only with text but nevertheless try to convey a whole range of emotions, without relying on non-verbal cues, e.g. tone of voice, that enable recognition of irony, sadness, or happiness. On the other hand, this disadvantage was supplanted by elements like emoticons which have an impact on message interpretation and are useful in intensifying a verbal message [5].

---

* Modelling-emotional-trajectories-of-individuals-in-an-online-chat.
[1] See data on Internet use 2001-2011 by the Internet Telecommunication Union. `http://www.itu.int/ITU-D/ict/statistics/` (all URLs retrieved 2012-07-01).

I.J. Timm and C. Guttmann (Eds.): MATES 2012, LNAI 7598, pp. 96–105, 2012.

The project CyberEmotions[2] deals with the role of *collective emotions* in creating, forming, and breaking-up of online-communities. As part of the CyberEmotions project, the development and experimental evaluation of affective dialog systems that interact with users online is undertaken: Affect Listeners [18]. Potential applications of such systems include support tools for online communities, e.g., current information on a group's affective state, or forecasting changes in groups' affective states or interaction dynamics.

In this paper, we present an effort to model the affective communication of individuals in chat-like internet communities as a tool for decision-support employed by these dialog systems. Based on the available datasets, the model is a step towards the support for decisions made by interactive bots that directly communicate with participants online [12,13,19,20]. In particular, the model should be able to accommodate new users joining a chat based on the dominant behaviour of other participants with a longer observed history.

Reference Data. Our modelling and simulation effort depends on available data from interaction logs of Internet Relay Chat (IRC) channels, in particular the support channels for the Ubuntu operating system. Even though these logs are in the public domain, our model does not keep track of complete utterances to be applicable in more privacy-sensitive application areas. The data is pre-processed by an anonymizing tool that introduces numerical ids and replaces utterances with annotations based on available classifiers and language processing tools described below.

The resulting features consist of a single *sender* and potentially a *recipient* of a message, as well as a *two-dimensional emotional evaluation* of the utterance. Further annotations are available but not used in the model described here. Recipients are not always directly known, as users do not need to explicitly target a message. Heuristics are used to determine whether a message is prefixed with the nickname of a user. Positive or negative polarity of an utterance as well as a value corresponding to the level of affective involvement of the author are based on two different classifiers: SentiStrength [22,21] and ANEW [2].

Based on these features, we model the affective communication between users and their emotional states by identifying triggers for affective action in the communication history. In the available datasets, we cannot identify all potential real-world triggers of an action, but only the users' online actions from which we derive emotional states. Some triggers necessarily remain unknown and the current work focuses on a simple model based on the available information. This kind of online modelling is complemented by the analysis of IRC datasets [6] indicating global measures of behaviour in chat environments which can be used to characterise and consequently mimic or violate typical behaviour in specific chat communities.

Goals. The model presented here aims to balance different requirements: suitable complexity to capture the details of affective communication online on the

---

[2] http://www.cyberemotions.eu/

one hand and fast response time on the other. The latter is a consequence of the application as online decision-support for interactive conversational systems. At this level, several questions relevant as a potential input for the systems' decision making mechanisms were identified [12]:

- Which individual will be most likely to provide an accurate response to probing about the group's emotional state, and which one will be most reliable?
- What influence can individuals have on the evolution of collective emotions, and which of the specific participants is likely to have the biggest influence?
- Can potential escalations, both negative and positive, be detected early on?
- What influence will a specific intervention of the system have at the current moment, and which style of intervention is most effective?

Running a simulation on demand to query about the above questions adds the requirement of timely, or possibly anytime, responses but also the need for a simulation that continuously adapts to the current state of an e-community. The model described here is intended to provide the foundation for answering these questions while interacting.

2   Related Work

The modelling of individual emotional behaviour has been an active research topic for some time, see [9,11] for an overview of computational models of emotion. Most of these models are based on psychological theories and targeted at the simulation of affective behaviour for a low number of individuals. Dealing with the emergence of collective emotions in large online groups is the focus of the CyberEmotions project. Different mathematical models have been created based on the datasets collected by the project, see e.g. [17,4,3]. For the current work, the framework described in [17] for modelling the emergence of collective emotions provides a reference point: Using the modelling tool of "Brownian agents" [16], the change of internal variables for valence and arousal is assumed to be mediated by a shared communication field described using stochastic dynamics.

Our model is dependent on affective classification of short text. The main classifier used for data annotation, *SentiStrength* [22], exploits the de-facto grammar and spelling style of cyberspace, to gauge the affective content of a text, providing a specialised variant of sentiment analysis [8,7].

3   Agent Modelling

Generally, agents communicate to achieve their goals in the society (system) in which they exist. Without semantic processing of utterances, we cannot explicitly relate actions to goals for individual agents. In our model, stand-ins for goals and motivations are derived solely from the affective activity of an agent inside the environment. The assumption is that the emotional value of agents' actions influences further development and behaviour of other agents. In comparison to

[17], we extend the modelling of individuals with concepts from cognitive modelling and emotion theory: expectations (for *appraisal*) and *coping strategies* to model the update of internal states based on affective relevance of external events and decisions for sending events based on detected relevance [13]. Appraisal and coping are terms introduced in cognitive appraisal theories of emotion. A typical definition of emotions in this context is:

> "episodes of massive, synchronized recruitment of mental and somatic resources allowing to adapt or cope with a stimulus event subjectively appraised as being highly pertinent to the needs, goals and values of the individuals" [15]

For our purposes, emotional events are represented using a two-dimensional model of *valence* and *arousal*. Note that this compromise is motivated mainly by available data annotation tools rather than a fit for modelling the particular domain. The emotional processes of appraisal and coping still provide a framework for modelling the state update of agents even when the representation of emotion is reduced to two-dimensional descriptions. Arousal, in this context, refers to user effort in expressing reactions in the online environment, while valence represents the positive or negative component of an emotion. For simplicity, valence is represented as a single positive-negative polarity of the written text.

Appraisal theories are based on the idea that emotions are elicited by a subject's evaluations (appraisals) of events or situations that cause specific reactions in different people. Since the earliest introduction of appraisal theories in [1], many variants have been proposed, e.g. [14,15]. The commonality between different appraisal theories lies in the idea of how individual differences in affective responses can be elicited by the same stimulus, explaining why two different people can significantly differ in their emotional response to the same event [10], a prerequisite for the purpose of modelling a population of heterogeneous agents.

Model Definition. In our model, an agent can send a message with 3 parameters: receiver, valence, and arousal. The receiver of a message is optional to allow messages directed at all agents in a channel. Valence and arousal describe the affective content of a message independently of receiver of the message and of its cause which could be an external event or an event in the channel. Thus, agents external actions can be defined formally as the following tuple:

$$A = \{\delta, a, v\} \tag{1}$$

$$\delta \in Agents \cup \{null\}, \quad a \in [-5...5] \ and \ a \in N, \quad v \in [-5...5] \ and \ v \in N \tag{2}$$

where δ defines the destination, i.e. the receiver of a message (which can be no one in particular), a defines the arousal value of a message, and v defines the valence value of a message. The environment in which agents operate, E, can be seen as an ordered history of all agents' actions, e_i, as message events:

$$E = e_0, e_1, ..., e_n \qquad e_i = T_i \delta_i A_i, \tag{3}$$

where T_i is a timestamp of the external action, δ_i is its author and A_i is the content of the external action expressed by this agent at that time. The index i ranges from 0 to n, the number of actions seen so far. A run of an agent in an environment is thus a sequence of self-dependent pairs of environment states (e_i) and agent's actions (A_i):

$$run : e_0 A_0, e_1 A_1, e_2 A_2, ... \qquad (4)$$

With the agent properties defined above, we have a representation of a reactive agent. To model the effect of the communication history on agent behaviour, we use an agent with state. The action-selection function action is denoted as a mapping from internal states I to actions. An additional function $next$ maps an internal state and a percept to a new internal state:

$$action : I \mapsto A, \qquad next : IxPer \mapsto I \qquad (5)$$

The internal state of our agent consists of a current emotional state, ϵ, as well as a "personality" table, Π, which consists of a set of rules:

$$I = \{\epsilon, \Pi\}, \qquad \epsilon \in [-5...5] \ and \ \epsilon \in R, \qquad \Pi = [r_0, r_1, ..., r_n] \qquad (6)$$

Where rule, r, is an n-tuple consisting of information abstracted from one or more trigger events that elicited a type of action in the history of the agent, and the agent's reaction to this trigger:

$$r = T_t, \epsilon_t, \delta_t, a_t, v_t, T_r, \delta_r, a_r, v_r \qquad (7)$$

The time units, T_t, T_r, are exact timestamps of the occurrence of trigger and reaction. The trigger parameters T_t, δ_t, a_t, v_t represent a class of situations that occurred in an environment. Thus a trigger event is represented by it's author, arousal, and valence of a message. The reaction parameters T_r, a_r, v_r show the specific reaction triggered, namely its reaction time, arousal, and valence. A personality table can be seen as a selection of, potentially abstracted, cases available for future decisions similar to case-based reasoning, while the rules themselves are derived from previous experience in the reference data similar to rule induction in machine learning applications.

Agent Initialization. During the initialization phase of a model, we derive agents' personality tables by the observation of available data for the history of a chat community. However, not all agents that will be encountered later appear in the data available during initialization. During the simulation phase, a model encounters new agents. One required feature of the model is to be able to readily account for new agents with suitable personality tables during the model run. This feature is provided by an Update function that is able to work on both types of personality tables: empty or already filled ones.

Agent's Update Function. In order to model participants of an online discussion in real time, the agent model needs to be updated as their actions are encountered. When training data, or recent changes in the channel, indicate that an agent reacts with an action A on a trigger in the environment, a rule r for a personality table Π is created as defined above. If the agent's personality table Π already contains a rule r_1 which is sufficiently similar to r, we increase the number of occurrences of this rule by 1. Two rules are same when

$$r(\epsilon_t, \delta_t, a_t, \delta_r, a_r, v_r) = r_1(\epsilon_t, \delta_t, a_t, \delta_r, a_r, v_r) \qquad (8)$$

$$||r(T_t)\text{-}r(T_r)| - |r_1(T_t)\text{-}r_1(T_r)|| < \epsilon_{TIME}, \qquad (9)$$

where ϵ_{TIME} is a number of seconds, e.g. 10, 60, 300, etc. If rule r does not exist in the agent's personality table Π, then the rule is added into the table.

People behave differently if they are in different emotional states. Therefore, one of the main features of this model, is direct influence of an agent's current emotional state, as inferred by the model, on action selection. Based on its communication history, we can observe the agent's behaviour for different events (new ones or similar ones) in different emotional states. Behaviour in a variety of situations can be used to approximate an agent's coping strategy for situations characterised by the emotional state, defining an agent "personality".

Agent's Workflow. The initial states of agents differ depending on whether there is no previous information about the agent, i0 = {}, or whether the agent has already been observed, yielding a non-empty personality table, i0 = {r1, r2, ...}. During its lifetime, an agent observes changes in the environment and generates percepts for every change. Based on percepts, the internal state is updated by the next function. In our case, the next function filters new events from the environment and takes into account just those that are related to the agent as indicated by the receiver of an event. Whenever updating the state of an agent, i.e. when a sufficiently similar rule was already in the personality table, its action module uses this information to perform an action thereby leading to a short-term prediction.

Use of Predictions. These kind of short-term predictions are only useful in small time-windows, but for those they can provide a conversational system with an overall characterisation of the level and emotional charge of activity to be expected in the channel. They further provide a hint as to which users might be active in the near future. As far as this information is concerned, the model is already useful. One way to evaluate these short-term predictions is a comparison with a purely stochastic model based on probabilities derived from the data. The performance of this model on the lowest level is measured by counting the number of predicted events that correspond to events actually encountered in the environment. The event is predicted correctly if the event is similar to a prediction: the authors of predicted and real event must be the same, the difference of valences and arousals between predicted and real event is small enough, and the time delta is small enough. This definition allows us to evaluate a model based on the number of correctly predicted events, the number of incorrectly predicted events (predictions for which there is no corresponding event) the number of events that were not predicted (events happened but were not predicted).

For a stochastic model with static probabilities based on a training set taken from the data, we also take into account the distribution of valence and arousal in the observed environment, since it is not evenly distributed. Using this distribution, we get probabilities for all possible types of events and a model with worse performance than the agent-based model on the reference dataset regarding correctly predicted events and slightly better performance regarding the avoidance of false positives. But more importantly the predictions are not traceable to identified agents. Similarly, the derivation of default personalities, as described in the following sections, is intended to quickly link predictions from the model used online with individuals.

4   Agent's Default Personality

When users join a chat room, we do not have any previous information about their behaviour or personality. Additionally, when a new user posts only few messages, there is not enough data for an agent to model the user's personality. By using the history of the channel, groups of typical user personalities can be derived and potentially associated to new users based on early behaviour patterns. Here we propose a perspective for a default personality implementation based on clustering all personalities into groups of typical behaviour specific to that online environment.

Calculation of Default Personalities. After the extraction of all agents' personalities from learning data, we can group all these agents into similar behavioural groups. As a key for grouping we use the number of similar rules in agents' personalities. Here we define a parameter ϵ_p, with $\epsilon_p in N$ and $\epsilon_p > 0$, for the number of similar rules that are needed to decide whether two agents should be in the same behavioural group or not. For an estimation, one can take into account the average number of messages per user according to the reference data. The parameter ϵ_p directly influences the number of behavioural groups created. When processing agent's personalities, we want to give preference to rules created early. We therefore rely on an ordering of the rules based on when they were created for that personality table and only consider the first K rules.

Usage of Default Personalities. When a totally new user joins the channel we wait for their first action in the channel to create an initial rule for the corresponding agents' personality. The agent then adopts rules from the most similar default personality. After a certain number of messages observed for that agent, the agent's personality table is re-created based on its actual history. While processing and predicting new emotional events, agents with adapted personalities tables do not take an author (sender) in rules into account.

5   Simulation and Results

A multi-agent simulation was initialized based on learning data taken from the timespan between 28.8.2006 up to 13.4.2007 in different IRC channels. This timeframe corresponds to the timewindow interval 0-3000 in the data, evaluation of prediction was done on the subsequent timeframe, 3000-3300. Figure 1 compares original (red) and predicted (blue) trajectories of arousal for the channel #ubuntu-irc. For every simulation we compare the emotional trajectories of the reference dataset events and the predicted events. Emotional trajectories are defined by the accumulation of absolute values for valence or arousal in a timewindow.

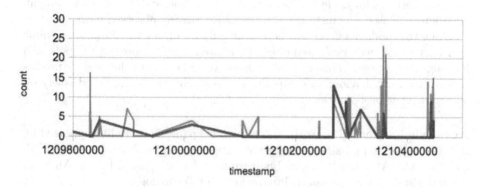

Fig. 1. Comparison of original and predicted arousals in #ubuntu-irc

The table in figure 2 shows overall simulation results for three channels, indicating that the model was mostly successful on some such as #ubuntu-website, with worse performance in others such as #ubuntu-irc, and with no correctly predicted events outliers such as #ubuntu-laptop. These varying results are due to data characteristics as the information about recipients of a message plays an important role for predictions. The final row of that table is indicative for this connection between recipient-data and prediction success.

6   Conclusion and Future Work

We have presented the design for an agent-based simulation of individuals' emotional interactions in an online chat environment, based on reference data that uses automatic annotation of the affective content of exchanged messages. This

Events	#ubuntu-irc	#ubuntu-website	#ubuntu-laptop
Total:	808	689	1384
Correctly predicted:	52	106	0
Incorrectly predicted:	106	109	25
Not predicted:	756	583	1384
Events with recipients:	136	75	15

Fig. 2. Simulation results for three IRC channels

model already proves useful as input for a decision mechanism of conversational systems. To further extend its usefulness, we propose using this model to derive a default settings for agents, a 'personality', that represent new users joining an environment based on clustering the agents for already observed users.

While the model as described here is already useful for the purpose of online decisions, it has been evaluated only to a limited extent regarding the potential for longer-term predictions. For this reason, we will evaluate the model's predictions of future behaviour in comparison to a stochastic model based solely on observed event probabilities.

Acknowledgments. The work reported in this paper is partially supported by the European Commission under grant agreement CyberEmotions (FP7-ICT-231323). The Austrian Research Institute for AI is supported by the Austrian Federal Ministry for Transport, Innovation, and Technology.

References

1. Arnold, M.B.: Feelings and Emotions As Dynamic Factors in Personality Integration. In: Arnold, M.B., Gasson, J. (eds.) The Human Person, pp. 294–313. Ronald Press, New York (1954)
2. Bradley, M., Lang, P.: Affective norms for English words (ANEW): Instruction manual and affective ratings. Tech. rep., Technical Report C-1, The Center for Research in Psychophysiology, Univ. of Florida (1999)
3. Chmiel, A., Sienkiewicz, J., Paltoglou, G., Buckley, K., Thelwall, M., Holyst, J.: Negative emotions boost users activity at BBC Forum. Physica A 390(16), 2936–2944 (2011)
4. Chmiel, A., Sienkiewicz, J., Thelwall, M., Paltoglou, G., Buckley, K., Kappas, A., Holyst, J.A.: Collective Emotions Online and Their Influence On Community Life. PLoSONE 6(7), e22207 (2011)
5. Derks, D., Bos, A.E., Grumbkow, J.V.: Emoticons and Online Message Interpretation. Social Science Computer Review 26(3), 379–388 (2008)

6. Garas, A., Garcia, D., Skowron, M., Schweitzer, F.: Emotional Persistence in Online Chatting Communities. Scientific Reports 2, 402 (2012)
7. Kim, S.M., Hovy, E.: Determining the Sentiment of Opinions. In: Gambäck, B., Jokinen, K. (eds.) Proc. 20th Int. Conf. on Computational Linguistics (COLING 2004), Geneva, Switzerland, p. 1367. Association for Computational Linguistics, Stroudsburg (2004)
8. Liu, B.: Sentiment Analysis and Subjectivity. In: Indurkya, N., Damerau, F.J. (eds.) Handbook of Natural Language Processing, 2nd edn., ch. 28. CRC Press, Taylor and Francis Group, Boca Raton (2010)
9. Marsella, S., Gratch, J., Petta, P.: Computational Models of Emotion. In: Scherer, K.R., Baenziger, T., Roesch, E.B. (eds.) A Blueprint for Affective Computing - A Sourcebook and Manual, pp. 21–46. Oxford Univ. Press (2010)
10. Mascarenhas, S., Dias, J., Prada, R., Paiva, A.: A Dimensional Model for Cultural Behavior in Virtual Agents. Applied Artificial Intelligence 24, 552–574 (2010)
11. Petta, P., Pelachaud, C., Cowie, R. (eds.): Emotion-Oriented Systems: The Humaine Handbook. Springer (2011)
12. Rank, S.: Designing an Agent-based Simulation of Collective Emotions. In: Trappl, R. (ed.) Cybernetics and Systems 2010 - Proc. Twentieth Meeting on Cybernetics and Systems Research. Austrian Soc. for Cybernetic Studies, Vienna (2010)
13. Rank, S.: Docking Agent-based Simulation of Collective Emotion to Equation-based Models and Interactive Agents. In: Oeren, T., Yilmaz, L. (eds.) Proc. of Agent-Directed Simulation Symposium at the 2010 Spring Simulation Conf. Spring Sim 2010, pp. 82–89. The Soc. for Modeling & Simulation Int. (SCS) (2010)
14. Roseman, I.J., Smith, C.A.: Appraisal Theory: Overview, Assumptions, Varieties, Controversies. In: Scherer, K.R., Schorr, A., Johnstone, T. (eds.) Appraisal Processes in Emotion: Theory, Methods, Research, pp. 3–19. Oxford Univ. Press, Oxford (2001)
15. Scherer, K., Wranik, T., Tran, V., Scherer, U.: Emotions in Everyday Life. Social Science Information 43(4), 499–570 (2004)
16. Schweitzer, F.: Brownian Agents and Active Particles - On the Emergence of Complex Behavior in the Natural and Social Sciences. Springer, Berlin (2003)
17. Schweitzer, F., Garcia, D.: An agent-based model of collective emotions in online communities. European Physical J.B 77(4), 533–545 (2010)
18. Skowron, M.: Affect Listeners: Acquisition of Affective States by Means of Conversational Systems. In: Esposito, A., Campbell, N., Vogel, C., Hussain, A., Nijholt, A. (eds.) Second COST 2102. LNCS, vol. 5967, pp. 169–181. Springer, Heidelberg (2010)
19. Skowron, M., Rank, S., Theunis, M., Sienkiewicz, J.: The Good, the Bad and the Neutral: Affective Profile in Dialog System-User Communication. In: D'Mello, S., Graesser, A., Schuller, B., Martin, J.-C. (eds.) ACII 2011, Part I. LNCS, vol. 6974, pp. 337–346. Springer, Heidelberg (2011)
20. Skowron, M., Theunis, M., Rank, S., Borowiec, A.: Effect of Affective Profile on Communication Patterns and Affective Expressions in Interactions with a Dialog System. In: D'Mello, S., Graesser, A., Schuller, B., Martin, J.-C. (eds.) ACII 2011, Part I. LNCS, vol. 6974, pp. 347–356. Springer, Heidelberg (2011)
21. Thelwall, M., Buckley, K., Paltoglou, G.: Sentiment Strength Detection for the Social Web. J. of the American Soc. for Information Science and Technology 63(1), 163–173 (2012)
22. Thelwall, M., Buckley, K., Paltoglou, G., Cai, D., Kappas, A.: Sentiment Strength Detection in Short Informal Text. J. of the American Soc. for Information Science and Technology 61(12), 2544–2558 (2010)

Using Time as a Strategic Element
in Continuous Double Auctions

Marcel Neumann, Karl Tuyls, and Michael Kaisers

Maastricht University, P.O. Box 616, 6200 MD Maastricht

Abstract. Numerous pricing strategies have been proposed and incorporated into software trading agents. Early simulation experiments have shown that markets are efficient even with only a few traders placing randomly priced offers at each time step using the *Zero-Intelligence* strategy. This article investigates the strategic effect of timing on the performance of trader profits and market efficiency. The trading strategies *Zero-Intelligence* and *Zero-Intelligence-Plus* are enhanced by new timing strategies, replacing their heuristics with random and strategic behavior. As expected, agents make less profit with random timing against the heuristic. However, market efficiency remains the same, confirming that continuous double auctions are highly efficient mechanisms even with traders placing profitable offers with random prices and timing. Furthermore, Zero-Intelligence-Plus agents also achieve high efficiency, but strategic timing reduces the risk of being exploited by trading far from the equilibrium price. Thus, there is a clear individual incentive to exploit timing strategically.

Keywords: Continuous Double Auctions, Zero-Intelligence, Timing.

1   Introduction

Brokers of the New York Stock Exchange (NYSE) exchange about 1.6 billion shares worth \$45 billion per day. The dominant market mechanism for the exchange of commodity goods is the continuous double auction. Each trader is assumed to have private valuations for the goods to be traded that are only known to itself. Traders place offers at self-elected times to indicate that they are willing to buy (bid) or sell (ask) a good at a certain price. Market clearing occurs each time a new offer arrives. The highest open bid is then tried to be matched with the lowest open ask.

Classic economic theory predicts that the price for one unit of a commodity settles at an equilibrium price where the quantity demanded is equal to the quantity supplied. Smith [8] showed that the transaction price time series has a tendency to converge towards the market equilibrium price even with a relatively small number of human traders. Gode & Sunder [4] introduced two types of "Zero-Intelligence" computer trading strategies that follow a random pricing scheme. Market efficiency was shown to reach values up to 99%. Cliff [1] followed with a more sophisticated trading strategy called "Zero-Intelligence-Plus". Traders are able to observe market activity and adjust their offer prices

I.J. Timm and C. Guttmann (Eds.): MATES 2012, LNAI 7598, pp. 106–115, 2012.
© Springer-Verlag Berlin Heidelberg 2012

accordingly. Both trading strategies apply the same implicit heuristic about the timing of offers. Offers are placed as soon as their price is being determined.

This article extends both trading strategies Zero-Intelligence and Zero-Intelligence-Plus with alternative timing strategies and compares their performance through a series of simulation experiments with their original counterparts. The complexity of the strategies used in this article is summarized in Table 1. The concept of random pricing by Zero-Intelligence agents is transferred and similarly applied to time in order to investigate the performance of agents that do not use time strategically. The complex form of pricing by Zero-Intelligence-Plus agents is enhanced with a sophisticated timing strategy to investigate the performance of agents that use time as a strategic element. This allows to evaluate the performance of traders and markets with varying strategic reasoning about time.

The outline of this paper is as follows. Section 2 introduces the trading strategies to be investigated together with their enhancements and performance measures. Section 3 describes the experiments. It gives a description of the simulation environment and the specific experimental setups together with their results. Finally, the last section draws the conclusions.

2   Background and Methodology

Trading Strategies

Gode & Sunder [4] introduced two *"Zero-Intelligence"* (ZI) trading strategies. A trader of the first version submits random offers independently, identically, and uniformly distributed over the range of feasible trading prices from 1 to the maximum trading price enforced by the market mechanism and is referred to as "ZI unconstrained" (ZIU). The second version is subject to a budget constraint that prevents it from engaging in loss making transactions. Thus, buyers submit the uniform random bids between 1 and the valuation of the unit in question. Sellers submit the uniform random asks between the cost of the unit in question and the maximum trading price of the market. It is referred to as "ZI with constraint" (ZIC). Both ZIU and ZIC submit offers as soon as they are computed.

ZI traders are considered to behave randomly. However, the originally proposed "Zero-Intelligence" traders submit offers at every round and thus implicitly use the heuristic *always submit*. *"Zero-Intelligence-Time"* (ZIT) traders combine the random pricing of ZI traders with random timing, picking a time t^* for the

Table 1. This table lists the sophistication of the strategies' reasoning about the price and time. Each of the strategies is explained in Section 2.

Price\Time	Random	Heuristic	Strategic
Random	ZIUT	ZIU	
Rational	ZICT	ZIC	
Heuristic		ZIP	ZIPT

submission of the intended offer, such that t^* is distributed uniformly over the anticipated remaining time of the auction.

The trading strategy *"Zero-Intelligence-Plus"* (ZIP) proposed by Cliff [1] allows agents to observe market activity and adjust future offer prices accordingly. Events in the market that suggest higher profit for a trader result in more profitable offer prices. Similarly, events that show the competitiveness of other traders results in less profitable offer prices. At last, offer prices converge towards unmatched offers in order to stay on a competitive basis. The reader is referred to [1] for a full specification.

"Zero-Intelligence-Plus Time" (ZIPT) enhances the trading strategy of ZIP with strategic timing behavior. The bid-ask-spread is defined by the difference of the price of the lowest open ask and the highest open bid. The size of this spread is used as an indicator of whether prices are going to change in the near future. Offers by ZIPT agents are only submitted when the size of the bid-ask-spread has fallen below a threshold value. The use of this threshold is inspired by the Kaplan strategy that has won the 1990 Double Auction Tournament despite being among the simplest strategies [7].

Performance Measures

The *profit* of a trader i considers all his successful transactions and measures them against the private values $\lambda_{i,j}$ of all units j. It is given by

$$pr_i = \sum_{j \in traded} k(\lambda_{i,j} - p_j),$$

$k = 1$ if $i \in Buyers$, $k = -1$ if $i \in Sellers$, where p_j denotes the transaction price of unit j.

The *coefficient of convergence* α introduced by Smith [8] measures how close a group of traders trades to the theoretical equilibrium. It is given in equation 1 and it is defined as the standard deviation of the actual trade prices p_i from the equilibrium price p_0 as a percentage of it.

$$\alpha = \frac{100}{p_0} \sqrt{\frac{1}{n} \sum_{i=1}^{n} (p_i - p_0)^2} \tag{1}$$

The *allocative efficiency* e is a measure of performance of an entire market. It is given by equation 2 and defined as the ratio of total actual profit and theoretical profit. Total actual profit is the sum of profits made by each trader while the theoretical profit is the sum of buyers' s_b and sellers' s_s surplus.

$$e = \frac{\sum_{i \in traders} pr_i}{s_s + s_b} \tag{2}$$

These three measurements give insight into the individual profit, the collective efficiency, and the convergence of the market to equilibrium prices. They provide the basis for the experiments presented in the following section.

3   Experiments

The experiments are conducted using a discrete-event simulation. A simulation process runs for six periods. During each period, traders are allowed to submit offers at every time step, and a period is closed after 20 time units without new offers. Traders receive a list of private values at the beginning of each period. The distributions of private values are given in Figures 1, 2, 3 and 4. Offers are for a single unit and subject to the NYSE spread improvement rule. Only one open offer is allowed per trader. A transaction occurs when the price of the highest open bid and the lowest open ask cross each other.

3.1   ZI vs. ZIT

A first set of experiments involves homogeneous populations of either ZIU, ZIC, ZIUT and ZICT traders. The population consists of six buyers and sellers

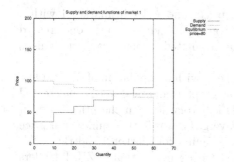

Fig. 1. Supply and demand functions introduced by Gode & Sunder [4]. Sellers' theoretical profit = 1050, Buyer's theoretical profit = 500.

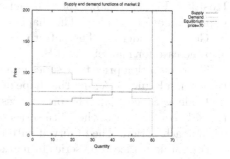

Fig. 2. Supply and demand functions introduced by Gode & Sunder [4]. Sellers' theoretical profit = 500, Buyers' theoretical profit = 1000.

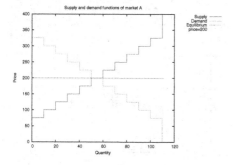

Fig. 3. Supply and demand functions introduced by Cliff [1]. Sellers' theoretical profit = 3750, Buyers' theoretical profit = 3750.

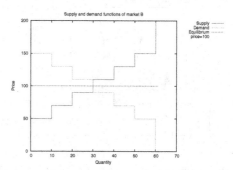

Fig. 4. Seller's theoretical profit = 900, Buyer's theoretical profit = 900

respectively. The simplification by Gode & Sunder [4] of dropping all open offers after a transaction is adopted for the sake of comparison.

Gode & Sunder [4] report that ZIU traders are able to achieve an allocative efficiency of 90% for market 1 and 2. ZIC traders are able to raise this value to 99.9% for market 1 and 99.2% for market 2. It is expected that the two types of traders will do equally good in this set-up of experiments. Parsons [5] noted that the efficiency depends on the distribution of private values only. Since ZIUT traders should be able to trade all their units, they should achieve the same efficiency value as ZIU agents. On the other ZICT traders should achieve lower values of allocative efficiency because of a higher risk of extra-marginal units to be traded.

A second set of experiments is concerned with heterogeneous populations of ZI and ZIT traders. ZIU traders are confronted with ZIUT traders while ZIC traders are confronted with ZICT traders. The population consists of twelve buyers and twelve sellers, equally divided into the respective type of traders.

Results. Figure 5 shows the transaction price time series in market 1 with a population of ZIU traders. The shape of the graph is identical to the one created by Gode & Sunder [4]. The pattern can be stipulated as being random. This is also the case for market 2 and B.

The transaction price time series in market 1 with a population of ZIC traders is shown in Figure 6. Again, the shape of the graph is identical to the one created by Gode & Sunder [4]. The price series is less volatile than the price series of the ZIU traders. Also, the price series converges towards the equilibrium price within each period. The observed pattern is similar for market 2 and B.

Transaction price time series in market 1 with a population of ZIUT traders is shown in Figure 8. The shape of the graph is similar to Figure 5. A random pattern can be observed while periods take longer to finish because traders do not submit offers as soon as possible anymore but randomly distributed over the least remaining time of the period. The pattern is similar for market 2 and B.

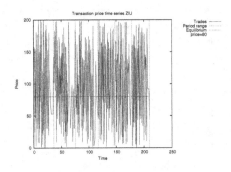

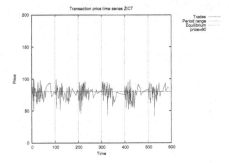

Fig. 5. Transaction price time series for market 1 with 6 buyers and 6 sellers of ZIU traders (heuristic timing)

Fig. 6. Transaction price time series for market 1 with 6 buyers and 6 sellers of ZIC traders (heuristic timing)

Traders	Market 1 $\bar{x}$ (s)	Market 2 $\bar{x}$ (s)	Market B $\bar{x}$ (s)
ZIU	90.32 ($\pm$ 0.00)	90.00 ($\pm$ 0.00)	0.00 ($\pm$ 0.00)
ZIC	99.17 ($\pm$ 0.23)	98.96 ($\pm$ 0.27)	97.21 ($\pm$ 0.61)
ZIU-T	90.32 ($\pm$ 0.00)	90.00 ($\pm$ 0.00)	0.00 ($\pm$ 0.00)
ZIC-T	99.12 ($\pm$ 0.24)	98.91 ($\pm$ 0.28)	96.95 ($\pm$ 0.67)

Fig. 7. Sample mean and sample standard deviation of the efficiency of ZI traders, sample size = 1000

Figure 9 shows the transaction price time series in market 1 with a population of ZICT traders. The price series looks similar than the one in Figure 6. It still converges to the equilibrium price but not as gradually as it was the case for ZIC traders.

Figure 7 shows the sample mean and the sample standard deviation of the allocative efficiency for the experiments above over 1000 runs. The designs of market 1 and 2 imply efficiencies of at least 90 % which occurs when all available units are being traded as it is the case for both types of unconstrained traders. The intra-marginal and the extra-marginal side of the symmetric market B are of equal size. Hence the allocative efficiency of the unconstrained traders in it is 0. Thus, Gode & Sunder [4] could have used truly ZIU agents for their experiments already. Introducing a timing heuristic does not increase the efficiency value. In the constrained case however, the introduction of a timing heuristic does lead to a slightly higher efficiency than it is the case with random timing.

The mean actual profits achieved by ZIC and ZICT traders per period in market B when placed in competition is shown in Figure 10. ZIC traders are able to achieve a mean actual profit of above 920 price units while ZICT traders are only able to achieve a mean actual profit of around 800 price units. Market theory predicts a theoretical profit of 900 units for this market. This shows that ZIC traders are more competitive due to their heuristic of time. ZICT traders

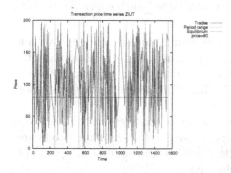

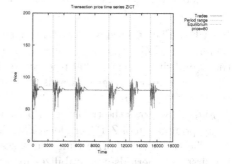

Fig. 8. Transaction price time series for market 1 with 6 buyers and 6 sellers of ZIUT traders (random timing)

Fig. 9. Transaction price time series for market 1 with 6 buyers and 6 sellers of ZICT traders (random timing)

are not able to achieve high profit values. They are even exploited by ZIC traders which explains their profit being above the predicted theoretical profit.

3.2   ZIP vs ZIPT

ZIP traders require the following set of parameters. During all experiments R is uniformly distributed over $[1.0, 1.05]$ for price increases and over $[0.95, 1.0]$ for price decreases. These values are suggested by Cliff [1]. The values for A are changed due to a larger scale for the price units. A is uniformly distributed over $[0.0, 5.0]$ for price increases and over $[-5.0, 0.0]$ for price decreases. The learning rate β is set to 0.3 and the momentum coefficient γ is set to 0.05 for all traders as suggested by Preist et al. [6]. At last, buyers start with profit margins that give a price of 0 as their first offer. Sellers on the other hand start with profit margins that give the limit price of the market as their first offer.

ZIPT traders start submitting offers when the size of the bid-ask-spreak has fallen below 5.0 price units. If the bid-ask-spread has not changed for 5 time units ZIPT traders start testing the market themselves before considering the size of the bid-ask-spread again. Also, ZIP traders adjust their profit margins in the direction of the best best open respective offer when there has not been a trade for 5 time units. This policy was introduced by Das et al. [2] and is necessary for ZIP traders to be applied in continuous double auctions.

Unlike the set-up in section 3.1 the list of offers persists after the occurrence of a transaction to provide a more realistic market place.

A first set of experiments is concerned with homogeneous populations of ZIP and ZIPT traders. Cliff [1] reports that transaction prices of ZIP traders converge to the equilibrium price during early periods and stays stable during later periods. The performance of ZIP traders in this set-up should be equally good. Transaction prices of ZIPT traders should also be able to converge to the equilibrium price since they employ the same pricing strategy as their original complement. However, clues for the profit margin adjustments of the traders are given less frequently which might lead to longer period lengths. In a second set of experiments ZIP traders are confronted with ZIPT traders. The performance of either trader is measured by their actual profit earned during any one period.

Results. Figure 11 shows the transaction price time series in market A with a population of ZIP traders. As can be seen the transaction prices scallop around the equilibrium price of 200 price units during the first four periods. However, the price series converges towards the equilibrium price where it stays stable for the last two periods.

Figure 13 shows the transaction price time series in market A with a homogeneous population of ZIPT traders. The shape of the graph looks similar to figure 11. The transaction price time series scallops around the equilibrium price for the first four periods and stabilizes in period five.

The mean allocative efficiency of markets with homogeneous populations of either ZIP or ZIPT traders are around 99% and summarized in figure 12. The efficiency value for ZIP traders conforms with the findings by Cliff [1].

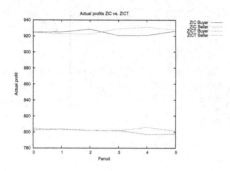

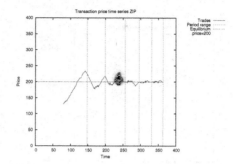

Fig. 10. Actual profits earned in market B by a heterogeneous population of ZIC and ZICT traders

Fig. 11. Transaction price time series for market A with 6 buyers and 6 sellers of ZIP traders (heuristic timing)

Traders	Market 1 $\bar{x}$ (s)	Market 2 $\bar{x}$ (s)	Market A $\bar{x}$ (s)
ZIP	99.79 ($\pm$ 0.24)	99.86 ($\pm$ 0.19)	99.86 ($\pm$ 0.30)
ZIPT	99.81 ($\pm$ 0.22)	99.83 ($\pm$ 0.22)	98.84 ($\pm$ 0.31)

Fig. 12. Sample mean and sample standard deviation of the efficiency of ZIP and ZIPT traders, sample size = 1000

The second set of experiments was concerned with heterogeneous populations of ZIP and ZIPT traders. Figure 15 shows the transaction price time series while Figure 16 shows the sample mean of the actual profits for each period. It can be seen that ZIPT traders trade closer to the equilibrium price and are therefore

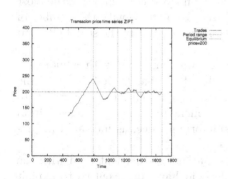

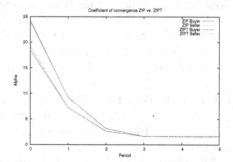

Fig. 13. Transaction price time series for market A with 6 buyers and 6 sellers of ZIPT traders (strategic timing)

Fig. 14. Course of the sample mean of the coefficient of convergence for heterogeneous populations of ZIP and ZIPT traders, sample size = 1000

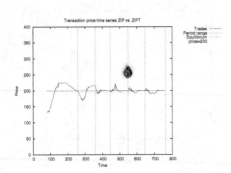
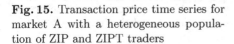

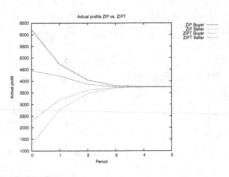

Fig. 16. Course of the sample mean of actual profits for a heterogeneous population of ZIP and ZIPT traders in market A, sample size = 1000

Fig. 15. Transaction price time series for market A with a heterogeneous population of ZIP and ZIPT traders

less vulnerable to being exploited. It is underlined by Figure 14 which shows the sample mean of the coefficients of convergence for each period.

4   Conclusions

This article expanded the horizon of timing strategies employed by trading agents. The implicit heuristic "sooner offers yield higher profits" was made explicit and has been investigated in two directions. First, the Zero-Intelligence trading strategy was enhanced with random timing. The efficiencies of these actual Zero-Intelligence agents does only differ by a very small margin in the case of constrained pricing and it does not differ at all in the case of unconstrained pricing in contrast to their original counterparts. However, when put in competition results of Figure 10 show that using the heuristic yields higher profit than placing random bids in time. This finding confirms that continuous double auctions are highly efficient mechanisms even with only a small number of the most random traders. This efficiency can be expected to increase with the number of traders, but additional experiments are necessary to quantify the scalability and efficiency gains of larger markets.

Second, the Zero-Intelligence-Plus strategy was enhanced with a more sophisticated timing strategy. Again, the results show that the efficiency of the enhancement does not differ from its original complement. In competition to heuristic timing, using time as a strategic element prevented the agents from being exploited by trading far from the equilibrium price, as indicated in Figure 16.

The outcome of this paper indicate that markets are efficient even with the most random traders, but individual traders do have an incentive to exploit timing as an essential part of their strategies. Intelligent timing strategies are indispensable and it can not be made standard practice to only consider timing strategies that place offers as soon as their prices are determined. We suggest to extend this strategic timing to more complex trading strategies such as Gjerstad & Dickhaut [3], and to discuss the effect explicitly.

References

1. Cliff, D.: Minimal-intelligence agents for bargaining behaviors in market-based environments. Technical report, School of Cognitive and Computing Sciences, University of Sussex (1997)
2. Das, R., Hanson, J.E., Kephart, J.O., Tesauro, G.: Agent-human interactions in the continuous double auction. In: Proceedings of the 17th International Joint Conference on Artificial Intelligence - Volume 2, pp. 1169–1176. Morgan Kaufmann Publishers Inc., San Francisco (2001)
3. Gjerstad, S., Dickhaut, J.: Price formation in double auctions. Games and Economic Behavior 22, 1–29 (1998)
4. Gode, D.K., Sunder, S.: Allocative efficiency of markets with zero-intelligence traders: Market as a partial substitute for individual rationality. Journal of Political Economy 101(1), 119–137 (1993)
5. Parsons, S., Marcinkiewicz, M., Niu, J., Phelps, S.: Everything you wanted to know about double auctions but were afraid to (bid or) ask. Technical report (in preparation)
6. Preist, C., van Tol, M.: Adaptive agents in a persistent shout double auction. In: Proceedings of the First International Conference on Information and Computation Economies, ICE 1998, pp. 11–18. ACM, New York (1998)
7. Rust, J., Palmer, R., Miller, J.H.: Behavior of Trading Automata in a Computerized Double Auction Market. In: Friedman, D., Geanakoplos, J., Lane, D., Rust, J. (eds.) The Double Auction Market: Institutions, Theories and Evidence. Addison-Wesley (1992)
8. Smith, V.: An experimental study of competitive market behavior. Journal of Political Economy 70 (1962)

Goal Delegation without Goals
BDI Agents in Harmony with OCMAS Principles

Alexander Pokahr and Lars Braubach

Distributed Systems and Information Systems
Computer Science Department, University of Hamburg
Vogt-Kölln-Str. 30, 22527 Hamburg, Germany
{pokahr,braubach}@informatik.uni-hamburg.de

Abstract. The BDI model is concerned with the rational action of an individual agent. At the multi-agent layer especially coordination among agents is an important factor that determines how overall system goals can be accomplished. Thus, from a software engineering perspective it is desirable to extend the BDI programming model to the multi-agent layer and make BDI concepts also useable for coordination among agents. A severe problem with existing approaches that tried to follow this path e.g. by proposing a BDI teamwork model is that they violate the OCMAS principles stating that no assumptions on agent architectures should be made on the multi-agent level. If OCMAS principles are violated the kinds of agents that can participate in coordination is limited ab initio to a specific sort such as BDI. In this paper we propose a new goal delegation mechanism that allows for both. On the one hand, BDI agents can delegate their normal goals to other agents and on the other hand these goals are not represented explicitly on the multi-agent level so that also non-BDI agents can act as receivers and help accomplishing a goal.

1 Introduction

The belief-desire-intention model (BDI) of Bratman [3] was inspiration source for one of the most successful agent architectures called PRS (procedural reasoning system) initially proposed in [9]. Main appeal of the BDI agent architecture is its folk psychological grounding that allows developers to naturally describe agent behavior in terms of beliefs (what is known of the world), goals (what is to be achieved), and plans (how goals can be achieved) in a similar way humans think that they think [12]. The traditional BDI architecture from [15] (cf. Fig. 1 left hand side) reduces the core process of BDI - called practical reasoning - to the means-end reasoning phase. Means-end reasoning refers to the process of deciding how to accomplish a goal or how to treat an event. Software-technically this is interpreted as plan selection and execution process, i.e. for a given goal the agent searches relevant plans (fitting to the goal type) and further inspects their applicability in the current context (referring to its beliefs). From this knowledge an applicable plan list is created and plans are executed one by one until the goal is achieved or no more plans are available causing the goal to be failed.

I.J. Timm and C. Guttmann (Eds.): MATES 2012, LNAI 7598, pp. 116–125, 2012.

Fig. 1. BDI deliberation

In previous work the traditional BDI architecture has been extended towards supporting the full practical reasoning cycle consisting of the phases goal deliberation and means-end reasoning (cf. Fig. 1 middle). In the upstream goal deliberation phase an agent deals with the question which of its goals it should pursue at the current point in time. The main aspect of goal deliberation consists in generating a conflict-free goal set for the agent as some of the existing goals interfere with each other. Prerequisites for supporting the full practical reasoning cycle consist in introducing explicitly represented goals [6,4], a goal deliberation strategy [14] and an extended BDI architecture with a new deliberation cycle [13]. These extensions allow for programming goal-driven agents that are able to autonomously deliberate about their goals and pursue them in flexible context dependent ways but do not touch the area of inter-agent dependencies.

Thus, in the envisioned BDI architecture (cf. Fig. 1 right hand side), besides the aforementioned intrinsic aspects of goal deliberation and means-end reasoning, also goal delegation should be covered. This transforms a multi-agent system into a distributed goal-oriented reasoning engine and allows for natural cooperation among cognitive agents. In contrast to previous extensions, goal delegation renders the deliberation process much more difficult. Basically, it has to be decided in which cases a goal should be delegated and to which agent. Furthermore, also timing aspects become more important because goal deadlines might influence the goal delegation decisions. In contrast to the aforementioned two-phased process of practical reasoning, goal delegation requires a new BDI deliberation approach.

As a first step towards such general architecture in this paper the foundations of goal delegation will be laid out. In the next Section related work is discussed. In this context, the concept of goal delegation is explained and contrasted with similar but nonetheless different approaches from the teamwork area. In Section 3 the principles and architecture of the new goal delegation approach are presented. Finally, in Section 4 some concluding remarks and aspects of planned future work are given.

2 Related Work

For the treatment of related work, first goal delegation is placed it into a larger context regarding the general coordination of BDI agents. Afterwards existing works with regard to goal delegation are presented.

Table 1. Comparison of coordination approaches

Example Approach \ Shared Attitude(s)	Beliefs	Goals	Plans
Hive BDI	X	-	-
Goal Delegation	-	X	-
Coordinated SaPa	-	-	X
Joint Intentions	X	X	-
Joint Responsibility	X	X	X
OCMAS	-	-	-

2.1   BDI Agents and Coordination

Coordination among BDI agents in a multi-agent system can take a number of forms. A fundamental property of BDI agents is their definition in terms of mental attitudes such as belief, goals and plans. Therefore an interesting question concerns the role of such mental attitudes in any coordination approach. A large family of BDI coordination approaches can be derived by following the general assumption that when some mental attitudes are shared, the individual reasoning processes will lead to coordinated behavior. This idea is appealing due to a number of reasons. On the one hand, using mental attitudes also for coordination purposes is conceptually in line with the intuitive, folk psychological interpretation of BDI. On the other hand, the BDI reasoning process is already quite sophisticated and it is expected that introducing extensions for sharing mental attitudes is technically less challenging than to develop a new reasoning process specifically for coordination.

Table 1 differentiates some existing coordination approaches with regard to the question, which mental attitudes are shared among agents. The approaches have been selected as examples for their respective category. The selection of approaches should not be considered exhaustive and an in-depth treatment of the individual representatives is out of the scope of this paper. Instead, the following descriptions try to elaborate the general implications of sharing some mental attitude(s). In particular, the criteria of coupling and communication are considered. Coupling refers to how directly one agent is able to influence the behavior of another agent. In addition, the communication overhead of coordination results from both the communication load (i.e. the amount of transferred data) and the communication frequency (i.e. how often agents need to engage in communication). The result of this analysis is illustrated in Figure 2.

In *Hive BDI* [1] agents can share some of their beliefs and thus induce indirect coordination similar to the way ant-like agents influence each other using digital pheromones. The approach aims at supporting large-scale agent systems composed of huge numbers of agents and features a high robustness and scalability. The sharing of beliefs represents a low coupling, because agents only influence each other indirectly. The communication overhead is relatively high, due to the communication frequency, which e.g. follows from the dynamics of the environment. *Goal delegation* has been defined in [2] as the *delegation of commitment*, i.e. an agent adopting a commitment of another agent, and the *delegation of*

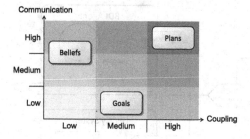

Fig. 2. Communication and coupling implications of shared mental attitudes

strategy, i.e. the agent on the receiving and has full control over how it pursues the delegated goal. In consequence, goal delegation incurs a rather low communication overhead, because at the start of the goal delegation, only the commitment needs to be communicated and after the delegated goal is achieved, some result might be passed back. Goal delegation allows medium influence on the behavior of other agents, because goal delegation states what the agent should achieve (commitment), but not how (strategy). Tight coupling can be produced by plan sharing approaches. E.g. *Coordinated Sapa* [10] allows resolving conflicts between plans, such that two cooperative agents can pursue their goals without accidentally executing actions detrimental to the other agent. This is facilitated by one agent sending its plan to the other and the other agent choosing its own actions in a way that avoids any conflict. Therefore tight coupling is established that requires communicating complete plan structures. There are also combined approaches that incorporate sharing of more than one attitude. E.g. in joint intentions [7], the notion of a shared goal is extended to require also shared knowledge about the state of the goal. Joint responsibility [11] takes these ideas further by also incorporating the plan level. These approaches lead to increased coupling, that may be advantageous, e.g. to improve the performance of teamwork, but comes with the cost of increased communication overhead.

2.2   Goal Delegation Approaches

The work presented in this paper aims at exploiting the intuitive BDI concepts for the development of open multi-agent systems. The above analysis shows that goal delegation represents a good trade-off between coupling and communication. With the initial delegation of the goal and the returning of some final result, it has clear interaction points with an intuitive semantics. Yet, for open and extensible systems the principles of organization-centered multi-agent systems (OCMAS) as laid down in [8] are considered very important as well. OCMAS advocates to treat agents as black boxes and therefore prohibits the use of mental attitudes at the MAS level. For a combination of both, two aspects are important. First, on the MAS-level, goal delegation needs to be represented in a standardized interaction that is open to non-BDI agents, too. Second, on the BDI-level, the standardized interaction scheme needs to be mapped to goals, which are delegated to and

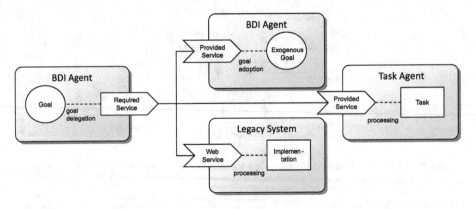

Fig. 3. Goal delegation concept

from other agents. Finally, the BDI reasoning cycle needs to be extended to incorporate decisions regarding the delegation and acceptance of goals. In the following, some existing goal delegation approaches are discussed with respect to their support for either of those aspects.

In [2] the authors propose a FIPA-compliant protocol for goal delegation. While being FIPA-compliant means that syntactically, any kinds of agents may engage into conversations according to this protocol, the motivation of the protocol is explicitly capturing the semantics of goal delegation in the protocol itself. It is therefore a heavy-weight approach that violates OCMAS principles in favor of a clearly defined semantics for each message. Furthermore, no suggestions regarding the implementation of BDI agents according to the protocol are made.

An explicit distinction between the MAS and the BDI level is considered by [16]. In addition to the goal inside an agent, the notions of task and service are introduced. A task represents a concrete goal instance to be delegated to another agent (i.e. on the delegator side), whereas a service describes the ability of an agent to receive task requests (delegatee side). To perform the actual delegation of tasks, the usage of a contract-net negotiation is proposed. Furthermore, a reasoning cycle has been conceived that triggers delegation of goals, when no local plans are found. The approach is interesting due to the explicit separation of the three aspects of goals (goal, task, service). Yet, the approach is not fully generic, because of the contract-net-oriented interaction and goal delegation being hard-coded into the reasoning cycle.

3   OCMAS Goal Delegation

There are two main requirements for our goal delegation approach. The first requirement is that BDI agents should be enabled to use the notion of goal delegation to outsource some of their goals to other agents. This means that the specification of BDI agents needs to be extended to incorporate details about which goals can be delegated at which moments to what agents. The second

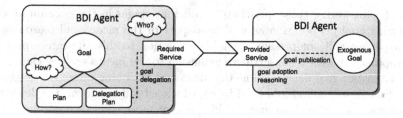

Fig. 4. Goal delegation with means-end reasoning

requirement mandates that the goal delegation approach should be in line with the OCMAS principles, i.e. the approach should not make any assumptions about the internal architectures of the participating agents. These two requirements seem to be naturally contradicting as using notions such as shared goals or plans requires all possible goal adopters to understand that notion and in this way restricts the heterogeneity of the participating agents.

The proposed solution path builds on the idea of having a common black-box view for all kinds of agents (BDI, task-based, etc.) that adds provided and required service specifications known from component based software engineering. These required and provided service descriptions are based on interface definitions with method signatures so that the interoperability of different components is clearly defined. The idea now is to treat goal delegation as a process of three perspectives that can be considered separately. From the perspective of the delegating agent, which is assumed to be a BDI agent, a mechanism is added to route a goal to another agent, After having delegated the goal it is guaranteed that a result of this delegation process is eventually received and the goal state is updated. From the perspective of the receiving agent goal delegation may lead to the exogenous creation of a goal from another agent. The receiving agent can reason about goal acceptance and afterwards can process the goal in the same way as it does with its own goals. In between the goal is not explicitly represented - hence "goal delegation without goals" - but is abstracted to a simple service invocation, i.e. the delegating agent invokes one of its required services. This required service is potentially dynamically bound to the provided service of another agent which if being BDI automatically maps the call to a goal.

This general invocation scheme is graphically depicted in Fig. 3. It further illustrates that on the receiving side the service must not recreate a goal but can also be perceived as normal service invocation. In this way also other types of agents, like task-based ones or even other types of systems such as web services can be naturally used as goal executors.

3.1 Reasoning Integration

As already presented in the introduction, goal delegation makes the BDI reasoning process of an agent more complicated, because 'who' and 'when' questions need to be answered and it is not clear at what points in the reasoning process this should be done. Rather, it seems that a very flexible approach is needed that allows for answering these questions at different stages in the decision process, i.e. during goal deliberation as well as as part of the means-end reasoning. In this paper we will not present a complete solution to this intricate aspect but will approach it with a conservative extension to the means-end reasoning part only. To install goal delegation at the mean-end reasoning phase a new generic delegation plan is introduced (cf. Fig. 4), which actually performs the delegation by automatically searching and invoking one or more services according to the user specification. In this way the means-end reasoning process determines if and when goal delegation in used. Plan priorities can be employed to determine the relation between own plans and goal delegation, i.e. if it should be tried to outsource a goal as soon as possible or rather as last available option. In addition pre- and context conditions can be used to define in which situations goal delegation is applicable. On the other side the incoming service call is handled by a generic goal creation service, which first checks if goal adoption is wanted by the agent and afterwards creates the exogenous goal for further processing.

In case the agent has decided to delegate a goal to another agent the question arises to which agent is should be sent if more than one option is available. It should be possible to base this decision upon functional as well as non-functional criteria. In our proposed solution the decision is not part of the goal delegation mechanism but belongs to the underlying service matching between required and provided services of agents. A required service specification is functionally defined via a service interface and additionally declares a search scope (e.g. platform or global scope) in which the search is performed. Depending on the required service specification, the search for suitable service providers (and hence goal delegation targets) can be done dynamically on each request or only once in case of a static scenario with fixed sets of service providers. Currently, non-functional criteria cannot be explicitly specified as part of the required service, but only by using custom classes that extend the search mechanism. Declarative specifications of non-functional criteria are an important part of future work.

3.2   Implementation

The goal delegation concept has been implemented using the Jadex agent platform [5]. The specification details will be presented in the following and they will be further illustrated by a small example application. The artificial scenario is called the money painter application. It consists of two agent types. The first, called rich agent, has the objective to become rich by getting a certain amount of money. It decomposes this goal to get the specified amount of money by creating a number of subgoals each responsible for getting one euro. To get one euro two different means are available. Either the agent can decide to paint one euro by itself or it can delegate the goal to paint one euro to another agent type called painter. It has to be noted that each agent can only paint one euro at the same time and it also needs some time to accomplish this task. In this scenario painter agents refuse to work on a new task as long as they are busy with an old one.

At the initiator agent side (i.e. an agent that wants to delegate a goal) merely a small extension to the plan element is necessary that allows for specifying a goal

```
01: <goals>
02:   <achievegoal name="get_one_euro" recur="true" recurdelay="1000">
03: </goals>
04:
05: <plans>
06:   <plan name="let_another_paint_one_euro">
07:     <body service="paintservices" method="paintOneEuro"/>
08:     <trigger>
09:       <goal ref="get_one_euro"/>
10:     </trigger>
11:   </plan>
12: </plans>
13:
14: <services>
15:   <requiredservice name="paintservices" class="IPaintService" multiple="true">
16:     <binding dynamic="true", scope="platform">
17:   </requiredservice>
18: </services>
```

Fig. 5. Cutout of the rich agent file

delegation plan. The delegation plan description differs from usual plan descriptions in the way the plan body is defined.[1] For normal plans, a class name is used to refer to the class that should be instantiated and executed. In case of a delegation plan, a service name and a method name have to be declared. The service name is a local name that corresponds to a required service definition from the services section of the agent and the method name is used to identify the method of the required service that should be called when a goal delegation is started.

In Fig. 5 a cutout of the rich agent is depicted. It can be seen that a goal to get one euro (lines 1-3), a delegation plan (lines 5-12) and a required service definition (lines 14-18) need to be specified. For each get one euro goal instance that agent possesses (creation not shown) it tries to accomplish it by executing the delegation plan (cf. the plan trigger in lines 8-10). This plan uses the new body description introduced above and links the delegation to the paintOneEuro method of the required service called paintservices. The required service specification defines the type of service should be bound (here of type IPaintService, line 15), that all instances of that services should be returned (multiple, line 15) and dynamic search should be applied (line 16) and that all components from the agent platform should be included into the search (scope platform, line 16). In case the delegation plan fails due to the fact that all painters are busy, the goal will pause and retry after one second (recur settings, line 2).

At the participant side (i.e. the agent that handles a goal delegation service call) an extension has been introduced to publish a goal as specific service method. Furthermore, a parameter mapping has been introduced that can be used to describe how a service argument is mapped to a parameter of a goal. In this way the method arguments can be passed to the goal also selectively or in a different order.

In Fig. 6 a cutout of the painter agent is shown. It owns a belief with name painting (line 1-3) of type boolean that indicates whether the agent is currently busy with painting a euro. Furthermore, it has one goal (lines 5-9) for painting a

---

[1] The plan body refers to the class that implements the domain logic of a plan. If the BDI interpreter executes a plan as first step it creates the plan body and afterwards executes it stepwise.

```
01: <beliefs>
02:    <belief name="painting" class="boolean">
03: </beliefs>
04:
05: <goals>
06:    <achievegoal name="get_one_euro">
07:      <publish class="IPaintService" method="paintOneEuro">
08:    </achievegoal">
09: </goals>
10:
11: <plans>
12:    <plan name="paint_one_euro">
13:      <body class="PaintOneEuroPlan"/>
14:      <trigger>
15:        <goal ref="get_one_euro"/>
16:      </trigger>
17:      <precondition>!beliefbase.painting</precondition>
18:    </plan>
19: </plans>
```

Fig. 6. Cutout of the painter agent file

euro and a corresponding plan (lines 11-19). The goal is equipped with the new publish declaration, which defines it as an exogenous goal that is instantiated when a method call ("paintOneEuro") to the IPaintService is received (line 7). Always when a new goal is created, goal processing will start and look for a suitable plan. In this example the agent only has one fitting plan that reacts to the goal (cf. plan trigger in line 15). Furthermore, a precondition is used to check whether the agent is already painting (line 17). The painting belief is modified by the painting plan itself when it starts and ends working. If a goal is created and the agent is busy the precondition evaluates to false and the plan cannot be used. As the agent has no other plan the goal is considered as failed and the service caller is automatically notified that goal delegation did not succeed.

4   Conclusion

This paper has tackled the question how goal delegation can be introduced without violating the OCMAS principles and forcing all agents of a multi-agent system to be BDI agents. The proposed solution distinguishes between the perspectives of the delegating agent, the multi-agent layer, and the receiving agent. Only at the delegating and possibly at the receiving agent goals are explicitly represented, whereas in between no goals occur and service calls are used as interaction means. As services are a common property of all kinds of agents (and especially of active components) the receiving side can interpret them in different ways, e.g. a BDI agent can recreate the goal, while a task based agent can execute a behavior. The contract between both sides is kept minimal and only requires the receiver to answer the service call with a result or an exception. This provides interoperability between BDI agents and other agent types as well as legacy systems, e.g. using web services. Taken together, the contributions of this paper therefore achieve *goal delegation transparency* on the intra-agent and inter-agent level. On the intra-agent level, transparency is achieved by treating endogenous and exogenous goals the same way. On the inter-agent level, goals are made transparent using service calls. In future work, especially the development of a new BDI architecture will be targeted, which is able to use goal delegation at different stages and not only as part of means-end reasoning.

References

1. Barbieri, M., Mascardi, V.: Hive-bdi: Extending jason with shared beliefs and stigmergy. In: Filipe, J., Fred, A. (eds.) Proc. Int. Conf. on Agents and Artificial Intelligence (ICAART). SciTePress (2011)
2. Bergenti, F., Botelho, L., Rimassa, G., Somacher, M.: A FIPA compliant Goal Delegation Protocol. In: Proc. Workshop on Agent Communication Languages and Conversation Policies (AAMAS 2002), Bologna, Italy (2002)
3. Bratman, M.: Intention, Plans, and Practical Reason. Harvard Univ. Press (1987)
4. Braubach, L., Pokahr, A.: Representing long-term and interest bdi goals. In: Proc. of (ProMAS-7), pp. 29–43. IFAAMAS Foundation (May 2009)
5. Braubach, L., Pokahr, A.: Addressing challenges of distributed systems using active components. In: Proc. of the Int. Symp. on Intelligent Distributed Computing (IDC 2011), pp. 141–151. Springer (2011)
6. Braubach, L., Pokahr, A., Moldt, D., Lamersdorf, W.: Goal Representation for BDI Agent Systems. In: Bordini, R.H., Dastani, M.M., Dix, J., El Fallah Seghrouchni, A. (eds.) PROMAS 2004. LNCS (LNAI), vol. 3346, pp. 44–65. Springer, Heidelberg (2005)
7. Cohen, P.R., Levesque, H.J.: Teamwork. Technical Report Technote 504, SRI International, Menlo Park, CA (March 1991)
8. Ferber, J., Gutknecht, O., Michel, F.: From Agents to Organizations: An Organizational View of Multi-agent Systems. In: Giorgini, P., Müller, J.P., Odell, J.J. (eds.) AOSE 2003. LNCS, vol. 2935, pp. 214–230. Springer, Heidelberg (2004)
9. Georgeff, M., Lansky, A.: Reactive Reasoning and Planning: An Experiment With a Mobile Robot. In: Proceedings of the 6th National Conference on Artificial Intelligence (AAAI 1987), pp. 677–682. AAAI (1987)
10. Hashmi, M., El Fallah Seghrouchni, A.: Coordination of temporal plans for the reactive and proactive goals. Web Intelligence and Intelligent Agent Technology 2, 213–220 (2010)
11. Jennings, N., Mamdani, E.: Using Joint Responsibility to Coordinate Collaborative Problem Solving in Dynamic Environments. In: AAAI, pp. 269–275 (1992)
12. Norling, E.: Folk Psychology for Human Modelling: Extending the BDI Paradigm. In: Proc. Int. Conf. Autonomous Agents and Multiagent Systems, AAMAS (2004)
13. Pokahr, A., Braubach, L., Lamersdorf, W.: A Flexible BDI Architecture Supporting Extensibility. In: Proc. of the Int. Conference on Intelligent Agent Technology (IAT 2005), pp. 379–385. IEEE Computer Society (2005)
14. Pokahr, A., Braubach, L., Lamersdorf, W.: A Goal Deliberation Strategy for BDI Agent Systems. In: Eymann, T., Klügl, F., Lamersdorf, W., Klusch, M., Huhns, M.N. (eds.) MATES 2005. LNCS (LNAI), vol. 3550, pp. 82–93. Springer, Heidelberg (2005)
15. Rao, A., Georgeff, M.: BDI Agents: from theory to practice. In: Lesser, V. (ed.) Proc. of the Int. Conf. on Multi-Agent Systems (ICMAS), pp. 312–319. MIT Press (1995)
16. Scafes, M., Badica, C.: Distributed Goal-Oriented Reasoning Engine for Multi-agent Systems: Initial Implementation. In: Papadopoulos, G., Badica, C. (eds.) Intelligent Distributed Computing III. SCI, vol. 237, pp. 305–311. Springer, Heidelberg (2009)

A Multi-robot Coverage Approach Based on Stigmergic Communication

Bijan Ranjbar-Sahraei[1], Gerhard Weiss[1], and Ali Nakisaee[2]

[1] Dept. of Knowledge Engineering, Maastricht University, The Netherlands
[2] National Organization for Development of Exceptional Talents, Shiraz, Iran
{b.ranjbarsahraei,gerhard.weiss}@maastrichtuniversity.nl,
ali.n123@gmail.com

Abstract. Recent years have witnessed a rapidly growing interest in using teams of mobile robots for autonomously covering environments. In this paper a novel approach for multi-robot coverage is described which is based on the principle of pheromone-based communication. According to this approach, called **StiCo** (for "Stigmergic Coverage"), the robots communicate indirectly via depositing/detecting markers in the environment to be covered. Although the movement policies of each robot are very simple, complex and efficient coverage behavior is achieved at the team level. **StiCo** shows several desirable features such as robustness, scalability and functional extensibility. Two extensions are described, including **A-StiCo** for dealing with dynamic environments and **ID-StiCo** for handling intruder detection. These features make **StiCo** an interesting alternative to graph-based multi-robot coverage approaches which currently are dominant in the field. Moreover, because of these features **StiCo** has a broad application potential. Simulation results are shown which clearly demonstrate the strong coverage abilities of **StiCo** in different environmental settings.

1 Introduction

In recent years there has been a rapidly growing interest in using teams of mobile robots for covering and patrolling environments of different types and complexities. This interest is mainly motivated by the broad spectrum of potential civilian, industrial and military applications of multi-robot surveillance systems. Examples of such applications are the protection of safety-critical technical infrastructures, the safeguarding of country borders, and the monitoring of high-risk regions and danger zones which cannot be entered by humans in the case of a nuclear incident, a bio-hazard or a military conflict. Triggered by this interest, today automated coverage is a well established topic in multi-robot research which is considered to be of particular practical relevance.

Currently available theoretical and algorithmic approaches to multi-robot coverage are typically of a computational complexity which excludes their usage in non-trivial application scenarios. Moreover, many of these methods are based

I.J. Timm and C. Guttmann (Eds.): MATES 2012, LNAI 7598, pp. 126–138, 2012.

on unrealistic assumptions. Examples of such assumptions are idealized sensors/actuators or sensors with infinite range (e.g. [1]), convexity and/or stationarity of the environment (e.g. [2]), the availability of unlimited communication bandwidth, and fully reliable direct communication links (e.g. [3]).

This article, which is an extension to the work reported in [4], presents a multi-robot coverage approach called **StiCo** ("Stigmergic Coverage") that avoids such type of assumptions. Specifically, **StiCo** is of a very low computational complexity and is designed for robots with very simple low-range sensors. Moreover, this approach does not rely on direct communication among robots. Instead, the covering robots coordinate on the basis of an indirect communication principle known as stigmergy. According to this principle, which was first observed in biological systems such as ant and termite colonies, natural entities improve their collective performance by influencing one another in their individual performance through local messages they deposit in their shared environment. In computer science, and especially in the field of ant algorithms (e.g., [5]), a number of computational variants of stigmergy have been developed and it has been shown that they allow for very efficient distributed control and optimization in a variety of problem domains (e.g., [6]). In addition to efficiency and distributedness, stigmergy-based coordination has several other properties which are also essential to multi-robot covering algorithms, including robustness, scalability, adaptivity and simplicity. In particular, a main advantage of stigmergy-based communication is its suitability for applications in environments with limited or intermittent network connectivity (e.g., in a devastated area after an earthquake or a military area under attack of jammers) [7,8]. This makes **StiCo** applicable in principle even in destructed environments where limited or no direct communication is possible. In addition to this, because robots use their environment for saving and transmitting messages no critical requirements are imposed on the storage memory of the individual robots.

The rest of this article is organized as follows. Related works is overviewed in Section 2. Section 3 gives a precise system description and problem formulation. **StiCo** is described in detail in Section 4. Simulation results are shown in Section 5 and Section 6 concludes the article.

2   Related Work

Our work is built on the notion of stigmergic communication introduced by Marco Dorigo [5]. The basic idea underlying this form of communication is that pheromones are used as a medium for transmitting messages among artificial ants. During the last years, computational variants of Dorigo's method (also known as ACO) have been developed and it has been shown that it allows for very efficient distributed control and optimization in a variety of problem domains [6]. Wagner et al. [9] were the first who invested stigmergic multi-robot coordination for covering/patrolling the environment. In their approach a group of robots were assumed which are able to (1) deposit chemical odor traces and (2) evaluate the strength of smell at every point they reach. Based on these assumptions, they used robots to model an un-mapped environment as a graph and they proposed basic graph search algorithms (such as Depth-First-Search and Breadth-First-Search) for solving robotic coverage problems. Many other researchers used this graph-based modeling scheme in order to design solutions for multi-robot patrolling/covering problems [10–14]. For example, in [10] Elor and Bruckstein mixed *cycle finding* algorithm with *spreading* algorithm in order to provide a finite-time cycle-based patrolling approach.

In contrast to all of the mentioned graph-based techniques, we use a geometrical framework which does not require to model the whole environment as a graph. Specifically, our geometrical approach is similar to Voronoi-based techniques that have recently been introduced for solving robot coverage problems (e.g., see Cortes et al. [3, 15] and Schwager et al. [2, 16]). These Voronoi-based techniques aim at devising coverage algorithms which work according to the following basic rule: *Each vehicle moves toward the center of its Voronoi region.* Based on this rule many researchers have proposed modified covering approaches which are adaptable to changes in the environment and are provably convergent (e.g., [2, 17]). However, all these geometrical algorithms require a group of robots with the capability of direct communication and in most of the cases also need very complex mathematical computations (e.g., calculating margins and center of mass for an individual Voronoi-region) which limits their potential real-world usage.

Another related research topic is focused on the "real" implementation of stigmergic communication in real world experiments. For example, chemical substances such as ethanol (C_2H_5OH) are already used instead of natural pheromones [18]. However, with recent developments in communication technology, electrical devices such as Radio Frequency Identification Devices (RFIDs) have gained much interest for such applications. In [7, 8] RFIDs are used for map building and simple pheromone-based explorations. Moreover, in [19] coordinated exploration and multi-robot SLAM for large teams of rescue robots is tackled by using RFIDs as environment features, which are detectable via UHF antennas. Based on characteristics of **StiCo**, it can be implemented on real robots with both chemical pheromones and digital markers.

3   Problem Formulation

The basic intention behind the work described here is to design a *motion policy* which enables a group of *robots*, each equipped only with simple *sensors*, to efficiently *cover* a possibly complex *environment*. Moreover, the basic idea pursued is to utilize the principle of pheromone-based coordination and to let each robot deposit *pheromones* on boundaries of its *territory* to inform the others about the already covered areas. This section defines and clarifies some key terms which are relevant to this intention and idea and will be used throughout this article.

- **Environment:** $\mathcal{Q} \subset \mathbb{R}^2$ is an *allowable environment* with area A, where "allowable environment" is defined as a closed and simply connected set which has a finite number of strict concavities [20].

- **Robot:** A *Dubins* vehicles [21] described by the dynamical system

$$\dot{x} = v \cos\theta, \quad \dot{y} = v \sin\theta, \quad \dot{\theta} = \omega, \tag{1}$$

where $x, y \in \mathbb{R}$ denote the vehicle position and $\theta \in \mathbb{S}^1$ denotes its orientation. The control inputs v and ω, describe the forward linear velocity and the angular velocity of the vehicle respectively, while v is set equal to v_0 (i.e. the nonholonomic vehicle is constrained to move at a constant linear speed) and the control input ω takes value in $[-1/\rho, 1/\rho]$; $1/\rho$ being the maximum curvature.

- **Sensor:** Each robot is equipped with two ant-antenna like sensors, placed on the front-right and front-left corners. These sensors have the ability to detect presence of pheromones from a predetermined distance called R_d, where R_d is considered to be very small.

- **Pheromone:** A chemical substance or an electrical marker placed at an arbitrary position (x_p, y_p). The pheromone is fully evaporated (naturally or artificially) after time T_e.

- **Territory:** Inspired by real ants, each robot considers a circular environment of area A_T as its territory and circles around this area persistently. The area of territory is related to angular and linear velocity of robot as: $A_T = \pi(v/\omega)^2$.

- **Motion Policy:** The motion policy tells a robot what to do at each iteration of time. Therefore, when a robot detects pheromone, it decides based on this policy what to do next.

- **Coverage:** We consider an environment to be covered, as a condition that no two robot territories share a common area of the environment. Therefore, the motion policy should guide the robots in a way that their territory intersections decrease as time passes. When the full coverage is achieved (i.e. no territories have intersection), each robot patrols its territory by moving on the territory border, persistently.

4 Design of the StiCo Approach

The basic notion underlying **StiCo** is to partition the environment into equal circular regions (also called territories) where each robot takes responsibility to guard one of these regions. The robots need not communicate directly, but deposit pheromones on the borders of their territory for instructing other robots to not enter it. In this way StiCo answers the core question *"How should robots move in order to decrease the intersections of their territories"*.

4.1 Basic StiCo

In **StiCo**, each robot starts to move with a constant forward linear velocity v_0, and a constant angular velocity w_0, which results in a circular motion on the border of a territory with radius v_0/w_0. The forward linear velocity remains constant during the whole mission. However, in different situations the angular velocity might increase or decrease based on the motion policy.

In order to adjust the angular velocity, based on the circling direction (CW or CCW), one sensor serves as the interior sensor (the one nearer to the center of territory) and the other one as the exterior sensor.

When the interior sensor detects a pheromone (Figure 1a), it indicates to the robot that it is about entering another territory, and therefore the robot changes its circling direction immediately (Figure 1b). In this way, the robot establishes its territory in a new region without any intersection with the other territory. Otherwise, if exterior sensor detects a pheromone (Figure 1c), this tells the robot that it is passing near another territory (however, not completely entering it as in Figure 1a). In this case the robot rotates (i.e., magnitude of w_0 is increased up to $1/\rho$) until it does not detect pheromone any more and then circles in the same direction with the constant angular velocity w_0 (Figure 1d). Therefore, the intersection between two territories is fully eliminated with a small displacement of territory.

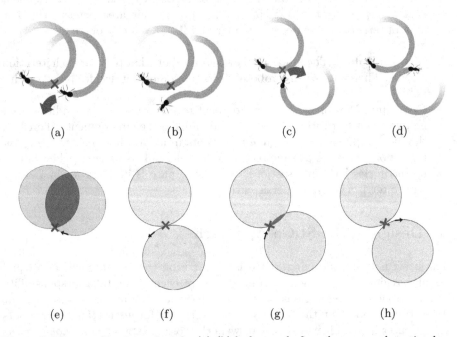

Fig. 1. StiCo coordination principle: (a)-(b) before and after pheromone detection by internal sensor. (c)-(d) before and after pheromone detection by external sensor. (e)-(f) covered area before and after pheromone detection by internal sensor. (g)-(h) covered area before and after pheromone detection by external sensor.

Figures 1e-1h, illustrate how StiCo works. As shown in Figures 1e and 1g, before pheromone detection there is an intersection between two territories. When one robot detects pheromone and changes its territory area the intersection is fully eliminated, as shown in Figures 1f and 1h. As a result, the robots keep their territories disjoint. In the case of a large swarm of robots, eliminating one intersection may cause the emergence of other intersections. However, as the simulation results of this article show, the statistical chance for decrement of intersections is significantly higher than the chance for its increment – and this makes **StiCo** a very efficient coverage approach.

StiCo is further detailed in Algorithm 1.

Algorithm 1. StiCo

Require: Each robot can deposit/detect pheromone trails
  Initialize: Choose circling direction (CW/CCW)
  loop
    while (no pheromone is detected) **do**
      Circle around
      deposit pheromone
    end while
    if (interior sensor detects pheromone) **then**
      Reverse the circling direction
    else
      while (pheromone is detected) **do**
        Increase the magnitude of angular velocity (Rotate)
      end while
    end if
  end loop

4.2 StiCo Extensions

By applying **StiCo** on a swarm of robots, complex behavior emerges and robots disperse in the environment homogeneously to cover the maximal possible area. Although this novel coverage approach generates very efficient coverage results based on relatively simple motion rules, it can be extended in two important ways. First, toward dealing with dynamically changing environments. In such environments it is difficult how to choose certain parameters of the multi-robot system such as motion speed of the individual robots. As a solution to this, **StiCo** can be extended by treating the territory area of each robot as an adaptable term: a robot can increase the size of its territory (by decreasing the magnitude of angular speed) when detecting large uncovered areas near its territory borders. We call this motion policy **A-StiCo** (for "Adaptive **StiCo** "). Second, **StiCo** allows to easily add intruder detection behavior: robots decrease their respective territories as soon as they detect the presence of an intruder. By adding this behavior to **A-StiCo**, the density of robots near the intruder increases automatically. The effective behavior of **ID-StiCo** (for "Intruder Detection **StiCo** ") suggests to use this coverage approach in surveillance missions of unknown environments.

5   Simulation Results

In this section, we demonstrate the evolution of **StiCo** on four simulation scenarios. In the first scenario robots are initialized in the center of an obstacle-free environment and disperse in it homogeneously in order to partition the environment into circular regions. In this simulation, the scalability of **StiCo** is demonstrated by using a unique motion policy for robotic swarms of different sizes. In the second scenario, obstacles are used to generate a non-convex coverage problem. The main goal of this simulation scenario is to demonstrate the robustness of **StiCo** in complex environments. Then, two possible extensions on **StiCo**, **A-StiCo** and **ID-StiCo**, are discussed and related simulations results are illustrated. A video presentation of different characteristics of **StiCo** is available at: http://youtu.be/DOlyqDN2a9o.

All of the simulations are implemented on a robotic swarm of identical members initialized in the center of a $40m \times 40m$ field. The pheromones are simulated with a high resolution, equal to 300×300 and the evaporation time is $T_e = 1.5s$. Moreover, we pay careful attention to numerical accuracy and optimization issues in the pheromones update policy.

5.1   Scenario 1: Convex Environment

Scenario 1 consists of a convex environment (a square of size $1600m^2$ shown in Figure 2). All of the robots are initialized in the center of this environment with different initial angles. The execution of **StiCo** on a group of 40 robots is illustrated in Figures 2a and 2b and its execution on a group of 80 robots is illustrated in Figures 2c and 2d.

The snapshots shown in Figure 2, confirm our predictions in Section 4 that the intersected area between territories is completely eliminated after a while and robots are dispersed in the environment homogeneously. It is intuitively clear that when robots are placed in a configuration that no two territories have intersection, then the whole configuration remains stable and the robots move on the borders of their territories, persistently.

In order to depict the coverage performance of this algorithm in respect of time, we run **StiCo** for 30 times with different initial positions. Then by averaging the overall covered area in each iteration over different simulation runs, we can compute the *estimated covered environment*. Moreover, based on basic geometry, the maximum possible fraction of a square which can be covered by a set of disjoint identical circles is 78.5%. Therefore, in the best case $1256m^2$ of the considered environment can be covered. Figure 3 shows a comparison of the estimated covered environment with this maximum possible coverage for both groups of 40 and 80 robots. As can be seen, **StiCo** converges to this maximum in both cases.

5.2   Scenario 2: Non-convex Environment

In order to demonstrate potential capabilities of the **StiCo** approach, we consider as a second scenario a non-convex environment as shown in Figure 4a. This

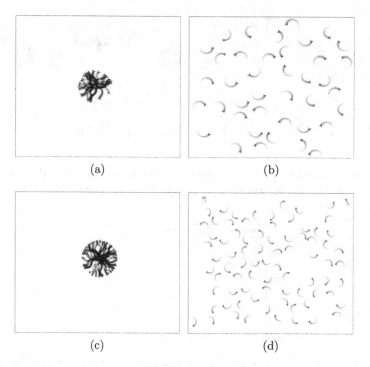

Fig. 2. The evolution of coverage achieved by **StiCo**: (a),(b) Initial and final position of the 40-robot group. (c),(d) Initial and final position of the 80-robot group.

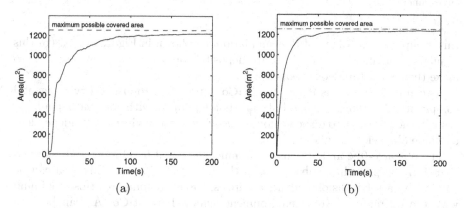

Fig. 3. The estimated covered environment: (a) 40-robot group. (b) 80-robot group

environment can represent, for instance, a devastated area after an earthquake, or a street map in an emergency condition.

For coverage of this environment, a group of 40 robots are initiated at the center of the environment with different initial angles. **StiCo** is executed on

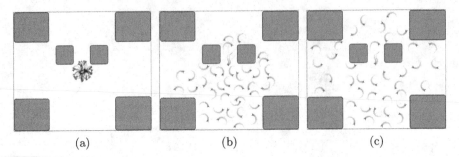

Fig. 4. Evolution of coverage of a non-convex environment achieved through **StiCo**: (a) Initial snapshot. (b) Intermediate snapshot. (c) Final snapshot.

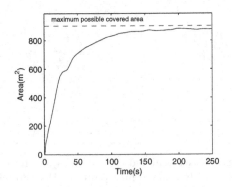

Fig. 5. The estimated covered environment for a 40-robot group in a non-convex environment

this group and snapshots of this simulation are shown in Figure 4(a-c). (In this simulation, artificial pheromones are deposited on the borders of obstacles to make them detectable for robots).

As can be seen in this figure, the **StiCo** approach is robust to environmental complexities. Although the robots are not equipped with any path planning system, they are able to disperse homogeneously in the environment independent of where obstacles are placed.

The obstacle-free area of this environment is equal to $1150m^2$ and, as mentioned in the preceding subsection, in the best case 78.5% of this area can be covered by a set if disjoint identical circles. Figure 5 compares this maximum with the estimated covered environment achieved by **StiCo**. As can be seen again, **StiCo** is able to reach the maximum possible coverage.

5.3   Extension 1: A-StiCo

In this simulation we show that by adding adaptive behaviors to the **StiCo** approach, even more efficient coverage results can be achieved. In **A-StiCo**, when a robot does not detect pheromones for a while, it decreases its angular velocity (w_0). Consequently, the territory area is expanded and the robot guards a larger region. Otherwise, when a robot detects pheromones very often (which means that many robots have been moving nearby), it increases its angular velocity. Consequently, the robot guards a smaller region. By adding this simple adaptive behavior to the **StiCo** approach, robots are able to cover the environment more adaptively. Figure 6 depicts the evolution of coverage for two swarms of 10 and 40 robots. In both simulations, robots start from the same initial conditions.

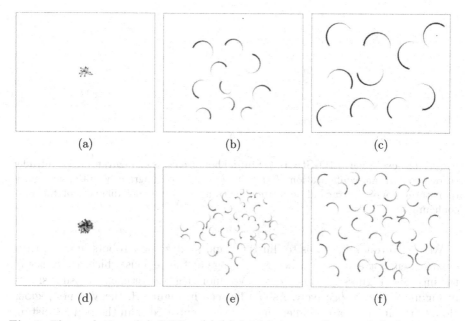

Fig. 6. The evolution of **A-StiCo**: (a)-(c) Initial, intermediate, and final snapshots after $250s$, for 10 robots. (d)-(f) Initial, intermediate, and final snapshots after $250s$, for 40 robots.

5.4   Extension 2: ID-StiCo

In Subsection 4.2 we suggested an extended form of **StiCo** called as **ID-StiCo** which realizes intruder detection behavior. According to **ID-StiCo** a robot decreases its territory area as soon as it senses an intruder. Integrating this behavior with the **A-StiCo** approach results in a very effective surveillance characteristic. Figures 7a-7c illustrates the evolution of the intruder detection behavior of this new approach for a group of 40 robots: Figure 7a shows an already achieved coverage of the environment, in Figure 7b a stationary intruder is added in the center of the environment which has resulted in an immediate reaction of nearby robots, and in Figure 7c the robots achieve a final stable configuration.

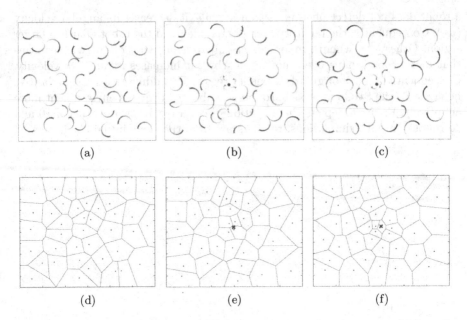

(a)   (b)   (c)

(d)   (e)   (f)

Fig. 7. The evolution of **ID-StiCo**: (a) Initial homogeneous configuration. (b) Intruder entrance. (c) Final configuration after $200s$. (d) Voronoi diagram of initial configuration. (e) Voronoi diagram after intruder entrance. (f) Voronoi diagram of the final configuration.

We use Voronoi diagrams to illustrate and analyze how robots move in their environment for achieving a better coverage of the regions which are closer to the intruder. Figures 7d-7f depict the Voronoi diagram for each snapshot shown in Figures 7a-7c, respectively. As can be seen in Figure 7f, the Voronoi regions close to the intruder are smaller and more concentrated than the regions distant from it – this is exactly the kind of behavior expected from an effective intruder detection approach.

6   Conclusion

This article addressed the multi-robot coverage problem in environments of different complexity and presented a new approach called **StiCo** which is based on indirect, stigmergic communication. **StiCo** is a fully distributed motion policy which allows for a very effective and efficient coverage performance. Compared to existing coverage approaches, **StiCo** shows several important advantages, including scalability, robustness, very low computational complexity and memory requirements, and easy functional extensibility (as shown with two extensions – **A-StiCo** and **ID-StiCo** – of broad practical relevance). This makes **StiCo** distinct from all other currently available multi-robot coverage approaches.

We think the experimental results justify to invest further research in **StiCo**. **StiCo** opens a promising new research avenue: the comparison of multi-robot stigmergy-based coverage and graph-based environmental coverage. Currently we are working on a mathematical framework for a formal analysis of **StiCo**, and we hope this framework will also contribute to a deeper understanding of how these two types of coverage approaches compare to each other in general. Moreover, we are currently working on an implementation of **StiCo** on a group of 30 e-puck robots in our SwarmLab (http://swarmlab.unimaas.nl/).

References

1. Roman-Ballesteros, I., Pfeiffer, C.F.: A framework for cooperative multi-robot surveillance tasks. In: Electronics, Robotics and Automotive Mechanics Conference, vol. 2, pp. 163 –170 (September 2006)
2. Schwager, M., Rus, D., Slotine, J.J.: Decentralized, adaptive coverage control for networked robots. International Journal of Robotics Research 28(3), 357–375 (2009)
3. Cortes, J., Martinez, S., Karatas, T., Bullo, F.: Coverage control for mobile sensing networks. IEEE Transactions on Robotics and Automation 20(2), 243–255 (2004)
4. Ranjbar-Sahraei, B., Weiss, G., Nakisaee, A.: Stigmergic coverage algorithm for multi-robot systems (demonstration). In: Proceedings of the Eleventh International Conference on Autonomous Agents and Multiagent Systems, AAMAS (2012)
5. Dorigo, M.: Optimization, Learning and Natural Algorithms. Thesis report, Politecnico di Milano, Italy (1992)
6. Dorigo, M., Birattari, M., Stutzle, T.: Ant colony optimization. IEEE Computational Intelligence Magazine 1(4), 28–39 (2006)
7. Johansson, R., Saffiotti, A.: Navigating by stigmergy: A realization on an rfid floor for minimalistic robots. In: IEEE International Conference on Robotics and Automation, ICRA 2009, pp. 245–252 (May 2009)
8. Herianto, Sakakibara, T., Kurabayashi, D.: Artificial pheromone system using rifd for navigation of autonomous robots. Journal of Bionic Engineering 4(4), 245–253 (2007)
9. Wagner, I.A., Lindenbaum, M., Bruckstein, A.M.: Distributed covering by ant-robots using evaporating traces. IEEE Transactions on Robotics and Automation 15(5), 918–933 (1999)
10. Elor, Y., Bruckstein, A.M.: Autonomous Multi-agent Cycle Based Patrolling. In: Dorigo, M., Birattari, M., Di Caro, G.A., Doursat, R., Engelbrecht, A.P., Floreano, D., Gambardella, L.M., Groß, R., Şahin, E., Sayama, H., Stützle, T. (eds.) ANTS 2010. LNCS, vol. 6234, pp. 119–130. Springer, Heidelberg (2010)
11. Elor, Y., Bruckstein, A.M.: Multi-a(ge)nt graph patrolling and partitioning. In: Proceedings of the 2009 IEEE/WIC/ACM International Joint Conference on Web Intelligence and Intelligent Agent Technology - Volume 02, WI-IAT 2009, pp. 52–57. IEEE Computer Society, Washington, DC (2009)
12. Glad, A., Simonin, O., Buffet, O., Charpillet, F.: Influence of different execution models on patrolling ant behaviors: from agents to robots. In: Proceedings of the Ninth International Conference on Autonomous Agents and MultiAgent Systems, AAMAS 2010 (2010)
13. Glad, A., Simonin, O., Buffet, O., Charpillet, F.: Theoretical study of ant-based algorithms for multi-agent patrolling. In: Proceeding of the 2008 conference on ECAI 2008: 18th European Conference on Artificial Intelligence, pp. 626–630. IOS Press, Amsterdam (2008)

14. Yanovski, V., Wagner, I.A., Bruckstein, A.M.: A distributed ant algorithm for efficiently patrolling a network. Algorithmica 37, 165–186 (2003)
15. Cortes, J., Martinez, S., Bullo, F.: Spatially-distributed coverage optimization and control with limited-range interactions. ESAIM: Control, Optimisation and Calculus of Variations 11, 691–719 (2005)
16. Schwager, M., Rus, D., Slotine, J.J.: Unifying geometric, probabilistic, and potential field approaches to multi-robot deployment. International Journal of Robotics Research 30(3), 371–383 (2011), doi:10.1177/0278364910383444
17. Breitenmoser, A., Schwager, M., Metzger, J.C., Siegwart, R., Rus, D.: Voronoi coverage of non-convex environments with a group of networked robots. In: Proc. of the International Conference on Robotics and Automation (ICRA 2010), pp. 4982–4989 (May 2010)
18. Fujisawa, R., Imamura, H., Hashimoto, T., Matsuno, F.: Communication using pheromone field for multiple robots. In: IEEE/RSJ International Conference on Intelligent Robots and Systems, IROS 2008, pp. 1391–1396 (September 2008)
19. Ziparo, V.A., Kleiner, A., Marchetti, L., Farinelli, A., Nardi, D.: Cooperative exploration for USAR robots with indirect communication. In: Proc.of 6th IFAC Symposium on Intelligent Autonomous Vehicles, IAV 2007 (2007)
20. Bullo, F., Cortes, J., Martinez, S.: Distributed Control of Robotic Networks. Applied Mathematics Series (2009), http://www.coordinationbook.info
21. Dubins, L.E.: On curves of minimal length with a constraint on average curvature and with prescribed initial and terminal positions and tangents. American Journal of Mathematics 79, 497–516 (1957)

Multi-Agent Systems Applied to the Field of Ornamental Plants

Francisco Javier Rodríguez-Martínez, Tito Valencia-Requejo,
and Lorena Otero-Cerdeira

Laboratorio de Informática Aplicada 2,University of Vigo, Campus As Lagoas,
Ourense, Spain
{franjrm,tvalencia,locerdeira}@uvigo.es

Abstract. The market of ornamental plants is very important and strategical in Galicia and yet is one of the sectors where fewer technological change has been incorporated in recent years. This paper describes a real solution applied to an enterprise of ornamental plant selling and distribution. The solution that we propose uses intelligent agent technologies and ontologies to meet the special needs of an enterprise of this kind. We present the architecture defined with the agents involved in both parties, the plant wholesaler and the plant producers. A description of the ontologies that these agents use to interact is also provided, as well an example of systems behavior. In the final section some relevant issues detected and conclusions will be presented.

1 Introduction

The market of ornamental plants has always been very important in Galicia (northwestern Spain) and yet it is one of the sectors where fewer technological change has been incorporated in recent years. This paper describes a real solution applied to an enterprise of ornamental plant selling and distribution. This enterprise, a plant wholesaler, needs to interact daily with the producers of the plants they sell and with the costumers that buy them. This plant wholesaler distinguishes between two types of producers, internal and external ones, making a total above 20 producers. Internal producers are those that are also partners in the enterprise, opposite to external ones which only have a trading relation with the enterprise. The costumers of the enterprise are also categorized, however this groups are not as clearly defined as producer's ones, and there are even costumers that lie on two different groups. Further details of enterprise's inner structure can not be discussed due to confidentiality reasons.

Our platform uses intelligent agent technologies and ontologies to meet the special needs of an enterprise of this kind. In business context it is essential to track all information and business processes, even more, since this enterprise is working with a perishable product as plants are, making an efficient and just-in-time control is crucial.

The platform that has been designed allows the enterprise to carry out tasks such as, *Production and Route Planning, Order Management Logistics* or *Catalog Processing*.

I.J. Timm and C. Guttmann (Eds.): MATES 2012, LNAI 7598, pp. 139–153, 2012.

Moreover, as this productive sector works with very tighten margins in both economic and time axis, it was essential for the designed platform to manage the whole production process covering from space or productive management to cost estimation, allowing a detailed tracking on the marketed products. Besides, to ensure enterprise's growth and to enable its interoperability with both producers of the plant and other plant wholesalers it has been necessary to define mechanisms to overcome the possible information heterogeneity of the different parties.

When taking into account all the requirements and issues of the enterprise, no software product or platform was found that integrated all of them in a fulfilling way. So there was the need to develop a completely new platform from scratch to satisfy all the requirements of such a system without the help or expertise that the existence of other software products or platforms would provide. Here lies the strength and the importance, but also the main difficulty of this project.

The development of such a platform was addressed as a multi-agent system (MAS), which we chose to divide as well in different smaller MAS for the sake of the design and categorization, obtaining this way a layered representation of the MAS.

MAS have usually been used in simulation applications, real-world interactions or adaptive structured information systems [1]. Within these contexts MAS have been used for fire accident detection[2], emergency evacuation simulation [3][4], meetings planning [5], etc., but never to develop a platform as the described in this paper.

It is important to state that not the whole system was addressed as a MAS, other pieces of software were developed to cover aspects of the system where the features of the MAS were not needed, such as human resources management or accounting. These pieces of the system where designed and implemented following traditional approaches. This part was developed taking an open-source platform, *OpenERP*, as a basis where the different modules where redesigned and customized.

For the purposes of this paper only the part of the system regarding the MAS will be described. In this paper a series of figures that depict the different components of the MAS will be presented. In these figures the part of the system that is not included in the MAS will be referred as *"other modules"* or *"rest of the system"*.

The MAS is divided into three different MAS. The *Plant Wholesaler MAS* is composed by the agents that take care of the enterprise's tasks mentioned above. The *Plant Nursery MAS* is composed by the agents that take care of all the processes related to plant producing, such as catalog processing or production following up. Both of these MAS are tightly related to the legacy systems existing in both types of organizations. The *Communication MAS* holds the agents that undertake the actions related to mutual exclusion preservation and information integration.

The rest of this paper is structured as follows, in Section 2 a detailed view of the system's goals will be provided. In Section 3 the builded platform will be fully analyzed. In Section 4 we will summarize the main conclusions of the development as well as further improvements that will be undertaken.

2   Project's Objectives

The project's main goal was to obtain a platform that could improve the production management, cost control in the producers and marketing support in foreign countries by using MAS and Business Intelligence algorithms.

Nowadays there are some commercial applications that centralize all the information related to plant nursing and plant selling processes allowing queries over this information. These applications are simply aggregative or storage systems and do not provide support to the enterprise's manager in relevant tasks such as production management, real-time order management, stock following up and production planning. Some of these solutions do have modules that take care of tasks such as field control, commercial invoices management and, customers and providers tracing.

From plant producers point of view, such applications do not achieve the requirements established, since they don't take into account the special characteristics of plants as products. Plants are a perishable item and so its production planning is not as straight and pre-established as other product's planning would be. Plants grow, die, bloom, etc., these kind of changes and others plants experience turn products into new ones. The same plant in the same flowerpot can be different products as it changes. Besides in these applications costs are stablished following financial and accounting parameters, which works fine in other types of productive areas but not on this one.

From the plant wholesaler point of view, there are several systems that do marketing management but that are simply Enterprise Resource Planning systems (ERP) which have been adapted from other productive areas and that do not consider the special circumstances of such an heterogeneous market as plant selling is.

The following needs have been identified as project goals as they don't coexist in a single software application in this environment: *Dynamic catalog processing, Dynamic price estimation, Dynamic route planning, Order processing, Production cost management, Production planning, Reservation of future products, Sales forecasting and Stock following up.*

Besides the functional requirements identified above, there were also other non-functional requirements that were tagged as mandatory for the final platform. Among them, the most remarkable are: *Efficiency, Expandability, Flexibility, Maintainability, Performance, Reliability, Robustness, Scalability, Security and Usability*

After analyzing all the requirements listed above, both functional and non-functional, the most suitable approach seemed to develop a multi-agent system, but a deeper analysis was necessary to confirm this hypothesis. We performed an evaluation of the project, its background and its environment to check whether the features that describe a MAS [6,7] could be identified in it.

The network connection in the rural areas where the plant nurseries and the plant wholesaler are set can not guarantee the correct timing in product order receipt, delivery confirmation, product reservation, etc. Besides, plant nurseries and plant wholesaler do not share the same timetables. This circumstances lead to an asynchronous behavior of the system. **Asynchrony**, is a feature that characterizes a MAS, meaning that agents communicate with messages which can be received at any time.

The different entities involved, plant producers and plant seller must both behave in two different ways, as independent enterprises that have their own processes, costumers and needs that must be taken care of, but also, as a conjoint entity which tries to maximize each part's benefits. So there is clearly the need to establish a coordination mechanism in order to guarantee that association's needs are satisfied without ignoring each part's needs. This must be done without implementing a global control system since each part must also behave independently. This situation is typical in a MAS, where agents must cooperate and interact to achieve the common goals, without an external entity that establishes a fixed execution algorithm. Each agent must decide on its own which actions to perform. In order to achieve a solution in a cooperative MAS additional coordination mechanisms need to be developed. This mechanisms would ensure that agents's individual decisions will lead to an accurate MAS state. The MAS feature that pops here is **Control.**

Plants are a living product that change almost every day and that need cares and attentions that other products do not require. This causes the environment to be continuously changing, and so, information about plants's production and plants's states must be updated at least a couple of times a day. As the number of plants increase, so does the catalog's modification rate. Besides, the system must serve requests along the day, causing system's supplies and stock to be in continuous modification. This steady updating causes the environment to be highly dynamic. **Dynamism** is one of the most remarkable features of a MAS. Agents have to deal with dynamic environments, they have to interact with environments that are continually changing due to the influence of other agents or external entities.

Plant nurseries have requirements and needs that are not crucial for the plant wholesaler and the other way round. Plant nurseries are mainly concerned about plant production costs, dynamic price estimation or plant preservation works, among others. On the other side, the plant wholesaler pays more attention to order processing, future products reservations or dynamic catalog processing. This types of entities are very heterogeneous, and **Heterogeneity** is another defining feature of a MAS. The various agents that comprise a MAS are heterogeneous. This condition can affect the very design of the agents, not only at hardware but also at software level. Besides we also consider heterogeneous those agents that even with the same hardware and software implement different behaviors or capabilities for problem solving.

The plant wholesaler's catalog is spread over the different plant producers, and so the plant wholesaler final catalog must be composed by gathering the information from all plant nurseries. The **Perception** of decentralized data is another defining feature of a MAS. The information that agents need to perform their actions is not stored in a single, centralized and unified repository. This means that the information that agents receive may appear at different locations, it may also arrive at different times and it may even require different interpretations due to a semantical difference. All these features cause the agents to have their own partial perception of the environment, and so an incomplete information.

At this point it is important to state that each plant nursery has its own information structure and confers different semantic meaning to the concepts of the plant nursing field. Information integration was one of the major problems that the legacy system had. People that first developed the legacy system were not experts in the field and so they used concepts without fully understanding its meaning. Without a common ontology over the concepts, the use and maintenance of the legacy system has turned incomprehensible. It is important to remark that the MAS itself will not cover for the information integration and so, means to overcome this information heterogeneity needed to be studied. Within the plant wholesaler, information is not updated in real-time, since they are not able to track the plants and products sold, and which is more dangerous, the legacy system can not link products to producers. In case an order returned, it would cause an stock of plant which could not be returned to its origin.

In order to achieve all the requirements listed above a MAS by itself could not replace the previously existing legacy system, it was also necessary a deep reengineering over the information system, due to the problems that it presented.

The causes for these problems in database's structure were found in:

- The technology that the databases used was obsolete.
- There was a bad initial design which has been exacerbated due to several years of poor maintenance.
- There were critical integrity problems due to technology misuse.
- When a conflict between several concepts at the semantic level arose, it was resolved manually.
- When the productive processes required of a data exchange between the plant nurseries and the plant wholesaler, it was performed in best cases by emailing a pdf file or raw text.

After considering several alternatives to rebuild the information system, the chosen one involves rebuilding the database structure for both types of entities. To perform the communication and data exchange between them the solution was found in ontologies. By using this approach, agents defined for the MAS would use an ontology to describe the meaning of concepts in the communication processes [8], avoiding this way the heterogeneity that exists between the involved knowledge sources.

3   Solution's Overview

The platform that we propose consists in the definition of a layered MAS whose agents use ontologies to provide interoperability between them.

The global MAS was divided into three MAS that will now be described. This is a logical division and it was made due to organizational reasons and not to physical ones. Although the different MAS will be described independently, the agents may accept requests from agents that belong either to its own MAS or to another MAS.

3.1 MAS Description

The plant wholesaler MAS consists of a group of agents performing tasks for which a traditional solution would not provide the appropriate functionality. Accordingly, intelligent behavior will accomplish tasks such as route planning, order processing or catalog processing. This part of the system was developed using C, for agents, and Python for forms and reports. Python modules were implemented to grant the interoperability of the MAS with the OpenERP platform that composes the rest of the system. At a certain timestamp the number of agents

In figure 1 the whole structure of the Plant Wholesaler MAS is depicted. The agents in these three MAS will interact with those defined in the Plant Nurseries MAS. In figure 2 the structure of the Plant Nurseries MAS is depicted. The whole structure, and interactions among all these MAS is reflected in figure 3.

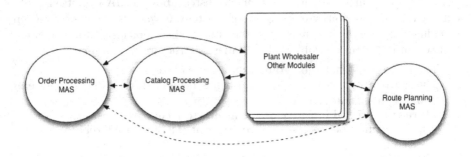

Fig. 1. Plant Wholesaler MAS

1. Order Processing

Order processing is a complex task and one of the most important for the plant wholesaler. To perform a proper order processing, there are some issues that impose strong restrictions on the defined MAS, which are:

- *Timeframes:* orders must be processed as soon as possible due to the very nature of the products, since they may loose value and quality very quickly.
- *Catalog:* plant's catalog is continuously changing due to sales, reservations and modifications from the producers.

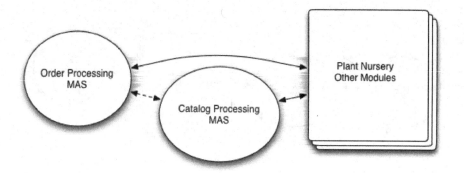

Fig. 2. Plant Nurseries MAS

- *Providers:* coordination among all the providers must be sharp, since to process a single order, several producers are always involved.
- *Transportation:* orders from the customers are not fixed every week, thus transportation routes must be continuously redefined and optimized to include new orders. To do so, some other orders may be renegotiated or rescheduled to assure the maximum profit. Besides, transportation routes range from Spain or Portugal, i.e., very close to the producers, to France, Holland or Germany.

Order processing subsystem involves several groups of agents. Those from the plant wholesaler compose its Order Processing MAS. The same happens in the plant nurseries, every agent involved in order processing integrates the Order Processing MAS.The agents defined for the plant wholesaler are of two different types, *Order Agent* and *Negotiator*. The number of agents that exist in the MAS at a certain timestamp can only be estimated, since it will depend on the number of orders received that day, the length of the orders and the number of providers.

Order Agent. *An order agent is responsible for splitting an order between its negotiators and composing the shipping with the results of each negotiator.* When a new order arrives to the plant wholesaler, a new order agent is created to manage it. This agent reports its existence to a mediator agent, which acts as an intermediary between the plant wholesaler's agents and the plant nurseries's agents. For every item in the order list, the order agent activates a negotiator agent to manage it. Once every negotiator is done, the order agent composes the final order with the information that each one of its negotiators provides. This information identifies every provider together with the product that it supplies, its cost, quality and further details.

Negotiator. *A negotiator agent is responsible for dealing with a provider to get a product.* A negotiator agent is responsible for getting the best offer for a product. The best offer might not only be determined by the price of the product. Indeed, it is necessary allowing that other constraints could

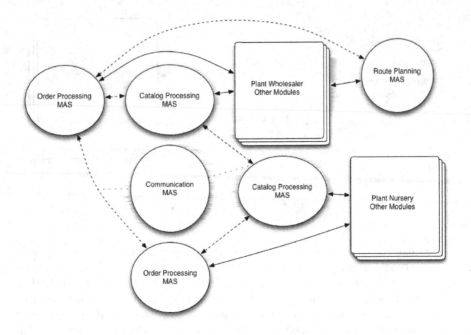

Fig. 3. Relation between the different MAS

be applied, such as provider's proximity or even constraints in the product. These constraints could be expressed with rules such as: *"plant color belongs to this group of colors"* or *"plant size is in the range (min, max)"*. To identify the agent from the plant nursery that each negotiator has to deal with, the different negotiators enquire the mediator agent.

For order processing, in the plant nurseries side two types of agents were defined, *Provider* and *Broker*.

Provider. *A provider agent supplies products from the plant nursery.* When a new provider is created it communicates its existence to a mediator agent. Since all mediator agents are federated, the knowledge about providers and negotiators is shared among all of them. A provider agent has a group of broker agents that negotiate the different products. A provider has at most a broker agent for each product that is sold in the plant nursery. The provider regularly reports its state to a mediator, so the mediators can optimize the distribution of requests from the negotiators among the different brokers. The provider reports on the products that their brokers are currently selling and on those that they have in stock for selling. If a provider receives a request from the mediator for a product that it's not being sold yet, it triggers a new broker for that product. If the broker for that product already exists, the provider adds the request to the broker's queue.

Broker or Delegate. *A broker agent is responsible for dealing with plant wholesaler's negotiators.* A broker agent sells to negotiator agents its product, respecting the boundaries that the provider agent may have established. If the broker belongs to an internal provider, it deals the conditions of the sale with the negotiator agent specified by a mediator. In this case we refer to it as *delegate*. If the broker agent belongs to an external provider, the selling process works as an auction between the negotiator agent and all the broker agents that sell the product.

The last type of agent involved in order processing is the *Mediator*. This type of agent does not belong to the plant wholesaler's MAS or to the plant nurseries's MAS, it belongs to the Communication MAS.

Mediator. *A mediator agent is responsible for linking negotiators to brokers.* In the communication MAS there are several federated mediators, which means that the knowledge that one of them has is immediately shared with the other mediators. A mediator agent is responsible for discovering the providers and for linking the negotiators to the brokers. When a new negotiator is created it consults a mediator agent. If the product that the negotiator needs is sold by one or several internal providers, the mediator links the negotiator to a free broker regardless of the plant nursery that the provider and broker belong to. However if the product is not sold by an internal provider, an auction with all the external providers is started. Each external provider assigns a broker agent for the auction and the mediator plays the role of referee in the auction. The negotiator agent is linked to the broker that wins the auction.

2. Catalog Processing

To grant enterprise's requirements and to adjust to their working procedure, catalog processing a distributed task performed asynchronously, that must balance in the producers the amount of plants that is set as available to ensure that a safety limit is not exceeded to prevent that the reservations over future products may be unattended. Another issue that must be considered is the evolution of the plants; they grow, bloom, die, etc., and with every change they suffer they become a new product in the catalog.

Catalog processing involves agents in the plant wholesaler and in the plant nurseries, additionally agents in the Communication MAS are necessary for mediation purposes. The types of agents involved in catalog processing are *Catalog Combiner* and *Seeker* for the plant wholesaler, and *Catalog Manager* for each plant nursery.

Catalog Combiner. *A catalog combiner is responsible for obtaining an updated catalog for the plant wholesaler.* The product catalog of the plant wholesaler must be daily revised and modified to provide the costumers with an updated version. The catalog combiner agent builds the catalog from the existing one, taking into account both internal and external information. As internal information, the sales of the day and the reservations must be considered, and as external information, the updates on every plant nurseries's catalog that is a provider for the plant wholesaler must be introduced. When the catalog combiner is created it checks the list of providers with the *mediator agent*, which offers and updated list of every provider that the plant wholesaler has. For each plant nursery identified as provider, the catalog combiner triggers a *seeker agent*. Together with the information that the seekers gather the catalog combiner will compose the new catalog.

Seeker. *A seeker agent is responsible for gathering the updated information about a provider's catalog.* A seeker agent is responsible for getting the updated version of a provider's catalog. Once a seeker is created it already knows the provider that it must deal with. By default the seeker gets the plant nursery's whole catalog, but it can also be configured to query the provider's *Catalog Manager* for an specific product o for a product that fulfills a set of requirements.

Catalog Manager. *A catalog manager agent is responsible for updating a plant nursery's catalog.* The catalog manager is responsible for updating a plant nursery's catalog by taking the existing one and modifying it with the sales of the day and the modifications that the products may have experienced. Since the kind of product plant nurseries have to deal with is a living one, it suffers changes that other products do not, such as growth, death, bloom, etc. This kind of changes turn the products into new ones. The catalog manager reports its existence to a mediator agent, so when a catalog combiner agent queries the mediator for the list of plant nurseries, it is included. From that moment on, the catalog manager is available for taking the requests from the seekers.

Mediator. *A mediator agent is responsible for providing indexing information.* A mediator agent holds the information over which catalog managers are available to be queried from the seekers. Since in the communication MAS several mediators exist, they must be federated so there is no difference in the information that they hold.

3. Route Planning

Another important task of the system is the dynamic route planning. It was also addressed as a *Multi-Agent Resource Allocation (MARA)* problem. In this type of problems a group of agents share a common resource which requires a coordination mechanism that will manage its usage [9].

In this case, the common resource would be the truck that carries the plants which must stop in several delivery locations. Depending on the truck's load, the features of the plants, the delivery time, etc., the different agents that represent the delivery locations must negotiate to determine the truck's best route. Dynamic route planning can be addressed as an independent task that lies outside the scope of this paper, and that will be developed in further papers.

3.2 Ontologies Defined

Some of the producers decided to accept the system as it was firstly designed, with a single ontology that was shared by wholesaler and nurseries. Problems showed up when some plant nurseries chose to use the platform but keeping their own information representation. Agents would be no longer able to interact correctly.

The existing information structure that the different entities had, was very different, causing the interaction between them to be very hard, and it turned non-viable, the option of keeping the original knowledge representation in those nurseries that were not willing to change. In addition we have identified several cases where the same term was used with different meanings, not only between the different entities but also within the same entity. The MAS defined in this project would not succeed if the problem of the semantic gap were not addressed. To accomplish this task, two different ontologies were defined, one for the plant wholesaler and the other one for the plant nurseries, this two ontologies share the semantic meaning over the concepts and so, agents are able to interact. In multi-agent environments ontologies are expected to complement mutual understanding and interactive behavior between such agents [10].

In figures 4 and 5, the global structure and properties of the Plant Wholesaler's ontology and Plant Nurseries' are respectively depicted. These ontologies are used by the agents in the plant wholesaler and plant nurseries to interact and thus assure the operational purposes of the enterprise. These ontologies reflect the specific situation of the enterprise that hosted the project and they may not be applied to every plant wholesaler and nursery, due to the peculiarities of the enterprise.

Further description about these ontologies, as well as their defining properties is deeply explained in [11].

In addition to defining these ontologies, to overcome the problem of the information heterogeneity it was necessary to take another step. In this situation, the most suitable one is to force an *ontology matching* process before agents start their communication. Imposing a single shared ontology would be, not only impractical because it would force the parties to use a standard communication vocabulary; but also limiting since it would not consider the requirements of agents that could be developed in the future.

Ontology matching is a way of guaranteeing the interoperability of the parties involved in a communication process, i.e, to ascribe to each important piece of knowledge the correct interpretation [12]. In our case, the purpose is to find semantic mappings between the concepts of the different ontologies that the agents use.

The problem of ontology matching has been extensively studied in recent years as stated in the works of [13], [14], [15] or [16]. And also its applications in Multi-Agent Systems [10] [8]. For generating the matches between ontologies

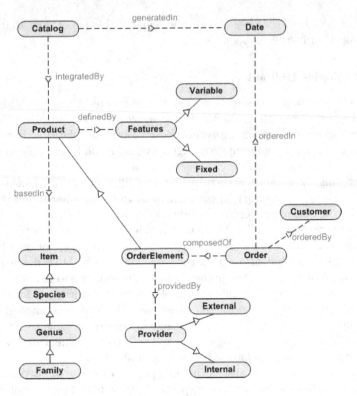

Fig. 4. Plant Wholesaler Ontology

several frameworks and techniques have been proposed, as those in the works of [17] [18] [19] [20] [21].

The next step of the development of this platform will be the integration of ontology matching techniques, to ensure the communication with agents that use an ontology different to the proposed one. The process that we will use to accomplish this challenge is as follows. First, the state of the art of ontology matching [22] will be deeply studied to identify the new trends and research fields. Then a framework will be developed to test different ontology matching algorithms, the purpose is to determine which set or combination works the best for this problem. Finally, once the algorithms are determined, they will be integrated in the system.

4   Discussion and Conclusions

After defining the MAS presented in this paper, it was evaluated by the experts in the plant wholesaler and plant nurseries. They confirmed that the system defined fully meets their expectations as far as its inner functioning is regarded. The plant nurseries that adopted the platform have described an improvement in their response times, cost estimation and production following up. On its side,

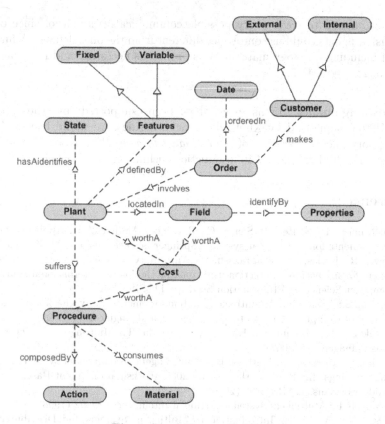

Fig. 5. Plant Nursery Ontology

plant wholesaler's managers are deeply satisfied with the reduction of the effort to keep the catalog updated and with the decrease in the time to process the customer's orders, besides, they have no longer experienced neither duplicate orders nor stock breaks, which were major issues with the previous system.

It is important to remark that the system being designed as a multi-agent system is not a major feature, from enterprise manager's point of view. Their concerns are more focussed on the daily operation of the system.

Nowadays, the system is in its first deployment state, where some measurements are being conducted to verify if the proposed solution with agent's technology is the most satisfying one.

To conclude, it is important to state that this paper we presented a Multi-Agent System applied to a new field, ornamental plant selling and distribution, where this technologies have never been used before. The MAS defined takes into account the particularities of this environment and it obtains the most profit of MAS features to deal with it. The system allows the different parties to operate not only coordinated but also independently. To allow this coordination two ontologies were defined in order to transmit the knowledge of this domain to the agents involved in the communication processes. This ontologies by themselves were not enough to cover every possible communicative scenario, since other systems, or agents could use ontologies different from the ones defined. A further step of including ontology matching was probed as necessary and it is the core of the ongoing research.

Acknowledgements. This work has been supported by the project 10MRU007E supported by Xunta de Galicia, besides, we would like to thank the support and cooperation of *Comercializadora de Plantas de Galicia. S.L* manager, Emilio Estévez and its production technician, Sandra Pereira.

References

1. Valckenaers, P., Sauter, J., Sierra, C., Rodriguez-Aguilar, J.A.: Applications and environments for multi-agent systems. Springer Science Business Media (2006)
2. Gowri, R., Kailas, A., Jeyaprakash, R., Anirudh, C.: Development of multi-agent system for fire accident detection using gaia methodology. International Journal of Computer Science and Information Security, IJCSIS (2010)
3. Sharma, S.: Avatarsim: A multi-agent system for emergency evacuation simulation. Journal of Computational Methods in Science and Engineering (2009)
4. Murakami, Y., Minami, K., Kawasoe, T., Ishida, T.: Multi-agent simulation for crisis management (2002)
5. Macho, S., Torrens, M., Faltings, B.: A multi-agent recommender system for planning meetings. In: Proc. of the Agents 2000 Workshop on Agent-Based Recommender Systems, WARS 2000 (2000)
6. Sycara, K.P.: Multiagent systems. Artificial Intelligence, 79–92 (1998)
7. Vlassis, N.: A Concise Introduction to Multiagent Systems and Distributed AI. Morgan and Claypool Publishers (2007)
8. Wiesman, F., Roos, N., Vogt, P.: Automatic ontology mapping for agent communication. ACM (2002)
9. Cicortas, A., Iordan, V.: Multiagent systems for resource allocation (2011)
10. Laera, L., Blacoe, I., Tamma, V.: Argumentation over ontology correspondences in mas (2007)
11. Otero-Cerdeira, L., Rodríguez-Martínez, F.J., Valencia-Requejo, T., Lueiro-Astray, L.: Multi-agent systems and ontologies applied to new industrial domains. Case study: Ornamental plants. In: 4th International Conference on Knowledge Engineering and Ontology Development (KEOD 2012), p. 8 (2012)
12. Euzenat, J.: Towards a principled approach to semantic interoperability (2001)
13. Noy, N.F.: Semantic Integration: A Survey Of Ontology-Based Approaches. SIGMOD 33(4) (2004)
14. Euzenat, J., Shvaiko, P.: Ontology Matching. Springer (2007)
15. Trojahn, C., Moraes, M., Quaresma, P., Vieira, R.: A cooperative approach for composite ontology mapping (2008)
16. Shvaiko, P., Euzenat, J.: Ontology matching: state of the art and future challenges. IEEE Transactions on Knowledge and Software Engineering (2012)
17. Falconer, S.M., Noy, N.F.: Interactive Techniques to Support Ontology Matching. Data-Centric Systemsand Applications. Springer (2009)
18. Klein, M.: Combining and relating ontologies: An analysis of problems and solutions (2001)

19. Shamsfard, M., Barforoush, A.A.: The State of the Art in Ontology Learning: A Framework for Comparison (2003)
20. Köpcke, H., Rahm, E.: Frameworks for entity matching: A comparison. Data and Knowledge Engineering. Elsevier Science (2009)
21. David, J., Euzenat, J., Scharffe, F., dos Santos, C.T.: The Alignment API 4.0., vol. 1, pp. 1–8. IOS Press (2010)
22. Kalfoglou, Y., Schorlemmer, M.: Ontology mapping: The state of the art. Science 2, 3 (2003)

An Argumentation-Based Approach to Cooperative Multi-source Epistemic Conflict Resolution

Mohammad Taghi Saffar[1], Fattaneh Taghiyareh[1], Sajjad Salehi[1], and Kambiz Badie[2]

[1] School of Electrical and Computer Engineering, College of Engineering,
University of Tehran, Tehran, Iran
{saffar,ftaghiyar,salehi.sajjad}@ut.ac.ir
[2] Iran Telecommunication Research Center, Department of IT, Tehran, Iran
k_badie@itrc.ac.ir

Abstract. An epistemic conflict is a situation when an agent receives a piece of information in contradiction with its own beliefs. To resolve conflicts, agents need to reason about how to update their beliefs regarding that conflict. In this paper we propose a deep cooperative multi-source epistemic conflict resolution method based on a version of preference-based argumentation. This method is based on the idea that the conflict resolution process should find the root cause of the conflict and the strength of some arguments shouldn't be sensitive to their providers' reputation. Our method formalizes several kinds of belief acquisition methods (e.g. deduction, communication and perception) and their sources and then uses it to provide arguments to support other arguments. It decides preference of some arguments by measuring their source reliability. It also enables the collaboration of other agents in the argumentation process.

Keywords: conflict resolution, epistemic conflict, belief revision, argumentation, belief source, belief acquisition.

1   Introduction

Argumentation is a well-developed theory for non-monotonic reasoning especially about conflicting knowledge. It is normally used to decide the epistemic state by considering which arguments support a particular belief [12]. Belief revision on the other hand, focuses on adapting the epistemic state in order to add a new piece of information to the knowledge-base. Some developments in argumentation [23][20][3][9] consider deductive justification as the only form for arguments. Recent developments combine argumentation and belief revision to provide *non-prioritized* [14] and *recoverable* [11] belief revision methods. In these works arguments can justify beliefs only by deduction and the certainties of all arguments are evaluated by the reliability of the providers of those arguments. In a cooperative multi-agent system, deduction is not the only way to support a belief. We believe that an explicit distinction should be made between truly deductive and non-deductive arguments, because the truly deductive arguments should be treated with no care about who provided them; just like we shouldn't consider who provides a proof for a theorem to accept or reject it. We also

I.J. Timm and C. Guttmann (Eds.): MATES 2012, LNAI 7598, pp. 154–164, 2012.

believe that there is a lot more to say about an epistemic conflict when agents consider their corresponding belief sources in the conflict resolution process. An ideal conflict resolution process would detect and resolve the root cause of contradictory statements. This desired *deep conflict resolution* method may reveal other more basic epistemic conflicts that may remain undetected in other methods. And finally there is a need for an argument-based epistemic conflict resolution method tailored for cooperative multi-agent systems where a team of agents collaborate in the argumentation.

In this paper we propose a new cooperative multi-source argumentation-based epistemic conflict resolution method in an effort to address the mentioned limitations. Our proposed method, introduces different types of arguments to justify beliefs based on *belief acquisition methods* and *sources*. *Deductive* arguments attacks are preference-independent because they are a sign of a more basic epistemic conflict between other beliefs of the agents. This is also the case for *communicative* arguments as they indicate epistemic conflicts between beliefs of other agents in the system. In order to decide the winner of preference-independent attacks, other *backing (supporting)* arguments should be provided and this process should be repeated until attacks are preference-dependent. The winner in preference-dependent attacks is decided with arguments strengths. In our method, the real sources of communicated beliefs collaborate in the conflict resolution by providing reinstating arguments.

The rest of this paper is organized as follows. The next section summarizes related works. Section 3 explains the motivation behind our proposed method followed by some preliminaries. Section 5 introduces belief acquisition methods and their corresponding sources. A formal definition of our epistemic conflict resolution method is presented in section 6. The last section is about conclusions and future work.

2   Previous Work

An argumentation-based practical reasoning method with three distinct argument frameworks about beliefs, desires and plans has been introduced in [23]. Conflict resolution between an agent's desires with norms of a society or with other agents' desires is the focus of study of another work [20]. Arguments in this work are constructed from the union of beliefs, desires and intentions. Merging conflicting knowledge-bases has been studied in several works. In [3] authors presented an argument-based solution for merging prioritized knowledge-bases.

Ma *et al* formalized an epistemic belief revision framework that can handle evidence of *partial epistemic state* form [16]. In another work [10] authors tackle the *iterated belief revision* problem by providing a parallel revision method for sets of formulas rather than a single formula. These works study *prioritized belief revision* and this differs from epistemic conflict resolution in its assumption of winning beliefs. Argumentation-based knowledge representation has been the focus of study of a large body of research. *Defeasible logic programming* (DeLP) [13] is a well-known formalism based on *logic programming* and *defeasible argumentation* to decide between contradictory conclusions. Capobianco *et al* extended DeLP to handle perceptions in dynamic environments with real-time issues [7]. As suggested by [11] a rational property of belief revision frameworks is the ability to recover previously discarded beliefs. The work of da Costa Pereira *et al* [9] is a recent approach to this problem. In their work a belief is an argument and the *fuzzy reinstatement* of arguments can recover previously discarded beliefs. More works are also explained in some surveys about argumentation and belief revision [12][21]. In all the above works, argumentation is used to either decide between conflicting beliefs or to incorporate new beliefs into the epistemic state. Deduction is the only form for arguments and all attacks are preference-dependent. Their strength is either associated with the reliability of their providers or the minimum certainty of the beliefs in the support set.

3   Motivation

To explain the general idea for deep collaborative multi-source epistemic conflict resolution we provide the following simple example.

Example 1. *Alice and Bob are talking about whether John is in Germany or not.*
Bob: "John is in Germany, Lisa told me so" = a (communicate)
Alice: "John is not in Germany, I saw him in the university today" = b (percept)
They ask Lisa about this, she joins in the dialogue.
Lisa: "John's paper was published in MATES proceedings, MATES regulation rule is that authors of accepted papers should attend the conference in Germany and the conference starts today, therefore John is in Germany" = c (deduct)
Alice knows about MATES regulation rules and dates but her previous observation (b) is now in conflict with one of the Lisa's assumption, the assumption that John's paper was published in MATES proceedings. Beginning with an argumentation about whether John is in Germany or not, another epistemic conflict about John's paper between Lisa and Alice is now detected. To resolve this conflict Alice asks Lisa how she knows about John's paper.
Lisa: "Frank told me about John's paper" = d (communicate)
They ask Frank about this, he joins in the dialogue.
Frank: "I have seen John's paper in MATES proceedings" = e (percept)
Alice (to herself): "Although I think I saw John in the university today, I know that Frank is a very reliable person. I have more confidence in Frank's observation than mine. Maybe I am wrong and John is in Germany" = f

As it's shown in example 1, the argumentation is done in a collaborative manner. Frank and Lisa collaborated in the conflict resolution by providing arguments to back other arguments. In previous conflict resolution methods, each person providing an argument is assumed to be the source of that argument, even if that person acquired the conclusion of that argument by communicating with others. This assumption is sometimes referred as the principle of *extending the scope of responsibility* [11]. In cooperative multi-agent systems this assumption can be dropped. Because of the nature of these systems, we can have access to the real sources of beliefs. Therefore instead of defining strength for all arguments we can ask real sources to justify their beliefs with additional supporting arguments.

Another interesting point in this example is the detection of another epistemic conflict during the course of argumentation. This is actually what we called *deep conflict resolution*, because it detects the root cause of the original conflict and tries to resolve it. Thanks to the introduction of different belief acquisition methods and belief sources, agents know how to make arguments to back other arguments, and when to finish argumentation simply because no more arguments can be made. Also they use belief sources to evaluate the strength of arguments to decide the winner between preference-dependent attacks with appropriate reliability measures (f).

4   Preliminaries

A classical propositional language $\mathcal{L}$ is used in this work to represent beliefs inside arguments; however we don't address the problem of representing epistemic states because we are only interested in the conflict resolution and not belief revision.

A revised version of *Extended Argumentation Framework* (EAF) formalized by Modgil [19] is used in this work. EAF is originally introduced to enable defeasible reasoning about preferences between arguments. This EAF is suitable for our deep conflict resolution method because it clearly distinguishes between *preference dependent* and *preference independent* attacks. This corresponds to the idea of our work that real deductive arguments *preference independently* attack other arguments but some other arguments *preference dependently* attack other arguments. In this work we revise the original EAF to include *preference independent* and *symmetric preference dependent* attacks but defeasible reasoning about preferences is not considered here. We also extended EAF with *backing relation* inspired by the work of Cohen *et al* [8].

Definition 1. *(Extended argumentation framework) An EAF is a tuple $(Args, \mathcal{R}_{pi}, \mathcal{R}_{pd}, \mathcal{R}_b, \prec)$ where*
- *$Args$ is a set of arguments.*
- *$\mathcal{R}_{pi} \subseteq Args \times Args$ is the preference independent (pi) attack.*
- *$\mathcal{R}_{pd} \subseteq Args \times Args$ is the preference dependent (pd) attack and it is symmetric.*
- *$\mathcal{R}_b \subseteq Args \times Args$ is the backing (supporting) relation.*
- *$\prec$ is a partial-order defined on $Args \times Args$. It is called the preference relation.*

From now on we use the following notations:

– We use $A \to B$ to denote $(A, B) \in \mathcal{R}_{pd}$ and $A \rightleftharpoons B$ to denote $(A, B), (B, A) \in \mathcal{R}_{pd}$.
– $A \hookrightarrow B$ represents $(A, B) \in \mathcal{R}_{pi}$. Also $A \Rightarrow B$ denotes $(A, B) \in \mathcal{R}_b$.

Definition 2. *(Defeat) A defeats B denoted by $A \twoheadrightarrow B$ iff one of the following conditions hold:*
- *$A \hookrightarrow B$; or $A \to B$ and $B \prec A$. (primary defeat)*
- *$A \to C$ and $B \Rightarrow C$ and $A \nprec B$; or $A \Rightarrow C$ and $B \to C$ and $A \nprec B$ (Implicit defeat[1])*

---

[1] Implicit defeat is used in our work similar to [8] to represent conflicts between supporting and attacking arguments that can't always be modeled explicitly with attack relations.

Definition 3. *(Conflict-free) A set of arguments $S \subseteq Args$ is a conflict-free set iff $\forall A, B \in S : (A \nrightarrow B)$.*

Definition 4. *(Acceptable argument) An argument $A \in Args$ is acceptable w.r.t. $S \subseteq Args$ iff $\forall B \in Args : (if\ B \rightarrow A\ then\ \exists C \in S, C \rightarrow B)$.*

Definition 5. *(Extensional semantics) Let $S \subseteq Args$ be a conflict-free set. Then*
- *S is admissible iff $\forall A \in S : (A$ is acceptable w.r.t. $S)$.*
- *S is preferred iff it is a set inclusion maximal admissible extension.*

5   Belief Acquisition Methods and Sources

The term 'source' in the literature usually refers to the agent or an active entity providing an argument to support a new belief or new evidence. We believe that this view of belief source can be broadened to cover belief acquisition methods. Intuitively, a *source* for a belief is an entity (either active or passive) that the agent acquires a belief from with some operations called *belief acquisition* methods. The idea of *keeping track* of belief sources can help conflict resolution process to find and resolve the root cause of epistemic conflicts. The most basic belief acquisition method is *perception* [1]. The source of a perceived belief is the corresponding sensor and the reliability of that sensor (e.g. accuracy, correctness) usually determines the certainty of that belief. Another belief acquisition method is *communication* [2][15]. The source of a communicated belief is the *communicator*. A communicated belief, when the agents are keeping track of their belief sources, is providing a hook for the collaboration of the real belief source (i.e. communicator) in the conflict resolution process. Therefore it is best to keep attacks with communicated beliefs preference-independent and let the communicators themselves, reinstate those beliefs. Another belief acquisition method is *reasoning* [2][6]. There are several approaches to reasoning but generally, logical reasoning methods can be classified into three major classes called *deduction*, *induction* and *abduction* [18]. In this work we limit our focus to deductive reasoning and we also assume that the deduction procedure of the agents is *sound* and *complete*. A deduced belief is obtained from a set of premises which can be seen as the source of that belief. Just like communicated beliefs, we believe it is desirable to treat attacks with deduced beliefs preference-independently, because when there is a conflict between a deduced belief and another belief, there are more basic epistemic conflicts between the set of premises and the source of the other conflicting belief, assuming that the deduction procedure is sound. Resolving those more basic conflicts automatically resolves the original epistemic conflict. Kolbel introduced perception, communication and reasoning as the belief acquisition methods [2]. In addition to that, in real applications an agent might have some pre-defined beliefs. Booth considered this kind of belief in [5] and he named it as *core* beliefs. A core belief is an innate belief with no associated source and because it has not been acquired explicitly within a process, we intuitively assign *embedding* as its belief acquisition method. To summarize this discussion, identified belief acquisition methods and their corresponding sources and also their strength semantics is shown in table 1.

Table 1. Belief acquisition methods, their source and argument strength

Belief acquisition	Source	Argument strength
Perception	Sensor	Sensor accuracy
Communication	Communicator	-
Deduction	A set of premises	-
Embedment	-	Reliability of argument provider

6 Deep Cooperative Epistemic Conflict Resolution

We now formalize our proposed argumentation-based deep multi-source cooperative epistemic conflict resolution method. An agent uses belief acquisition method and its source to provide arguments to justify its beliefs.

Definition 6. *(Argument) An argument $A \in Args$ is exclusively one of the following:*

- *Deductive argument is a pair $< \phi, \psi >$, with $\phi \subset \mathcal{L}$ is the set of premises and $\psi \in \mathcal{L}$ is the conclusion such that*
  (a) ϕ is consistent.
  (b) $\bigwedge_{\phi_i \in \phi} \phi_i \vDash \psi$. (We use $\vDash$ to denote propositional entailment.)
  (c) ϕ is minimal w.r.t. set inclusion.
- *Perceptive argument is $< s, \psi >$ where s is the sensor and ψ is the conclusion.*
- *Communicative argument is $< ag, \psi >$ where ag is the communicator and ψ is the conclusion.*
- *Embedded argument is $< \emptyset, \psi >$ where ψ is the conclusion.*

The provider of an argument A is the agent who puts up A and is denoted by $\mathcal{P}(A)$ and the conclusion of A is denoted by $conc(A)$. It should be noted that the communicator of a communicative argument is different from its provider. An agent $ag1$ might provide a communicative argument that ψ is true because $ag2$ says so. $ag1$ is the provider and $ag2$ is the communicator for that argument.

Definition 7. *(Argument strength) The preference relation between arguments is decided by argument strength. The strength of an argument A is denoted by $\mathcal{S}(A)$ and is defined as follows:*

- *If A is perceptive then $\mathcal{S}(A) = sensor\ accuracy(s(A), \mathcal{P}(A))$.*
- *If A is embedded then $\mathcal{S}(A) = reliability(\mathcal{P}(A))$.*
- *$\mathcal{S}(A)$ is not defined for communicative and deductive arguments.*

Argument strengths are defined with the help of two abstract functions called *sensor accuracy* and *reliability*. The internals of these two functions are not regarded in our work as they are domain dependent. *Reliability* can represent an aggregated value of all the applicable factors in a domain such as reputation, expertise, etc. These functions are global and shared between agents in the system; therefore they always agree about arguments strengths and consequently about the winner of attacking arguments.

Definition 8. *(Undercut/Rebuttal) Let A and B be two arguments. A rebuts B iff* $conc(A) \wedge conc(B) \equiv \bot$. *Let* $B = <\phi, \psi>$ *be a deductive argument. A undercuts B iff* $\exists \phi_i \in \phi : (\phi_i \equiv \neg conc(A))$.

Definition 9. *(Attack) Let A and B be two arguments then*
1. *A* ↪ *B iff at least one of the following conditions hold:*
   — *A undercuts B.*
   — *A rebuts B and at least one of the two arguments are either communicative or deductive.*
2. *A* → *B iff*
   — *A rebuts B and both arguments are neither communicative nor deductive.*

Definition 10. *(Backing) Let A and B be two arguments. A backs (supports) B iff one of the following conditions hold:*
- $B = <ag, \psi>$ *is a communicative argument and* $\mathcal{P}(A) = ag$ *and* $conc(A) = \psi$.
- $B = <\phi, \psi>$ *is a deductive arguments and* $\mathcal{P}(A) = \mathcal{P}(B)$ *and* $conc(A) \in \phi$.

Dialogue games have been widely used to define communicative behaviors for argumentation [22]. We now formalize a *persuasion dialogue* model for our epistemic conflict resolution method. This dialogue is between two initiator agents at first, but the initiators of the dialogue might ask other agents to join in the dialogue by asking them some questions. Intuitively, the participants of a dialogue are on two sides according to their attitude towards the topic of a dialogue. One group called *defenders* tries to justify the topic and the other group called *attackers* tries to prove otherwise.

Definition 11. *(Dialogue) A dialogue D is a sequence of moves* $[m_1, ..., m_t]$ *such that a move is either*
- *An atomic move which is a tuple* $m = <p\ell(m), pr\!f(m), arg(m), trg(m)>$ *where* $p\ell$ *is the player,* $pr\!f \in \{why, assert, open\}$ *is the performative,* $arg \in Args$ *is the argument and* trg *is the target of that move.*
- *A parallel dialogue move* $m = \{D_1, ..., D_n\}$ *which is a set of dialogues that are being undertaken simultaneously.*

A dialogue D also has the following condition:
   — $\forall i, m_i \in D$ *and is atomic,* $pr\!f(m_i) = \begin{matrix} assert \\ open \end{matrix} : \left(p\ell(m_i) = \mathcal{P}(arg(m_i)) \right)$.

The above condition states that if an agent asserts an argument during a dialogue, it should be considered as the provider of that argument. From now on we use $\mathcal{D}$ to denote the set of all dialogues. $\mathcal{I}$ is the set of all agents and $\mathcal{M}$ is the set of all moves. Also $last(D) = m_t$ represents the last move in D. A dialogue in this definition can have *nested parallel sub-dialogues* [4][17]. In order to define a dialogue game we need to define some rules to determine when a dialogue terminates and some rules to define which move to make at every stage in a dialogue (i.e. strategy). *Strategies* unlike *protocols* are personal to agents and depend upon their epistemic state. As mentioned previously we don't detail internals of epistemic states. However we assume each agent is a track-keeper and maintains a consistent knowledge-base. In other words an agent i has a function $belief_i : \mathcal{L} \rightarrow \{\top, \bot, \emptyset\}$ and a function $source_i : belief_i^{-1}(\top) \rightarrow Args$ that provides a justifying argument for a belief based on its acquisition method and source. From now on we use the term *source* to refer to a justifying argument based on acquisition method of that belief.

Definition 12. *(strategy) A conflict resolution strategy is a function* $\Omega: \mathcal{D} \to \mathcal{M}$.

$$
\Omega = \begin{cases}
< i, open, source_i(\phi), j > where \\
belief_j(\phi) = \bot \ and \ belief_i(\phi) = \top & if \ D = [\,] \\
< j, open, source_j(\neg\phi), i > & if \ D = [< i, open, source_i(\phi), j >] \\
\{D_{deep}(m_1), D_{deep}(m_2)\} & if \ D = [m_1, m_2]
\end{cases}
$$

A conflict resolution dialogue D starts with a pair of opening moves about ϕ which we call the topic of the dialogue. In the opening moves, initial arguments about ϕ and $\neg\phi$ are provided. The third move is a parallel dialogue move in which two separate *deep sub-dialogues* about the topic and its negation begins. In a deep sub-dialogue the attacker starts questioning the defender about its last move until the root cause of conflict is found. Agent i is the attacker in one of the deep sub-dialogues and it is the defender in the other deep sub-dialogue. Sometimes it is also needed to project a move with deductive argument so that the argument contains only a specific proposition from the set of premises as its conclusion. Projection is used to address a specific belief in the set of premises of a previous move and to directly question it.

Definition 13. *(Projected move) Let* $m = < p\ell(m), pr\!f(m), < \phi, \psi >, trg(m) >$ *be a move with a deductive argument and* $\phi_i \in \phi$, *then* $m[\phi_i]$ *is equal to* m *except for its argument which is* $< \phi_i, \phi_i >$.

Definition 14. *(deep dialogue) A* $D_{deep}(m) \in \mathcal{D}_{deep}$ *is a deep sub-dialogue about a move* m *in the parent dialogue between defender* $p\ell(m)$ *and attacker* $trg(m)$. *A deep strategy is a function* $\Omega_{deep}: \mathcal{D}_{deep} \times \mathcal{M} \to \mathcal{M}$.

$$
\Omega_{deep}(D_{deep}, m) = \begin{cases}
\Omega_{question}(m) & if \ D_{deep} = [\,] \\
\Omega_{answer}\left(last(D_{deep})\right) & if \ pr\!f\left(last(D_{deep})\right) = why \\
\Omega_{question}\left(last(D_{deep})\right) & if \ pr\!f\left(last(D_{deep})\right) = assert
\end{cases}
$$

$$
\Omega_{answer}(m) = < trg(m), assert, source_i\left(conc(arg(m))\right), p\ell(m) >
$$

$$
\Omega_{question}(m) = \begin{cases}
< trg(m), why, arg(m), ag(arg(m)) > & if \ arg(m) \ is \\
& communicative \\
\left\{ D_{deep}(m[\phi_i]) \mid \phi_i \in \phi \ and \atop belief_{trg(m)}(\phi_i) = \bot \right\} & if \ arg(m) = < \phi, \psi >
\end{cases}
$$

A deep sub-dialogue $D_{deep}(m)$ starts with a *why* statement provided by the attacker $trg(m)$ about the move m which defender $p\ell(m)$ played in the parent dialogue. Defenders play answering moves in response to questioning moves. The attacker plays questioning moves to ask for more backing arguments. If the last asserted argument is communicative, attacker asks the communicator about its belief. If it is a deductive argument, attacker starts a set of deep sub-dialogues which are about other more basic epistemic conflicts in the set of premises.

Definition 15. *(Terminated dialogue) A conflict resolution dialogue D is a terminated dialogue iff all of its deep sub-dialogues are terminated. A deep dialogue $D_{deep}(m)$ is terminated iff one of the following conditions hold:*

- *Either $last(D_{deep})$ or $m = < i, \begin{smallmatrix} assert \\ open \end{smallmatrix}, A, j >$ and A is perceptive or embedded.*
- *$last(D_{deep}) = \{D_1, ..., D_m\}$ $\forall D_i : D_i$ is a terminated deep sub-dialogue.*

A terminated conflict resolution dialogue is a dialogue that participants can't provide more backing arguments about the topic or its negation. The first condition in the above definition shows a deep dialogue that attacker can't ask for more arguments from defenders, because they have reached to a perceptive or embedded argument and the sources for these arguments, sensors and empty set respectively, can't join in the dialogue to provide reinstating arguments. The second condition shows that all deep sub-dialogues about other conflicts detected during a deep dialogue have terminated.

During the course of a conflict resolution dialogue, participants assert some arguments with *assert* and *open* performatives. The *outcome* of a terminated conflict resolution dialogue is then the set of all asserted arguments along with their backings and attacks to form an instantiation of our conflict resolution framework. We now show all conflict resolution dialogues terminate with the assumption that the number of agents in the system is finite and each agent has a finite knowledge-base. The proof also relies on the following axioms about belief sources.

Axiom 1. *A belief can't have a chain of communicative sources that has cycles in it.*

Axiom 2. *If an agent has a belief with deductive source, it believes in the premises.*

Axiom 3. *A belief ϕ can't have a chain of deductive sources that one of them has ϕ in its set of premises.*

Proposition 1. *Every belief of the agents in the system eventually has a set of perceptive or embedded sources.*

Proof. *According to axiom 1 a communicative belief eventually has a perceptive, embedded or deductive source from the union of the beliefs of all agents in the system. Every belief ψ with a deductive source is deduced from a set of promises ϕ that are believed by an agent in the system and have their own sources (axiom 2). Now consider every belief $\phi_i \in \phi$ in the set of premises. If ϕ_i has a deductive source, then ψ can't be in its set of premises (axiom3). Therefore every deductive source in a chain of sources needs to have new beliefs as its set of premises. Because there are a finite number of agents in the system with finite knowledge-bases, there are only a finite number of beliefs that deductive arguments can be constructed from; therefore every belief with deductive sources eventually has a set of perceptive or embedded sources.*

Proposition 2. *All conflict resolution dialogues terminate.*

Proof. *Every belief eventually reaches to perceptive or embedded sources (proposition 1). Question and answering moves in deep sub-dialogue finds these sources. Also only a finite number of conflict-resolution sub-dialogues can exist in a deep dialogue,* *because a deduced belief can't have an infinite number of premises. Therefore every deep dialogue terminates hence all conflict resolution dialogues terminate.*

Example 2. *In order to show how the conflict resolution dialogue works, we take example 1 to describe how agents play moves during the course of a dialogue in figure 1. The agents' names are Alice, Bob, Lisa and Frank. The propositions are named as follows: "John is in Germany"=Ger, "John is in university"=¬Ger, "John's paper was published in MATES proceedings"=Pr, MATES regulation rules=Rl.*

Current move	Current dialogue
$m_1 = $ <Bob, open, <Lisa, Ger>, Alice>	$D = [\ ]$
$m_2 = $ <Alice, open, <see, ¬Ger>, Bob>	$D = [m_1]$
$m_3 = \{D_{deep}(m_1), D_{deep}(m_2)\}$	$D = [m_1, m_2]$
$D_{deep}(m_2)$ terminates with no moves	$D_{deep}(m_2) = [\ ]$
$m_3 = $ <Alice, why, <Lisa, Ger>, Lisa>	$D_{deep}(m_1) = [\ ]$
$m_4 = $ <Lisa, assert, <{Pr, Rl}, Ger>, Alice>	$D_{deep}(m_1) = [m_3]$
$m_5 = \{D_{deep}(m_4[Pr])\}$	$D_{deep}(m_1) = [m_3, m_4]$
$m_6 = $ <Alice, why, <Pr, Pr>, Lisa>	$D_{deep}(m_4[Pr]) = [\ ]$
$m_7 = $ <Lisa, assert, <Frank, Pr>, Alice>	$D_{deep}(m_4[Pr]) = [m_6]$
$m_8 = $ <Alice, why, <Frank, Pr>, Frank>	$D_{deep}(m_4[Pr]) = [m_6, m_7]$
$m_9 = $ <Frank, assert, <see, Pr>, Alice>	$D_{deep}(m_4[Pr]) = [m_6, m_7, m_8]$
$D_{deep}(m_4[Pr])$, $D_{deep}(m_1)$ and finally D terminates at this point	

Fig. 1. Conflict resolution dialogue and its steps for the situation in example 1

7   Conclusions and Future Directions

In this paper we have proposed a new argumentation-based cooperative multi-source epistemic conflict resolution method based on the idea that a conflict resolution method should find and resolve the root cause of conflicts. We have introduced different belief acquisition methods. Our method enables agents to use belief sources to collaborate in the argumentation by providing reinstating arguments about their beliefs. We have also used an abstract notion of reliability and sensor accuracy to define strength for embedded and perceptive arguments respectively. Finally we have formalized a persuasion dialogue game for our conflict resolution method and we have proved that this dialogue game terminates eventually.

This work can be extended in several directions. One important extension could add a definition of epistemic state and a suitable belief revision operator to our work. Also we can determine argument strength by defeasible reasoning about preferences which frees us from limiting our system with the assumption that arguments strengths are globally defined.

References

1. Armstrong, D.M.: A Materialist Theory of the Mind. Routledge, London (1968)
2. Kolbel, M.: Truth WithoutObjectivity. Routledge, London (2002)
3. Amgoud, L., Kaci, S.: An Argumentation Framework for Merging Conflicting Knowledge Bases. International Journal of Approximate Reasoning 45(2), 321–340 (2007)
4. Black, E., Hunter, A.: A generative inquiry dialogue system. In: Proc. of the 6th International Joint Conference on Autonomous Agents and Multiagent Systems, Honolulu, Hawaii, pp. 1–8 (2007)
5. Booth, R.F.: On the Logic of Iterated Non-prioritised Revision. In: Kern-Isberner, G., Rödder, W., Kulmann, F. (eds.) WCII 2002. LNCS (LNAI), vol. 3301, pp. 86–107. Springer, Heidelberg (2005)
6. Broome, J.: The Unity of Reasoning? Spheres of Reason 1(9), 62–93 (2009)
7. Capobianco, M., Chesnevar, C.I., Simari, G.R.: Argumentation and the dynamics of warranted beliefs in changing environments. J. AAMAS 11(2), 127–151 (2005)
8. Cohen, A., García, A.J., Simari, G.R.: Backing and Undercutting in Abstract Argumentation Frameworks. In: Lukasiewicz, T., Sali, A. (eds.) FoIKS 2012. LNCS, vol. 7153, pp. 107–123. Springer, Heidelberg (2012)
9. da Costa Pereira, C., Tettamanzi, A.G.B., Villata, S.: Changing one's mind: Erase or rewind? possibilistic belief revision with fuzzy argumentation based on trust. In: Proc. of IJCAI, pp. 164–171 (2011)
10. Delgrande, J., Jin, Y.: Parallel belief revision: Revising by sets of formulas. J. AI (2011)
11. Dragoni, A.F., Giorgini, P.: Distributed belief revision. J. AAMAS 6(2), 115–143 (2003)
12. Falappa, M.A., Garcia, A.J., Kern-Isberner, G., Simari, G.R.: On the evolving relation between Belief Revision and Argumentation. Knowledge Engineering Review 26(1), 35–43 (2011)
13. Garcia, A.J., Simari, G.R.: Defeasible logic programming: An argumentative approach. Theory and Practice of Logic Programming 4(2), 95–138 (2004)
14. Hansson, S.O., Ferme, E.L., Cantwell, J., Falappa, M.A.: Credibility limited revision. Journal of Symbolic Logic, 1581–1596 (2001)
15. Liau, C.J.: Belief, information acquisition, and trust in multi-agent systems: a modal logic formulation. J. AI 149(1), 31–60 (2003)
16. Ma, J., Liu, W., Benferhat, S.: A belief revision framework for revising epistemic states with partial epistemic states. In: AAAI 2010, pp. 333–338 (2010)
17. McBurney, P., Parsons, S.: Games That Agents Play: A Formal Framework for Dialogues between Autonomous Agents. J. of Logic, Lang. and Inf. 11(3), 315–334 (2002)
18. Menzies, T.: Applications of abduction: knowledge-level modelling. Int. J. of Human-Computer Studies 45(3), 305–335 (1996)
19. Modgil, S.: An abstract theory of argumentation that accommodates defeasible reasoning about preferences. Symbolic and Quantitative Approaches to Reasoning with Uncertainty, 648–659 (2007)
20. Modgil, S., Luck, M.: Argumentation Based Resolution of Conflicts between Desires and Normative Goals. In: Rahwan, I., Moraitis, P. (eds.) ArgMAS 2008. LNCS, vol. 5384, pp. 19–36. Springer, Heidelberg (2009)
21. Paglieri, F., Castelfranchi, C.: Revising Beliefs Through Arguments: Bridging the Gap Between Argumentation and Belief Revision in MAS. In: Rahwan, I., Moraïtis, P., Reed, C. (eds.) ArgMAS 2004. LNCS (LNAI), vol. 3366, pp. 78–94. Springer, Heidelberg (2005)
22. Prakken, H.: Coherence and flexibility in dialogue games for argumentation. Journal of Logic and Computation 15(6), 1009–1040 (2005)
23. Rahwan, I., Amgoud, L.: An argumentation-based approach for practical reasoning. In: Proc. of ArgMAS, pp. 74–90 (2007)

The Importance of Being Accurate
in Agent-Based Models – An Illustration
with Agent Aging

Julia Schindler

Center for Development Research, Bonn University,
Walter-Flex-Str. 3, 53113 Bonn, Germany
julia.schindler@uni-bonn.de
http://www.julia-schindler.de

Abstract. Sometimes, descriptive and empirical agent-based models
contain sub-models of variables whose change over time cannot be easily
modelled. Due to a frequent lack of long-term data, especially on demographic change, often logical design principles are used for modeling
such changes. The problem with these modeling principles is that many of
them exist and the choice is a difficult one. We would like to illustrate in
this article that this choice has consequences, using the example of farm
agent aging sub-models in an existing land-use change model. We will
show that different design principles lead to different long-term changes
in age pattern. The problem here is that one cannot be sure where the
change in age structure comes from, i.e. whether it is an account of real-
world change and/or whether it is caused by model assumptions. Then,
we will show that simulated land-use change is highly sensitive to the
type of aging sub-model. As a solution, we develop an alternative aging
sub-model that exactly maintains an age pattern externally prescribed,
but still allows individual aging.

Keywords: agent-based modelling, accuracy, critique, agent age,
demography.

1 Introduction

Empirical agent-based models have often been rigorously built on snapshot survey data (e.g. [10], [13], [2]). There, a common difficulty is how to model agent
variables whose changes over time cannot be easily modelled using snapshot data.
Especially demographic variables, such as agent age, household size, household
labor, but also animal stocks, etc., are difficult to model without a long-term
database. Many approaches to circumvent this difficulty exist, and nearly every
model has its own approach. However, we believe that the way we modellers
circumvent the problem of unknown data can have consequences for model credibility and accuracy. In this article, we aim to demonstrate that different approaches to model aging of farm agents can have far-reaching consequences for
simulation results. First, we will show that different existing models of agent

I.J. Timm and C. Guttmann (Eds.): MATES 2012, LNAI 7598, pp. 165–177, 2012.
© Springer-Verlag Berlin Heidelberg 2012

aging converge to different age structures using the same database. Here, we do not claim that these models are wrong, but the problem is that we cannot prove whether they are right. That is, it is not clear whether real-world change was simulated, and/or whether the change was caused by model assumptions. Finally, we will illustrate that, as a case study, the choice of aging model in an existing empirical agent-based model of land-use change can have drastic consequences for simulation results. We offer a solution to this problem, which is an aging model that is able to control assumptions made.

In section 2, we review models of aging for farm agents, the problem is described, and we offer an improved model to deal with the described problem. In section 3, we present the case study and the consequences of choice of aging model in the case-study model. Finally, we conclude that modellers should be more self-critical when developing algorithms for unknown variable change.

2   Aging Models and Problem Analysis

2.1   Existing Aging Models

We reviewed existing algorithms to model the change of age of farming agents. Thereby, we constricted ourselves to simple algorithms whose dynamics consist of agents' aging, death and replacement, not including algorithms that explicitly model mating and reproduction during lifetime. We excluded the latter because these can be regarded as sophisticated enough to replicate human reproduction explicitly - a quality that we think the former does not have. For each reviewed algorithm class we identified the underlying modelling principle. We used this modelling principle to adapt the corresponding algorithm to our case study. Since in peer-reviewed articles the aging algorithm is often not explained in sufficient detail, the review was mainly limited to dissertations and master theses.

We start with the simplest idea of modeling the aging process of farming agents. None of the reviewed models in fact implemented it, but we found it worth including, because it sounds straightforward but has an oblique rub in it. The algorithm consists of the replacement of agents that reach a certain age by young agents (equation 1). For simplicity, we only reset the age of the "dying" agent instead of deleting and recreating an agent. This applies to all algorithms in this article.

$$\text{If } H_{age} > Age_{old} \text{ then } H_{age} \mapsto Age_{young} \tag{1}$$

where Age_{old} is the death age and Age_{young} the age of agents starting farming.

The rationale behind this algorithm is that in many real-world systems the role an agent has assumed during lifetime does not vanish with agent death. Instead, it is often only refilled with a younger agent in reality. The question therefore seems to be only where to set the death age and the age of the succeeding agent. But the more subtle problem is that this algorithm is not able to maintain the age distribution of the agent population when the distribution is non-uniform.

Non-uniform distributions are as such maintained but simply shift with age over time, while disappearing at old age and reappearing at young age (Figure 1).

In reviewed models on farming agents, this issue has been approached differently. We identified three different principles that suggest how to model aging more realistically. The first has been applied by the LUDAS (Land Use DynAmic Simulator) family (e.g. [10], [6]), where agents, when reaching the maximum age, are assigned an "average" age. This average age is uniformly randomly drawn from the range consisting of the mean age plus and minus the standard deviation (equation 2).

$$\text{If } H_{age} > Age_{max} \text{ then } H_{age} \mapsto Age_{mean} - Age_{std} + rand(2 \cdot Age_{std}) \qquad (2)$$

where H_{age} is an agent's age, Age_{max}, Age_{mean}, and Age_{std} are maximum, mean, and standard deviation of the original empirical age dataset, respectively, and $rand()$ is a function that draws a uniformly random floating number between zero and the assigned number.

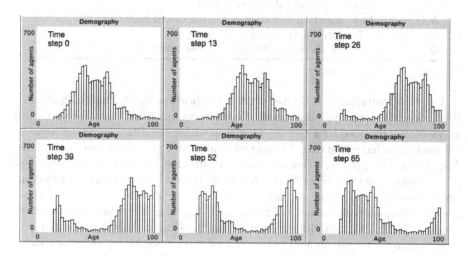

Fig. 1. Shift of age structure over time in terms of number of agents per age class for simple replacement algorithm (death age = 95, young age = 15)

The next modeling principle that we identified is drawn from a series of publications on regional structural change in Canada (e.g. [3], [15], [1]). Here, agents die with death probabilities derived from empirical life tables and are replaced by agents with age one generation younger (equation 3). The idea of replacing agents by agents of age minus the generation-cycle interval is a widespread strategy. The widely used AgriPoliS model for simulating agricultural policies (e.g. [4], [8]) also uses this idea. However, in none of the reviewed AgriPoliS publications the specific generation-cycle value was explicitly given. In all three reviewed publications on regional structural change, the generation-cycle interval was set to 30 years, which the authors concede is an assumption.

$$\text{If } rand(100) < D_{age} \text{ then } H_{age} \mapsto H_{age} - G_{int} \tag{3}$$

where D_{age} is the death probability for the agent's age class, and G_{int} the generation-cycle interval.

Table 1. Parameter values used for implementing the selected principles for the Ghanaian case study

Parameter	Value (years)	Explanation and Source
H_{old}	75	mean death age calculated from D_{age} over all ages
H_{young}	21	mean of minimum age Age_{min} and reproduction age G_{init}
Age_{max}	95	maximum age derived from [12]
Age_{min}	15	minimum age derived from [12]
H_{mean}	46.3	mean age calculated from [12]
H_{std}	14.1	standard deviation of age calculated from [12]
G_{int}	27	rural marriage age of males by [7]
D_{age}	—	death probability per age class using [5]

The third principle was derived from a publication by Millington et al. [11]. Here, death is also modelled using life-table probabilities, but the deceasing agent is only replaced by a new agent with younger age if the deceasing agent is old enough to have offspring. Millington et al. define this minimum age to have offspring as the minimum age an agent can become farmer plus the empirical generation length [11]. Accordingly, the age of the new agent is assigned a random age between this minimum age and the minimum age plus one generation. In case the deceasing agent is not old enough to have offspring, it is replaced by another random agent. Although Millington et al. also implemented other reasons to stop being a farmer, we use an adapted version of this principle that only focuses on death as a cause, which is sufficient for our purpose (equation 4).

$$\text{If } rand(100) < D_{age} \begin{cases} \text{If } H_{age} > Age_{min} + G_{init} \text{ then } H_{age} \mapsto Age_{min} + rand(G_{init}) \\ \text{else } H_{age} \mapsto H_{age} \text{ of another random agent} \end{cases}$$
$$\tag{4}$$

where Age_{min} is the minimum age at which agents can be farmer.

2.2   Problem Analysis

In order to test these modeling principles, we implemented each of them and calibrated them for a Ghanaian case study, which is the Atankwidi Catchment

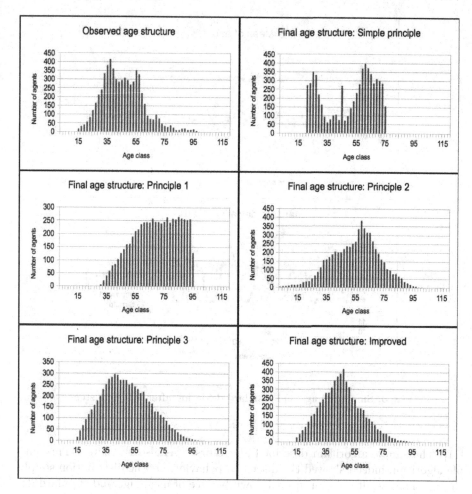

Fig. 2. Initial observed age structure and simulated age structures after 300 time steps

in Upper East Ghana (Table 1). We used own data collected in the field [12], and used life tables from the district from the same year by [5]. The complete death probabilities were derived from the life tables via extrapolation. In addition, we used the generation length of males cited by [7]. Unfortunately, the source seems somewhat outdated, but given the fact that cultural change was slow during the last decades in the study area, and since we believe that generation cycles of males are still high in rural West Africa, we decided to stick to the reported value (Table 1).

We simulated each principle five times for 300 time steps (years) (the simulation period was set this high to enable convergence of the age structures and to identify their limits (see Figures 2 and 3)). Henceforth, with principle 1 we will refer to the principle of LUDAS by [9] with principle 2 to that of the Canadian group (e.g. [3], and with principle 3 to that largely following Millington et al.

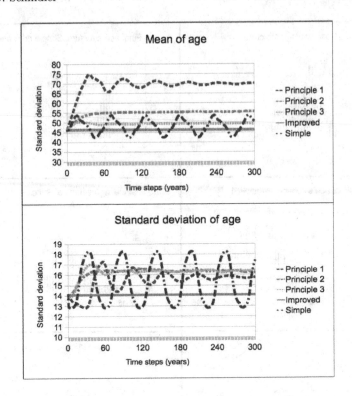

Fig. 3. Simulated age and standard deviation after 300 time steps

[11]. The simple algorithm described above first was also simulated. This simple algorithm indeed showed the discussed behavior, i.e. the distribution simply shifted. This resulted in an up-and-down bounce of mean age and standard deviation (Figure 3). Implementing principle 1, on the other hand, resulted in a convergence to a significantly higher mean age and standard deviation over time (Figure 3). The reason is that the algorithm assigns to new agents only *average* values, thus removing the lower age values in the long term but maintaining higher values. This leads to a shift of mean age in the positive direction over time. Furthermore, the shape of the age structure converged to a significantly changed structure over time (Figure 2). One of the causes for this significant change in age-structure shape is that agent life was designed to end at the same age for all. Principles 2 and 3 solved this issue by using death probabilities for age classes, resulting in a smooth curve of the right-hand side of the age structure (Figure 2). But both of them also showed an increase of mean age and standard deviation (Figure 3).

The problem with these modeling principles is that one cannot determine where the change in age structure comes from. Is it an account of real-world change or is it caused by model assumptions, or is it even a bit of both? As long as one does not model demographic change in detail (e.g. through reproduction and mating), the model is prone to forcing the modeller to make (possibly weak) assumptions. We do not claim that these models are wrong, but the problem is that one cannot be sure whether and which one is right. We neither claim that one is not allowed to make assumptions, but that one should keep control what happens with these assumptions. That is, whether the emergent age structure is in line with our understanding of real age-structure change. The solution that we propose is to externalize assumptions in such as way that the shape of the age structure itself can be controlled. This implies for us to develop a model that enables individual aging of agents on the one hand, but on the other is able to adjust death and youth ages in such a way that the age structure changes the way prescribed, as e.g. by expert opinion. This way, we aim to offer a model that has been cleared from internal and potentially inaccurate assumptions.

2.3 An Improved Model

For developing such an improved model we decided to use principle 3 as a basis, since it comes closest to the observed structure in shape. We extended the algorithm of principle 3 in such a way that the simulated mean and standard deviation coincide with the prescribed mean and standard deviation. However, please note that the observed age structure is **not** exactly normally distributed (significant at 0.001 level with Kolmogorov-Smirnov test). But in the absence of other simple measures that can describe the observed age structure, we went for the simplest available. Though, we must concede that other important characteristics such as kurtosis of the age structure may not be maintained this way.

We extended the modelling principle 3 by an algorithm that adjusts death ages and newcomer ages to match the prescribed mean and standard deviation. It consists of two consecutive parts. The first part does adjustments when the simulated mean age is too high, and the second when it is is too low. The first part is depicted in NetLogo 4.1.3 code (Figure 4), while the second part has the same code except that the "larger than" and "lower than" signs in the first four lines are to be reversed. In the first part, as long as the simulated mean age is higher than the prescribed mean (in the algorithm: mean-age), a random agent with non-minimum age is selected and its age is changed to the age of a random agent with lower age. Then, the age of this adjusted agent is again adjusted to match the prescribed standard deviation as closely as possible. That is, the age is repeatedly adjusted in steps of one year until a minimum difference between simulated standard deviation and prescribed standard deviation (in the algorithm: std) is achieved. Thereat, the age is not allowed to fall below 15 years, which is the minimum age boys can be household heads in the study area. The explanation of the second part is analogous, given the reversal of the signs in the first four lines.

We implemented this algorithm for the case-study age-structure data set (Table 1), and conducted five test simulations for 300 years like for the other modeling principles. Results verify that the simulated mean and the standard deviation remain constant at the prescribed mean and standard deviation, respectively (Figure 3), which we set to the initial observed values. Also, the shape of the

```
If (mean [age] of turtles > mean-age) [
  while [mean [age] of turtles > mean-age] [
    ask one-of turtles with [any? turtles with [age < [age] of myself]] [
      set age [age] of one-of turtles with [age < [age] of myself]
      ask turtles with [age != nobody] [set age-1 age set age+1 age]
      set age-1 age - 1 set age+1 age + 1
      while [
        (abs(standard-deviation [age] of turtles - std) >
        abs(standard-deviation [age-1] of turtles - std) and age > 15) or
        (abs(standard-deviation [age] of turtles - std) >
        abs(standard-deviation [age+1] of turtles - std))
      ] [
        ifelse (abs(standard-deviation [age-1] of turtles - std) <
        abs(standard-deviation [age+1] of turtles - std)) [
          set age age - 1
        ]
        [
          set age age + 1
        ]
        set age-1 age - 1 set age+1 age + 1
      ]
    ]
  ]
]
```

Fig. 4. First part of algorithm extension for equation 4 for improved aging modelling

age distribution seems to mimic the age structure better than the other models (Figure 2, bottom right).

3   The Importance of Being Accurate: A Case Study

In order to illustrate that the choice of modeling principle for aging of farm agents is relevant in real-world studies, we implemented the selected algorithms in a fully-fledged model for simulating land-use change in the selected study area. The model is one of the model versions described in detail in [14] (version Ord-L) and follows the modelling framework of the LUDAS family. To remind the reader, this was the model family from which we derived modelling principle 1.

The core of the LUDAS framework is the representation of the human-environment feedback loop. This loop involves the bidirectional feedback between human land-use activities and ecological dynamics. In addition, the framework integrates feedback at several scales and speeds. As such, it considers both long-term change of farm livelihood strategies and short-term changes in human land-use choice (for details see [10], [14]). In detail, the framework is implemented through household agents running a land-use choice phase, in which landscape

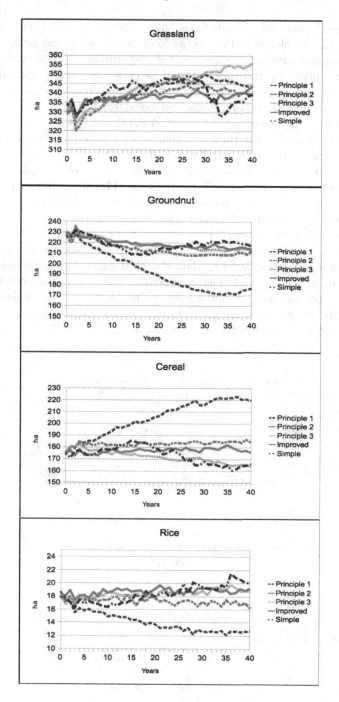

Fig. 5. Simulated land-use areas (ha) over time

patches are selected and evaluated (i.e. their location, land-use type, and management mode is selected). That is, as long as the agent has sufficient spare labor for management, patches are selected and evaluated. Thereby, first owned patches are cultivated, and then external patches are searched for cultivation. The choice of land-use type is represented via a multinomial logistic regression model using environmental and household variables. The preference coefficients of the model are dependent on the so-called livelihood type of the agent. These livelihood types represent farm agent archetypes with typical livelihood strategies. Each time step, which usually consists of a year, the livelihood type is updated for each agent, dependent on the agent's changes in explanatory variables. In the version presented here, the last type of land-use choice, the choice of patch management, is simply modelled via assignment of categorical values dependent on agent and patch characteristics. Models of ecological returns to these decisions complete the model. These usually feed back into both the choice of agent's livelihood type and the agent's short-term land-use decisions. All used data and sub-models are based on data collected during two household surveys conducted in 2006 ([13], [12]). The simulated land-use types comprise grassland for grazing and the main cropping systems in the area, i.e. cropping systems based on either cereals, groundnut, and or rice. The simulated area comprises an area of 918 ha located in the Atankwidi Catchment.

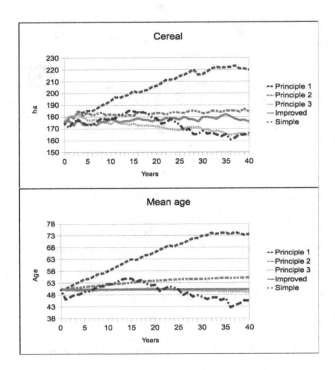

Fig. 6. Simulated mean age (years) and cereal area (ha) over time, rescaled

Table 2. Overall correlation between mean age (years) and land-use area (ha)

Land-use type	Correlation coefficient	R^2
Grassland	0.066	0.004
Groundnut	-0.678	0.460
Cereal	0.710	0.504
Rice	-0.601	0.361

We simulated each modelling principle 20 times for 40 years, which is the time period that we believe the model can more-or-less reproduce. Results clearly show how sensitive the model is to the choice of aging sub-model (Figure 5 and 6), where simulated areas of land use, in specific the cropping systems highly correlated with simulated mean age (Table 2). The reason for this correlation is that the land-use choice model contains age as an explanatory variable. The selection of explanatory variables for the land-use choice model was based on hypotheses collected in the field, which were (partially) confirmed statistically (see [14]). Age was insofar selected as the field study indicated that younger farmers tended to favor the more cash-oriented staples groundnut and rice, while older individuals rather opted for the traditional but subsistence-oriented cereal crops such as millet and sorghum. This is also indicated by the results, where the large increase in age under principle 1 is accompanied by an accordingly lower area of rice and groundnut, and an accordingly larger area of cereal (Figure 5).

4 Discussion

A review and test of aging models for farm agents showed that they, using the same database, converge to different age structures over time. Each of the simulated age structures differed from the observed age structure in a different way. The problem is that it is not clear whether simulated emergent change is an account of real-world change and/or a result of inaccurate assumptions. And one cannot identify for which algorithm which of these causes apply. Further, it is not clear whether authors tested the assumptions made in their models, i.e. whether the resulting age structure is in line with their global understanding of how the structures would evolve. Therefore, we argue that assumptions for variables whose change over time is not or little known should be held under control at the emergent global level. In this article, we aimed to offer such an algorithm for aging of farm agents, and showed that it is able to match the age distribution prescribed over time, but also lets agents age by one year every annual time step. We finally illustrated what effects the choice among presented algorithms can have, using a case-study model for land-use change in Northern Ghana. Results suggest that the selection of aging model is one of the major factors that determines both the direction and extent of land-use change in the case-study model.

Some readers may think that the developed model became very specific at
the cost of losing generality. However, we would the like to point out that the
developed aging model is not more specific to its case study than the models
reviewed. It can be applied to the same domain of case studies as the reviewed
models. The aim of developing the aging model was neither to increase its prediction accuracy for the case study. On the contrary, the goal was to eliminate
prediction while preserving the feature of individual aging. Instead, the predic-
tive part was externalized to be specified by expert opinion. The reason for that
was, as stated above, that the simpler reviewed models contradicted each other
and one had no theoretical means to decide which model to choose. One may
equally argue that the reviewed models impressed by their simplicity, which got
lost in the presented aging model. But when we claim to provide empirical agent-
based models of land-use change, we need to provide realistic aging sub-models,
be they a bit more complicated or not. And the reviewed publications all had
the pretension to be empirical.

References

1. Arsenault, A.M.: A Multi-Agent Simulation Approach to Farmland Auction Markets: Repeated Games with Agents that Learn. Master thesis. University of
   Saskatchewan (2007)
2. da Feitosa, F.F.: Urban Segregation as a Complex System: An Agent-Based Simulation Approach. Dissertation. University of Bonn. Ecology and Development Series
   70 (2010)
3. Freeman, T.R.: From the ground up: An agent-based model of regional structural
   change. Master thesis. University of Saskatchewan (2005)
4. Happe, K., Kellermann, K., Balmann, A.: Agent-based Analysis of Agricultural
   Policies: an Illustration of the Agricultural Policy Simulator AgriPoliS, its Adaptation and Behavior. Ecology and Society 11(1), 49 (2006)
5. Khagayi, S., Debpuur, C., Wak, G., Odimegwu, C.: Socioeconomic status and
   elderly adult mortality in rural Ghana: Evidence from the Navrongo DSS. African
   Population Studies Journal (2011)
6. Kaplan, M.: Agent-based modeling of land-use changes and vulnerability assessment in a coupled socio-ecological system in the coastal zone of Sri Lanka. Dissertation. University of Bonn. Ecology and Development Series 77 (2011)
7. Lamptey, P., Nicholas, D.N., Ofosu-Amaah, S., Lourie, I.M.: An Evaluation of
   Male Contraceptive Acceptance in Rural Ghana. Studies in Family Planning 9(8),
   222–226 (1978)
8. Lobianco, A.: The Effects of Decoupling on Two Italian Regions. An Agent-based
   Model. Dissertation. Polytechnic University of Marche (2007)
9. Le, Q.B.: Multi-agent system for simulation of land-use and land-cover change:
   A theoretical framework and its first implementation for an upland watershed in
   the Central Coast of Vietnam. Ecology and Development Series, vol. 29. Cuvillier
   Verlag, Göttingen (2005)
10. Le, Q.B., Park, S.J., Vlek, P.L.G., Cremers, A.B.: Land use dynamic simulator
    (LUDAS): A multi-agent system model for simulating spatio-temporal dynam-
    ics of coupled human-landscape system. 1. Structure and theoretical specification.
    Ecological Informatics 3(3), 135–153 (2008)

11. Millington, J., Romero-Calcerrada, R., Wainwright, R., Perry, G.: An Agent-Based Model of Mediterranean Agricultural Land-Use/Cover Change for Examining Wildfire Risk. Journal of Artificial Societies and Social Simulation 11(4), 4 (2008)
12. Schindler, J.: Household surveys July and November 2006. For questionnaire see [13] (2006)
13. Schindler, J.: A multi-agent system for simulating land-use and land-cover change in the Atankwidi catchment of Upper East Ghana. Dissertation. University of Bonn. Ecology and Development Series 68 (2010)
14. Schindler, J.: The difficulties in justification of agent design and their effects: An illustration with a land-use model (submitted, 2012)
15. Stolniuk, P.C.: An Agent-Based Simulation Model of Structural Change in Agriculture. Master thesis. University of Saskatchewan (2008)

Author Index